PRAISE FOR
TROUBLED

T0370161

"A fascinating memoir and an analysis of the 'luxury beliefs' gripping American elites . . . Targets the stupidity of what now passes for orthodoxy, but [Rob Henderson] does so without penning an angry culture-war screed."

—*The Economist*

"Henderson's story of self-discovery, growth, and resilience is a valuable contribution to the conversation about how our society must contend with the forever problem of kids who get separated from their parents—a subject shrouded in darkness."

—*Los Angeles Review of Books*

"A memoir of hardscrabble living . . . [Henderson] traces the contours of his remarkable and often-harrowing life. . . . [He] is at his best in the frank observations about his trip up the 'American status ladder.'"

—*Kirkus Reviews*

"Affecting . . . intriguing . . . heartbreaking . . . This eye-opening account lays bare the realities of America's deep economic and social divides."

—*Booklist*

"I defy you to read *Troubled* and not come away in equal parts outraged and inspired."

—Thomas Chatterton Williams, author of *Self-Portrait in Black and White*, contributing writer at *The Atlantic*

"[S]uperbly composed memoir . . . Deserves careful attention."

—Christy Carlson Romano, actress, cofounder of PodCo

"*Troubled* is an extraordinary document. . . . Henderson's story is breathtaking but all too familiar in this county."

—Dr. Drew Pinsky, author of *The Mirror Effect*

"[Henderson] is a keen observer of both the world he came from and the world he now inhabits. . . . Read this book. It will challenge both your heart and mind. A rare feat."

—J.D. Vance, author of *Hillbilly Elegy*

"*Troubled* reads at times like *Hillbilly Elegy* or Tara Westover's *Educated*. . . . [A] remarkable book."

—Naomi Schaefer Riley, *Commentary*

"[A] powerful description of the predicament of countless foster children, and a sophisticated social critique . . . *Troubled* is magnificent."

—Nicholas A. Christakis, author of *Blueprint,* Sterling Professor of Social and Natural Science at Yale University

"A captivating memoir."

—Jordan B. Peterson, author of *12 Rules for Life*

"[A] profound account of a foster child overcoming severe adversity and achieving the unthinkable."

—Yeonmi Park, author of *While Time Remains*

"[A] breakout memoir . . . Henderson, a brilliant young psychologist, illumines how harmful childhood instability is by reflecting on his own experience. . . . His eye is as keen as his intellect."

—Judge Stephanos Bibas, *The University of Chicago Law Review*

"[A] powerful, moving, and necessary book."

—John Lewis Gaddis, Pulitzer Prize–winning author of
George F. Kennan: An American Life, Robert A. Lovett
Professor of Military and Naval History at Yale University

"[As] a product of a single mother raised in public housing, I see so much of my story in Rob's insightful book. . . . As you see the world through Rob's eyes, you won't be able to pull your eyes off the page."

—Ed Latimore, author of *Hard Lessons from the Hurt Business*

"A tour de force that in a more rational world would be required reading for all incoming college students at elite schools."

—Kay S. Hymowitz, *City Journal*

"A work of art—one that deserves to become a classic."

—Emily Yoffe, author of *What the Dog Did*

"Searing and brutal, but utterly articulate. Devastating, yet full of hope: *Troubled* is a masterwork."
                    —Stephen P. Hinshaw, author of *Another Kind of Madness*

"*Troubled* is impossible to put down. . . . One of the best memoirs I've ever read."
                    —Polina Marinova Pompliano, author of
                    Hidden Genius and founder of The Profile

"A refreshing voice . . . This memoir is a testament to the path that has shaped Rob's unique perspective."
                    —Chamath Palihapitiya, founder and
                    CEO of Social Capital, co-host of the *All-In* podcast

"Absorbing and deeply moving."
                    —Emily Esfahani Smith, author of *The Power of Meaning*

"Truly extraordinary."
    —Will Storr, *Sunday Times* bestselling author of *The Status Game*

"[A] must-read."
                    —Naval Ravikant, cofounder of AngelList

"An astonishing story . . . It will make readers wiser, more humble, and above all, more compassionate."
                    —Jonathan Haidt, NYU Stern School of Business

"A tremendously promising debut by an already important young American thinker."

—Greg Lukianoff, coauthor of
The Coddling of the American Mind

"One of the most compelling stories I've ever read."

—Anthony B. Bradley, author of *Heroic Fraternities,*
professor of religious studies, The King's College

"Brilliant . . . Reveals a resounding antidote to a life of chaos and instability for boys and young men: love."

—Melanie Notkin, author of *Otherhood:*
Modern Women Finding a New Kind of Happiness

"One of the most insightful thinkers I follow."

—Chris Williamson, host of the *Modern Wisdom* podcast

"Henderson . . . toggles seamlessly between a personal narrative of Dickensian horrors and . . . an encyclopedic recitation of all the relevant social scientific research pertaining to the outcomes witnessed on either side of the vast class divide he traversed . . . Intriguing and effective."

—Wesley Yang, author of *The Souls of Yellow Folk*

"*Troubled* is a tragedy in gripping story form."

—Amy Alkon, award-winning applied
science columnist and author

Troubled

A MEMOIR OF FOSTER CARE, FAMILY, AND SOCIAL CLASS

ROB HENDERSON

G

GALLERY BOOKS

NEW YORK   AMSTERDAM/ANTWERP   LONDON   TORONTO   SYDNEY   NEW DELHI

G

Gallery Books
An Imprint of Simon & Schuster, LLC
1230 Avenue of the Americas
New York, NY 10020

First Gallery Books trade paperback edition February 2025

GALLERY BOOKS and colophon are registered trademarks
of Simon & Schuster, LLC

For information about special discounts for bulk purchases,
please contact Simon & Schuster Special Sales at 1-866-506-1949
or business@simonandschuster.com.

The Simon & Schuster Speakers Bureau can bring authors
to your live event. For more information or to book an event,
contact the Simon & Schuster Speakers Bureau at 1-866-248-3049
or visit our website at www.simonspeakers.com.

Manufactured in the United States of America

10 9 8 7 6 5 4 3 2 1

The Library of Congress has cataloged the hardcover edition as follows:

Names: Henderson, Rob Kim, author.
Title: Troubled : a memoir of foster care, family, and social class / Rob
    Henderson.
Description: First Gallery Books hardcover edition. | New York : Gallery
    Books, 2024. | Summary: "Rob Henderson, a doctoral candidate in social
    psychology at Cambridge, reflects on his childhood in foster care, how
    he narrowly escaped a broken system, and the only hope for
    disenfranchised kids across America: family"—Provided by publisher.
Identifiers: LCCN 2023008344 (print) | LCCN 2023008345 (ebook) | ISBN
    9781982168537 (hardcover) | ISBN 9781982168551 (ebook)
Subjects: LCSH: Foster children—United States.
Classification: LCC HV881 .H46 2024 (print) | LCC HV881 (ebook) | DDC
    362.73/30973—dc23/eng/20231127
LC record available at https://lccn.loc.gov/2023008344
LC ebook record available at https://lccn.loc.gov/2023008345

ISBN 978-1-9821-6853-7
ISBN 978-1-9821-6854-4 (pbk)
ISBN 978-1-9821-6855-1 (ebook)

For Carmen L.H.J.

From time to time I meet with a youth in whom I can wish for no alteration or improvement, only I am sorry to see how often his nature makes him quite ready to swim with the stream of the time; and it is on this that I would always insist, that man in his fragile boat has the rudder placed in his hand, just that he may not be at the mercy of the waves, but follow the direction of his own insight.

—Johann Wolfgang von Goethe,
1749–1832

CONTENTS

PREFACE

As someone who never really had one, maybe I am the least qualified person to defend the importance of family. But as someone with more education than I ever expected to receive, maybe I'm more qualified to say we give education more importance than we should. I am grateful for the miraculous trajectory of my life, but I had to experience upward mobility firsthand and reach the summit of education to understand its limitations. I've come to understand that a warm and loving family is worth infinitely more than the money or accomplishments I hoped might compensate for them.

Throughout the past eight years, I've learned that educated and affluent people tend to focus on credentials when deciding whether or not to listen to someone. But whatever authority I have to speak about the matters contained within this book comes from the origins of my name itself, not the credentials after it.

My name is Robert Kim Henderson.

Each of my three names was taken from a different adult. Robert was the name of my biological father, who abandoned my mother and me when I was a baby. I have no memory of him. In fact, the only information I have about him is contained in a document given to me by the social worker responsible for my case when I was being shuffled around to different foster homes in Los Angeles.

My middle name, Kim, is from my birth mother. It was her family name. She succumbed to drug addiction soon after I was born, rendering her unable to care for me. I have only two memories of her. I haven't seen her since I was a child.

And my last name: Henderson, which comes from my former adoptive father. After my adoptive mother separated from him, he severed ties with me to get back at her for leaving him. He figured that this would hurt me, and that my emotional pain would transmit to my adoptive mother. He was right.

These three adults have something in common: All abandoned me. None took responsibility for my upbringing. When I was in foster care, doctors, psychologists, social workers, and teachers would often use the word *troubled* to describe me and the other kids who were overlooked, abandoned, abused, or neglected.

When educated Americans discuss what's best for kids, we tend to talk about education as the be-all and end-all, when it should be seen more as the fortunate benefit of a warm and loving upbringing. Elites are simply too quick to equate education with well-being. Yale sociologist and physician Nicholas Christakis has written, "almost every innovation in child welfare in the United States, including orphanages and subsidized childcare, has been driven primarily by adult concerns. Of secondary importance were convictions about what was best for children." Educated people ask how we can get more underprivileged kids into college. That is a laudable goal. But education is a red herring. For many kids, having the kind of childhood I had takes a toll in ways that a college degree will never fix.

Education is meant to be a ladder toward a better life, and often, it is. But even if every abandoned, abused, and neglected kid graduates from college as I did and earns a comfortable income, they are still going to carry the wounds, or in the best-case scenario, the scars, from their early life. Unstable environments and unreliable caregivers aren't bad for children because they reduce their future odds of getting into college or making a living; they are bad because the children enduring them experience pain—pain that etches itself into their brains and bodies and propels them to do things in the pursuit of relief that often inflict even more harm. Credentials and money are not antidotes to the lingering effects of childhood maltreatment.

I've met some well-heeled people who have attempted to imagine what it's like to be poor. But I've never met anyone who has tried to imagine what it would have been like to grow up without their family. If you're born into wealth, you take it for granted. If you're born with loving parents, you'll take them for granted, too. In one of my classes at Yale, I learned that eighteen out of the twenty students were raised by both of their birth parents. That stunned me, because none of the kids I knew growing up was raised by both of their parents. These personal discoveries reflect broader national trends: in the United States, while 85 percent of children born to upper-class families are raised by both of their birth parents, only 30 percent of those born to working-class families are.[1]

My friends from high school grew up in garden-variety broken

---

1   C. Murray, *Coming Apart: The State of White America, 1960–2010* (New York: Crown Forum, 2012).

homes, and the trajectories of their lives align with data indicating that boys raised by single mothers or by caregivers other than their parents are five times more likely to be incarcerated than boys raised by both of their parents.[2] The majority of jail inmates report being raised by single parents or non-parental guardians. Two of my childhood friends landed in prison, and another one would have if he hadn't been shot to death first. Studies indicate that in the US, 60 percent of boys in foster care are later incarcerated,[3] while only 3 percent graduate from college.[4] What this means is that for every male foster kid like me who obtains a college degree, twenty are locked up.

Some have suggested that the school system should be held responsible for childhood outcomes. But the schools I attended (and often ditched) in California weren't that bad. Several of my teachers urged me to apply myself and encouraged me to explore my potential. But my home life was such a mess that I didn't have the desire to put in the effort. I preferred sleeping in class and getting into trouble with my friends. I had little supervision at home and no one who took an interest in my grades. When adults let children down, children learn to let themselves down.

Two days after I graduated from college, the *New York Times* published a widely read op-ed titled "College Does Help the Poor."[5]

---

2   C. C. Harper and S. S. McLanahan, "Father Absence and Youth Incarceration," *Journal of Research on Adolescence* 14 (2004): 369–397.

3   P. Fessler, "Report: Foster Kids Face Tough Times After Age 18," NPR, April 7, 2010.

4   Y. A. Unrau, R. Hamilton, and K. S. Putney, "The Challenge of Retaining College Students Who Grew Up in Foster Care," *Retention Success* (2010): 1–5.

5   T. Bartik and B. Hershbein, "College Does Help the Poor," *New York Times*, May 23, 2018.

I agree with the headline and believe education is crucial for social mobility. Nevertheless, the article is emblematic of the narrow way elites think about poverty and instability. The authors share research indicating that Americans who grow up poor and then graduate from college earn about $335,000 more in their lives compared with their peers who did not attend college. In contrast, college graduates from wealthy backgrounds go on to earn about $901,000 more than comparable individuals who did not complete college. In other words, wealthier individuals receive higher gains from college than those from more modest backgrounds. These disparities are worthy of consideration. What is behind them? Before reading on, I already knew what the authors were going to suggest: people from wealthier backgrounds "tend to go to more selective colleges." Like many of its kind, the article is centered on money and education. There is no discussion of trauma, neglect, feelings of worthlessness, and stressful interpersonal relationships that accompany an already impoverished upbringing. The discussion is framed as if the main challenge kids from deprived backgrounds face is that they don't attend good enough colleges and don't earn high enough incomes.

Or consider a popular article in *The Atlantic* titled "Marriage Makes Our Children Richer—Here's Why" by the sociology professor W. Bradford Wilcox.[6] He presents compelling evidence that, relative to kids living in single-parent homes, kids with married parents are more likely to graduate from college and obtain higher-paying jobs. In fact, he calculates that young adults are at least 44 percent more likely to graduate from college if they are raised

---

6 "Marriage Makes Our Children Richer—Here's Why," *The Atlantic*, October 29, 2013.

by married parents, relative to being raised by single parents. Wilcox then goes on, "This is important because a college degree is associated with better work opportunities, lower odds of unemployment, and a substantial wage premium." All good things, but like many others of its kind, the article implies that the main reason stable families are good for kids is because it sets them up to go to college and earn more money. The article takes the position that the only kind of impoverishment worth focusing on is educational and financial, not social or emotional. In other words, to persuade highly educated people—readers of periodicals like *The Atlantic*—about the importance of families for children, the author had to frame his argument in the language of economic and professional benefits.

Finally, take a recent paper led by the economist and Nobel laureate James J. Heckman. The authors compared childhood outcomes in the United States and Denmark and found that "Despite generous Danish social policies, family influence on important child outcomes in Denmark is about as strong as it is in the United States." Even though public assistance in Denmark is widely available and university education is free, disparities in test scores and educational mobility between children raised in wealthy versus low-income families are virtually identical to the US. One interpretation is that having access to educational and economic opportunities doesn't mean much when kids come from impoverished or tumultuous family backgrounds. In Denmark, the out-of-wedlock birthrate is 54 percent, higher than the US, which is 40 percent.[7] And in Den-

---

7   J. Chamie, "Out-of-Wedlock Births Rise Worldwide," Yale Global Online, March 16, 2017, https://archive-yaleglobal.yale.edu/content/out-wedlock-births-rise-worldwide.

mark and the US, the number of children raised by single parents is virtually identical.[8]

Heckman and his coauthor reviewed research indicating that children are powerfully affected by their interactions with their families. They go on to state, "However, public policy and social analysts often ignore these fundamental points and neglect the central role of family influence and family response to policy."[9] Kids from attentive families are in the best position to take advantage of educational benefits. Neglected or maltreated kids seldom respond to such opportunities in the same way.

Making good choices is hard enough, even in the best of circumstances. Just because you know something will benefit you doesn't mean you'll actually do it. As a kid, I knew a lot of the choices I was making in the moment were unwise. I just didn't care. Knowledge alone isn't enough. For children, having a stable environment with two parents who implement rules, provide attentive care, and cultivate a sense of security goes a long way. Even when you present opportunities to deprived kids, many of them *will decline them on purpose* because, after years of maltreatment, they often have little desire to improve their lives.

Others suggest that economic forces are the key factor for the disparity in outcomes among my peers from different periods of my life. My childhood friends and I did grow up poor and did

8   "How Many Single-Parent Households Are There in the EU?," Eurostat, June 1, 2021, https://ec.europa.eu/eurostat/web/products-eurostat-news/-/edn-20210601-2.

9   J. J. Heckman and R. Landersø, "Lessons from Denmark About Inequality and Social Mobility," National Bureau of Economic Research (2021), https://www.nber.org /system/files/working_papers/w28543/w28543.pdf.

experience the stress of material deprivation. But money is not the whole story. There's something else going on.

An important clue comes from a widely cited 2012 paper in the scientific journal *Developmental Psychology*. A team of psychologists found that compared to children raised in wealthier families, children raised in lower-income families are no more likely to engage in risky behaviors or commit crimes as adults. However, compared with children raised in stable environments, children raised in *unstable* environments are significantly more likely to engage in harmful or destructive behaviors later in life. Holding family income constant, the researchers found that the association between childhood instability and harmful behaviors in adulthood remained significant.[10]

Plainly, being poor doesn't have the same effect as living in chaos.

As part of their studies, the researchers administered a childhood instability scale. I completed it out of curiosity. Among other questions, it asked how often I relocated, how frequently others moved in and out of the homes I lived in, and how much uncertainty there was in my daily life. I scored well into the top 1 percent of the most unstable childhoods in the US.

My views have been fashioned by the hardships I've encountered and the lessons I've derived from them: foster care, extreme instability, divorces, separations, gaining parents, losing parents, gaining siblings, losing siblings, and all the pain, numbness, thrill-seeking, violence, and substance abuse that results. These experiences have led

---

10   J. A. Simpson, V. Griskevicius, S. I. Kuo, S. Sung, and A. W. Collins, "Evolution, Stress, and Sensitive Periods: The Influence of Unpredictability in Early Versus Late Childhood on Sex and Risky Behavior," *Developmental Psychology* 48 (2012): 674–686.

me to reflect on what environments are best for children. Certainly not the ones I came from.

I've heard variations of the phrase "I'm grateful for what I went through because it made me who I am today." Despite what I'm proud to have accomplished, I strongly disagree with this sentiment. The tradeoff isn't worth it. Given the choice, I would swap my position in the top 1 percent of educational attainment to have never been in the top 1 percent of childhood instability. Much of my own life has been an unsuccessful flight from my childhood. Each time I moved, each time another adult let me down, and each time I let myself down, it was like tossing a Mentos into a Coke, sealing it, and believing everything would be fine.

I've written each chapter of this book from the perspective of myself at various ages. Much of the language I'll recount would today be considered uncouth or offensive. That's how my friends and I talked to each other in the not-too-distant past spanning the 1990s and mid-2000s. My aim is to share a firsthand view of what life was like for a kid growing up in disorder during that era. With each chapter, I try to bring to more mature expression the lessons I learned. To this end, I relegate much of my reflective commentary to later chapters. This is because, quite frankly, as a kid going through what I went through, I simply didn't have many profound insights about my situation. When kids are in survival mode, they don't have much energy left for contemplative thought. It wasn't until later, when I was in a more stable environment, that I began to think more deeply and realized that I'd spent most of my youth in a relentless state of fight-or-flight. I share those lightbulbs and the context surrounding them as they went off. As a kid, it would have been useful to have an older version of myself helping me to understand the events I experienced and the reasons behind my reactions to them. I didn't have that, but you, to some extent, will.

I've come to believe that upward social mobility shouldn't be our priority as a society. Rather, upward mobility should be the side effect of far more important things: family, stability, and emotional security for children. *Even if* upward mobility were the primary goal, a safe and secure family would help achieve it more than anything else. Conventional badges of success do not repair the effects of a volatile upbringing.

I grew up poor, encountered the middle class in the military, and later found myself ensconced in affluence at Yale. My story would be incomplete without reflecting on these different groups. I'll reveal what it was like for me to come from a deprived and dysfunctional background and move along the American status ladder. Throughout these experiences, I learned a lot about those who sit at or near the apex of that ladder, which led me to develop the concept of "luxury beliefs"—ideas and opinions that confer status on the upper class at little cost, while often inflicting costs on the lower classes.

I began writing this book in 2020, a little over a year after arriving as a PhD student at Cambridge University. At this point, I have lived a life that my seventeen-year-old self would have found both absurd and hilarious. On a typical day, I wake up at around 6:00 a.m. and pedal an overpriced bicycle to my college boathouse. The air in Cambridge is so frosty that by the end of the twenty-minute ride I can no longer feel my face. There I join a crew of seven other guys and row in the River Cam for two hours. Later, I go to my office at the university, which I share with another doctoral student. He usually arrives a little later than me and has asked, "Why do you row when it means you have to wake up so early?" The reason, I explained, is that it imposes structure in my life. I grew up in disorder and later discovered that stability helps me to retain my focus and achieve my goals. In my office, I write, read, do statistical analyses, track down research papers, take meetings, and do other academic stuff that my teenage self would not believe. In the evenings, I spend time with my girlfriend, do a bit more work before bed, and call it a day. During the COVID-19 lockdowns, my routine was interrupted, so I created a new one by dedicating time to this memoir.

Revisiting my childhood by mentally traveling back in time and, later, physically visiting the places where I grew up to jog old memories was more exhausting than I'd anticipated. Returning to the present after a stretch of writing felt like entering the kind of tranquil paradise I'd only dreamed about as a kid, even under the unusual conditions of 2020 and 2021.

Lastly, I want to make clear that all these stories are true, though some names and dates have been changed. I share early memories that were initially stored in the mind of a child, and I try to communicate them to the best of my ability, though of course they may not mirror reality perfectly. I suspect, considering how stress affects young children, my brain may have dimmed some of the details for my own protection.

RKH
Cambridge
2023

Troubled

CHAPTER ONE

Until Your Heart Explodes

I graduated with a BS in psychology from Yale University on May 21, 2018. Shortly before the commencement ceremony, I walked through the idyllic campus one last time with my sister. A friend from class loudly called my name as we passed. He and his boyfriend joined us, saying they needed a short break from their families. My sister snapped photos of the Gothic architecture for her Instagram story.

My friend grinned and wrapped his arm across my shoulder, whispering "So who is she?" and tilting his head toward Hannah.

"Matthew," I replied, "that's my sister."

"What? You guys don't really look alike."

"I'm adopted. I've told you this." Matthew was right. Although my adoptive sister and I share a similar ethnic background—both of us are half Korean—there isn't much of a resemblance.

"Oh, right. Wow. Yale and now Cambridge. And you're like the only foster kid I know. Dude, your family won the adoption lottery!"

I laughed with him. "Yeah, maybe they did."

If you ask most people to recall their earliest memory, it's usually from when they were around age three. Here is mine.

It's completely dark. I am gripping my mother's lap. Burying my face so deeply into her stomach I can't breathe. I come up for air and see two police officers looming over us. I know they want to take my mom away, but I'm scared and don't want to let her go. I fasten myself to her as hard as I can.

My internal alarms are going off and I'm sobbing. I want the strange men in black clothes to leave.

The memory picks up, like a dream, in a long white hallway with my mother. I'm sitting on a bench next to her drinking chocolate milk. My three-year-old legs dangle above the floor. I sneeze and spill my chocolate milk. I look to my mom for help, but she can't move her arms. She's wearing handcuffs.

My mother came to the United States from Seoul, South Korea. Her father, my grandfather, was a former police detective who had grown wealthy after starting a fertilizer company. My mother moved to California as a young woman and completed one semester of college before dropping out. Her parents supported her while she studied. After I was removed from her care, she was asked by a forensic psychologist if she had taken drugs in college. She replied, "It was a psychedelic age." Several years after arriving in the US, she met my father, and became pregnant with me. As an adult, I took a DNA test that revealed that my father was Hispanic, with ancestry from Mexico and Spain. He abandoned my mother shortly after her pregnancy, and I have no memories of him. According to the social worker responsible for my case, my mother had two sons with two other men before becoming pregnant with me. I've never met my half-brothers. I've never tried or wanted to. From a young age, I wanted to distance myself from any reminder of my origins.

When I was a baby, my mother and I lived in a car. About a year later, we moved into a slum apartment in Westlake, a poor neighborhood in Los Angeles. Documents from social workers report that my mother would tie me to a chair with a bathrobe belt so that she could get high in another room without being interrupted. She left bruises and marks on my face. While my mother did drugs, I would cry from the other room as I struggled to break free.

Eventually, after many instances of this, neighbors in the apartment complex overheard my screams. They called the police. Later, I obtained a report from a Los Angeles County forensic psychologist:

> I have received reports from her apartment manager that she has been associating with known drug users. There have been many people, mostly men, in and out of her room at all hours, and allegations that she is exchanging sexual favors for drugs. She denies these accusations.
>
> In view of the above, I cannot recommend she have custody of her son at this time. While I do not doubt her love for her son,

3

the atmosphere in which she has chosen to live is not conducive to child-rearing. Furthermore, she may soon be homeless again.

After her arrest, my mother was deported to South Korea. I never saw her again. It's funny, many nonadopted people have asked me if I've tried to find her, and when I say I haven't, they often react with surprise. But other adopted people seldom ask me about whether I've tried to find my birth parents, and when they do, they're never surprised when I say I haven't. Why try to find someone who did not want you in their life?

No father, no mother. I was three years old when I entered the Los Angeles County foster care system.

One in five foster kids are placed in five or more homes throughout their time in the system. Three-quarters of foster kids spend at least two years in foster care. Thirty-three percent stay five or more years. One in four are adopted. The median age for leaving foster care is seven years old.[1] I am a data point for each of these statistics. I am often asked why foster kids are moved into so many different homes, even when things are going relatively well. One reason is that, oftentimes, a birth parent or family member will later become available to care for the kid. But if the child has grown too attached to their foster parents, this can create problems. So, kids preemptively get shuffled around

[1] "Foster Care Statistics 2019." US Department of Health and Human Services, Children's Bureau, https://www.childwelfare.gov/pubPDFs/foster.pdf.

so that they don't get too attached to any one particular home. But there are plenty of kids like me, with no possibility of being taken in by a family member, whom this strategy needlessly deprives of stability.

According to documents from my social workers, I lived in seven different foster homes in Los Angeles in total. In two of the placements, my stays were brief—less than a month—and nothing noteworthy occurred. In two others, I can't report what happened because, to my dismay, I simply can't remember. It's possible that these experiences were so upsetting that the memories weren't encoded. It's also conceivable that I stayed in these homes for such a short amount of time that my recollections of them blended with the placements I do remember—this is what I hope occurred. I have substantive memories of three of my foster homes.

After I was taken from my mother, there was a blur of different adults buzzing around me. I felt confused and terrified. On the way to my first home, still distressed over my separation from my mother, I vibrated in my car seat as my social worker drove. Eventually I fell asleep from physical and emotional exhaustion and woke up in a foster home.

It was a small and crowded duplex. There were seven kids in my new home, mostly Black and Hispanic, plus one white kid. Race wasn't a big deal in any of my homes, though. Size was more important. An older kid, around twelve years old, was the ringleader. He controlled the television channel with the threat of violence if any of us tried to watch what we wanted. We spent most of our time watching TV, roughhousing without much adult supervision, and scrounging around for food. MTV was usually on in the background, and it seemed like "Waterfalls" by TLC played every day.

After a few months of this, I got used to living there. One day, I was playing with the other kids under a table, pretending to be a dinosaur. Suddenly, an adult trespassed on our fantasy. This was rare. Typically, the adults in this home left us alone, except to feed and bathe us. I reluctantly peered out from under the table. A Black woman knelt down and said it was time for us to go. I recognized her as Gerri, the woman who first drove me here to my new home. Instinctively, I knew she was taking me somewhere else, and I would not return. Some part of me suspected that my arrangement was not meant to last. Even at four years old, I remember being confused that the people on-screen had different kinds of families than we did. The TV families were all the same. The kids always lived with the same parents; they never had to live with others. I'd also seen some of my foster siblings leave, and new ones had come to join us.

Gerri repeated that it was time to go. I started crying. The kind of crying where kids lose control of their bodies and forget how to breathe. I gripped one of the table legs, refusing to let go. My foster parents told me it was okay, that I would join a new foster family. Their words weren't registering. I didn't want a new family; I wanted to stay with what was familiar.

They were the only parents I had really known, even though I barely saw them. I had no idea where I was going next. I bawled the entire way to the new foster home. And when we arrived, I clutched Gerri, unwilling to let go of her leg. She was my new anchor. She was the only familiar thing in this strange new home, full of strange children and adults speaking a language I couldn't understand. The house was located in West Covina, a working-class area of LA County composed mostly of Hispanic and Asian families.

I didn't eat much for my first couple of days. Anytime my new foster parents, the Dela Peñas, tried to feed me, I'd push the food away, saying I had a stomachache. I did, from the distress of being taken from my previous foster placement. But I was also, without realizing it, on a hunger strike. I thought if I didn't eat for long enough, maybe Gerri would reappear and I could ask her to take me back to my last home. She didn't, and eventually my appetite returned.

My new foster parents were from the Philippines. The dad spoke English well, but he was rarely home. Mrs. Dela Peña had some challenges with English, which created challenges for me. This was the first home I was at when I started attending school. On my first day at school, I stood in the lunch line. The lunch lady asked me for my lunch card. I didn't have one. She gave me a form and said I couldn't have lunch until it was signed.

I brought this form to Mrs. Dela Peña. She glanced at the form and said I should get free lunches without her having to pay. She thought the form required payment, when it was simply to register me into the free lunch system, so she ignored it. I didn't understand the mix-up at the time and just figured I wouldn't be able to eat lunch at school. I was hungry a lot.

I went through the lunch line each day, hoping maybe I'd magically be registered in the system. Sometimes I'd fantasize about sneaking through to get some chicken nuggets or a slice of pizza. Each day, the lunch lady would apologize and ask for the form. So, I'd sit and watch other kids eat lunch. At first, I didn't think it was a big deal. But slowly, I realized other kids thought it was weird that I didn't have anything to eat. My classmate Anthony brought lunches his mom packed. He would sometimes give me half of his bologna sandwich. Once, a kid asked him if he could trade his sandwich for some chips. Anthony said no because he was going to give me half his sandwich.

"Why are you giving Robert half? Let's just trade. I don't like Fritos."

"Nah, I can't," Anthony said, tilting his head toward me. "He ain't got no lunch." This kid Anthony also let me use his coloring pencils and would invite me to his house to watch cartoons.

One day, as I stood in line, the lunch lady smiled.

"I have a surprise for you," she said. She pulled out a lunch card and handed it to me, instantly becoming my favorite person in the school. I made sure to thank her each time I went through the line. I never did learn how she managed to do this for me. I was an unsophisticated little kid, just grateful to be able to eat like everyone else. I felt like less of an outsider. And it was easier to pay attention in class when I wasn't so hungry.

Food was sometimes hard to come by in my foster home. There were my five or six foster siblings, plus members of my foster parents' extended family, many of whom were teenage boys. They often plowed through most of the food before the younger foster kids had a chance to eat anything. One of my foster brothers and I would sometimes conspire to sneak snacks from the pantry. One day I came home from school, and he was gone.

"His mommy took him home, Robert," Mrs. Dela Peña explained.

"Okay," I said. I wanted to ask if that would ever happen to me. But I hoped it wouldn't, and I was afraid asking might make it come true.

An older man, Mrs. Dela Peña's father, lived in the home as well. He was nice to me. He would spend weekends in the kitchen, cooking chicken. I always offered to help, and he gave me portions of the food. I loved this chicken, especially the legs. I spent a lot of time hanging around the old man, even though we couldn't communicate because of the language barrier. Like me, he was mostly ignored in the house.

Although the everyday experiences of my foster siblings and I were already confusing, I suspect a coincidence in the mid-nineties made it an especially perplexing period for any five-year-old. I would hear "Simpson" on the television in the living room. So, the other kids and I would think it was *The Simpsons* cartoon and get excited. But then we'd see it was just the news talking about a guy in a courtroom, and we'd walk away disappointed.

A few weeks after he left, my foster brother returned to live with us. He said his mom "got into trouble again." I was so glad he was back and gave him half of a stale Zebra Cake I had hidden under my bed. I would sometimes wonder if, like my foster brother, my mom would ever come back for me. It didn't even occur to me that my father might, because I had never known him. Later, I'd realize how lucky I was that my mom had moved back to South Korea and didn't know who my dad was. I did not have to experience the revolving door of toxic biological parents continually entering and exiting my life the way so many of my foster siblings did.

. . .

There were a lot of teenage boys in this home. Some were relatives and nephews of my foster parents, who spoke Tagalog as well as English, and others were older foster boys.

They usually hung out in the garage, drinking and smoking. They played music videos on MTV or listened to the radio. The music was so loud that sometimes it physically reverberated throughout the house. I heard songs like "Gangsta's Paradise" by Coolio and "Tha Crossroads" by Bone Thugs-N-Harmony.

One day I wandered into the garage. The music video for "Keep Their Heads Ringin'" by Dr. Dre was playing on the TV. Whenever I walked in, the boys usually ignored me. I saw a small glass with a golden-brown liquid on a table. It looked like apple juice. I grabbed it and took a sip. It tasted awful. I spilled the glass, which got the guys' attention. They laughed and asked what I was doing.

"I wanted juice," I said.

"Yo, I got you," one of the guys said. He muted the TV and pressed some buttons on a boombox radio. "Gin and Juice" by Snoop Dogg played.

Another guy popped the tab of a soda can and handed it to me.

"Here, try this," he said.

I smelled it. It wasn't soda.

"It's beer, give it a try."

I took a small sip. It tasted bad. I made a face and ran off when they started laughing.

One boy in the house was my foster parents' birth son. He was the cousin of the guys in the garage and was a little older than me. I told him what had just happened.

"I asked them to try beer once and they tickled me until I ran away. They said my mom would get mad," he said. I figured this meant the guys liked me, and that made me want to get their approval.

I came back and tried their beer again. They all looked at me, waiting to see what would happen. I took a sip and started coughing.

"It's okay, you'll get the hang of it," one of them said, smirking as he grabbed the can from me and took a swig.

They taught me some swear words—my favorite was *motherfucker* because it was the word my teacher reacted to the most when I said it.

Some of them had tattoos. I announced that I wanted to get lots of them when I had big muscles like them.

"Isn't that how Angel got caught?" one said.

"Yeah, man," said another. "Tattoos make it easier for the cops to catch you."

"Why?" I asked.

"They learn what tattoos you have, so they know who you are and that makes it easier to find you."

That made sense. I still wanted one, but not as much anymore.

One of my older foster brothers told me why he moved in with us. He said his mom had gone off for several days on a bender, getting high with one of her boyfriends. He was twelve years old and left to fend for himself. A teacher discovered that he'd been living alone and reported it to the authorities. They placed him with us. Later, he and some other kids at their middle school lured a boy into a hallway and stabbed him to death. I didn't see my foster brother after that. I asked my older foster sister what had happened to him, because nobody mentioned why he had suddenly vanished. She paused, and then said that he had gone off to "juvie." I sort of knew what juvie was. It was where the bad kids went. I asked if we'd ever see him again. She replied that she didn't know, but a few weeks later she said that he had hanged himself. That was the first time I'd learned about suicide.

Months later, Gerri, my social worker, came to the house. It was time for me to go live somewhere else, she said. I'd just turned seven, and this time I didn't cry. I was dejected, but the tears didn't come. I'd learned to shut down, sealing myself off from my emotions. Gerri helped me gather my clothes and put them into a black garbage bag. She picked up a shoe box next to my bed, and a bunch of cards fell out.

"What are these, Robert?" she asked.

I picked up a Sonic the Hedgehog card, not responding.

"These are from Valentine's Day?" she asked, flipping through them.

"Yeah, kids in class gave one to everyone, and I play with them." I swung the Sonic card around to show Gerri how fast he was.

We packed up and walked out to her car. I wondered if this was how the rest of my life would be: moving to a home, staying for a while, and Gerri putting me somewhere else. By this point I knew that other kids didn't have to do this.

No matter which foster home I lived in, Gerri visited to check in on me every few weeks, which to me indicated that she cared about me, and on each occasion she would take me to lunch. At the time, I thought Gerri's favorite place to eat was In-N-Out Burger because that's where we would always go, but it's also likely she went there because she was always busy with her social worker caseload. Her visits were the only time I ate fast food, which I always looked forward to. By this point, I felt great affection for Gerri, and I hoped she felt the same way about me. She was the only stable, familiar adult figure in my life. My appreciation for Gerri and the restaurant became intertwined. To this day, when I walk into an In-N-Out, I feel a pleasant sense of nostalgia—of serenity. It's still my favorite restaurant.

After our pit stop at In-N-Out, Gerri took me to my next foster home, in a town in the San Gabriel Valley. This new foster home was in a neighborhood that was a little more run-down than the one I lived in before. The houses were closer together, the yards more unkempt, the cars older.

Still, the house seemed big because there were no other kids living in it. I peered around as Gerri and my new foster mom, Mrs. Martínez, spoke with each other. I dropped my bag of clothes and wandered into the hallway.

"Not too far, Robert," Gerri said.

The house was nicer on the inside than the outside. The kitchen was pretty small, but there were three bedrooms and a tube TV in the living room. Everything was *clean*. This was because, again, there were no other kids here. I had mixed feelings about this. I liked having other kids around to play with. But I was happy to not have to fight with other kids over food or what TV shows to watch. I wondered aloud why the Martínezes, my new foster family, didn't have more kids living with them.

"We like things quiet," Mr. Martínez said. "We like things clean." The adults smiled knowingly. I didn't realize it yet, but the Martínezes took young foster boys because we were ideal for performing chores.

"We only need one kid," Mrs. Martínez told me. She and Gerri went on to say that I'd have plenty of time with other kids in school, and there were lots of kids on the block.

This created opportunities for trouble.

There was this kid who lived on my street named Jason. He was a big kid, or at least bigger than me. One day I was roller-skating by his house and he started calling me names. The roller skates belonged to Mrs. Martínez's adult son from back when he was a little older than I was at this point (seven), so they were too big for me. It was tricky to keep my balance. I returned the favor to Jason and called him names as I skated by. Suddenly he started chasing me. I rolled fast but tripped over a garden hose on the sidewalk and he caught up to me. He kicked me in the face a few times as I struggled to get up. It turns out dodging kicks to the head while trying to stand up on oversized roller skates is not easy. I kept slipping back down, catching more kicks. I managed to kick him once as hard as I could in the shin with my roller skates, putting an end to things.

I staggered up, wiping my face with my arm. I saw my blood smeared across my sleeve and panicked. I sat down on the edge of the sidewalk in front of the Martínez house, tears running down my face. A few minutes later, a girl named Rosa who lived next door saw me. She yelled for her parents, and they helped me clean up. They asked me why I didn't go to my foster mother, Mrs. Martínez, for help. It was a confusing question. It hadn't occurred to me to ask her for help. I was actually thinking of ways to hide my wounds from her. I dreaded asking Mrs. Martínez for anything. I didn't trust her.

The reason was because of an incident that occurred about two weeks after I'd been placed in the home. The Martínezes had a swimming pool in their backyard. I still remember my excitement when I learned about this. Unfortunately, most of my pool time was limited to cleaning and maintaining it. I was a seven-year-old pool boy. One afternoon, after a long day of school and chores, Mrs. Martínez said I could spend five minutes in the pool. I was thrilled. I didn't know how to swim, but I decided to spend the few minutes trying to learn. Mrs. Martínez told me to stay on one specific end of the pool, without explaining why.

I splashed around with my legs planted to the bottom of the pool, and then decided to venture to the other end, not knowing that it was the deep end. I grabbed the wall of the swimming pool, edging along to the other side, and then pushed off and tried to do what I'd been doing in the shallow end. Suddenly, I realized I couldn't feel the bottom of the pool with my feet. I didn't know that pools had shallow ends and deep ends. I panicked, swallowing mouthfuls of water as I gasped for air. Through splashes, I saw Mrs. Martínez talking on the phone, standing at the edge of the pool. She furrowed her brows at me and walked away.

As I continued kicking my feet and reaching for the edge of the pool, my arms grew weary. I screamed for help. Mrs. Martínez reappeared. She held out an extendable pool net. I grabbed onto the net while she pulled me to the edge, phone still tucked between her shoulder and her ear. I climbed up, sobbing. She walked inside the house and closed the door without saying a word to me. I stood outside, stunned, rubbing my eyes and heaving from the chlorinated water I'd swallowed. Later, I told Mrs. Martínez my stomach hurt from swallowing the pool water. She replied, "You see? Listen to me. Stay on that side of the pool. Next time I'll drop the net and you can drink up the whole pool!"

Mrs. Martínez never laid a hand on me. I would come to learn that she was well-practiced in designing creative and cruel punishments.

I had a friend named Julian who lived down the block. He had cable, unlike the Martínezes, so we'd sometimes watch cartoons together. My favorite was *Doug* on Nickelodeon, especially the Quail Man episodes. Doug would daydream of being a tough superhero, which I also did. We'd listen to music, too, blaring "No Diggity" by Blackstreet or whatever else was on the radio. I hung out with Julian and other friends as often as I could to avoid Mrs. Martínez. But after the roller-skate fight, Mrs. Martínez said I couldn't go to my friends' houses anymore. I'd told Rosa's parents that I was scared to tell Mrs. Martínez about Jason injuring me. They relayed this to Mrs. Martínez, which spooked her. She was afraid I'd tell other parents about how she treated me.

One day I was outside pulling weeds in the front yard. Julian's stepdad was walking their family dog. He stopped and said, "Hey, Robert, nice job there," pointing his chin toward the pile of weeds. "You haven't visited in a while, and I know Julian would like to see you."

Mrs. Martínez stepped outside, smiling and waving. Julian's

stepdad continued on his walk. I wondered whether he could detect the menace beneath Mrs. Martínez's pleasant exterior. I had a strange feeling just then. It was familiar, but it hit me that time in a way that I was able to consciously realize for the first time: *I'm all alone out here.* The feeling of utter isolation just washed over me.

Mrs. Martínez said I wasn't allowed to see Julian "for a while," and whenever I asked when I could hang out with him again, she always replied "soon." Eventually, just as I was about to give up asking, she let me visit his house again.

One night I heard Mrs. Martínez's adult daughter, who sometimes stayed over, on the phone saying, "No, she doesn't take teenagers. She prefers young boys." I eavesdropped as I mopped the hallways, thinking that I might be getting a new foster brother. I missed having foster siblings to talk to. But on the bright side, I also realized that I didn't have to see any of my foster siblings leave for new homes anymore. And I wouldn't miss any of them when I'd eventually have to go to another home. Saying good-bye got easier each time, but it still hurt.

Mrs. Martínez was controlling and severe. It didn't surprise me that she didn't take older boys who might be tempted to rebel. She had a routine for me. I spent a lot of time doing chores around the house. There were two dogs I had to feed every morning and evening. I took out the trash and put the bins at the curbside once a week. I cleaned the pool and swept the patio. Later, confirming my hunch that she was an eccentric woman, Mrs. Martínez bought a parrot, which she named Carlos but insisted I refer to as

Mr. Carlos. Sometimes I would purposely call him Carlos just to upset Mrs. Martínez. I was scared of this bird but still had to feed him. And as long as I did my chores, Mrs. Martínez didn't seem to care if I got into trouble at school.

One day a psychologist came to visit the foster home to give me a few tests, I guess because I was doing so badly in school. She asked me if I wanted Mrs. Martínez to stay in the room or not. I said I wanted her to stay because I was wary of strangers. Really, though, both adults were strangers to me. But I wanted the adult I knew for ten weeks to stay because she was more familiar to me than the adult I had only known for ten minutes. I was a kid surrounded by strangers who thought that maybe I had a learning disability or some condition that inhibited my academic progress. I don't know if they'd considered that never having had a family and moving all the time was a big part of why I wasn't doing well. Placing a label on my poor academic performance would have helped to absolve adults of responsibility, I guess. The psychologist showed me pictures and asked me to describe them.

"This is a man combing his hair," I said.

She paused and asked if I noticed anything unusual about the image. The man in the picture was bald. He was combing air over his hairless head. I knew she wanted me to say yes, there was something odd about this picture. I said no.

After a few more questions, she asked if I knew what "parrot" meant. I said no. Mrs. Martínez glared at me. I glared at the psychologist. *Who is this person?* I thought to myself. Another adult with a sing-songy voice trying to be nice to me while knowing neither of us was ever going to see the other again. The psychologist asked what grade I was in. I said second grade. She asked if I remembered any of my first-grade teachers' names. I said no. She asked if I remembered the names of any of the schools I attended last year. I said no. I made an effort for some of the other questions—like measuring a pencil using a paper ruler. That part was fun. For the easier questions, I gave vague or wrong answers because I knew what she wanted me to say. I was being purposely defiant—this was an outlet for my barely contained anger. Generally, I was either morose, incensed, or just totally emotionally numb at having to move so frequently or from seeing my foster siblings move. After a while, I zoned out. I didn't care about this psychologist's questions. I didn't care about school. Adults didn't seem to take my needs seriously. *So why*, I thought, *should I take their tests and questions seriously?*

I had been enrolled in six different elementary schools before entering the third grade. One day in second grade I was in the bathroom at school. As I washed my hands, some boys were huddled nearby, snickering. One of them showed me a quarter, which they had apparently picked from my pocket. Sure enough, I'd had two quarters, but when I reached into my pocket, I found only one. I chased them out of the bathroom and tackled one. This boy didn't have the quarter, but I grabbed his fingers and twisted them back until he yelped in pain. I got up and kicked him in the head. Another kid ran up behind me and punched me in the back of the neck, making me drop forward.

It was Jason—the kid who had beaten me up when I was

roller-skating. I leapt up and kicked him between the legs. Two of the other boys instantly tackled me and held me down.

Jason limped toward me. He surprised me by saying he was sorry about what he'd done. He said his mom had wanted him to come over to apologize, but Mrs. Martínez wouldn't let him see me. Then he shifted gears and said they were planning to steal a purse.

Mrs. Martínez would sometimes say that there were a lot of "bad kids" in the neighborhood and that she made me do chores so that I would "learn discipline" and wouldn't have enough time to get into trouble. I couldn't tell if she was sincere or if that was just self-serving reasoning—maybe both. Still, her adult daughter said she avoided driving over alone at night because there were older boys in the neighborhood who shouted at her.

"You're a liar," I said, as the boys let up from holding me down.

"Don't call me a liar, bitch," Jason said.

I slapped him across the face and tried to kick him again. We resumed fighting while the other boys watched.

He was a big kid, so he got me in a headlock pretty fast.

"We're gonna nab that fucking purse," he said, squeezing my neck while both of us panted from exhaustion.

"Prove it, motherfucker." I tried to bite his arm while struggling to break free.

"Come with us," he said, letting me go.

We walked to a classroom, which the boys had noticed earlier was unlocked. We peered inside, and it was empty because of recess. On the teacher's desk was a purse. One of Jason's friends grabbed it, and we ran back into the bathroom. We split the money and left the purse there. I hung out with these boys a few more times and learned to pickpocket from them. We taught each other swear words that we'd learned; I had a lot from the garage crew in my last foster home.

Two of the kids in my new friend group, Vinnie and Alonzo, were brothers who lived in my neighborhood. I had to cross a street to visit them, which led to a disagreement between Mrs. Martínez and me.

"You can only visit those boys if I walk with you there. No crossing any streets unless an adult is there to walk with you," she said firmly.

"Why? I can look both ways first," I replied.

"Because it's dangerous. You could get hit by a car," she said.

"I don't care if I get hit by a car." I shrugged.

It took five minutes to walk to Vinnie and Alonzo's, and I walked there all the time. Mrs. Martínez thought I was at Julian's, who lived on the same block as us. Usually, at Vinnie and Alonzo's, we played songs on their Walkman ("Mo Money Mo Problems" by Biggie was a favorite) or watched movies on VHS (*Space Jam*, *Kazaam*). The first time I visited their house, I was in the living room with Vinnie and Alonzo. From the window, we saw their mom outside in the street yelling at some other woman who was sitting in the driver's seat of her car drinking a soda. Suddenly, their mom grabbed the driver by her hair and began punching her in the face. Then she grabbed the soda from the woman's lap and hit her a few times with it, and shouted, "Have a Coke and a smile, bitch!"

"Dude." I looked over at Alonzo and Vinnie. "Your mom is a fucking badass," I said.

"Yeah, she's tough," Alonzo replied. "Used to fight our dad all the time before he left."

Their older sister, who was around nine, walked in and tried to put on *The Lion King*.

Vinnie threw a Hot Wheels car at her and narrowly missed. "Get that bullshit off the TV!" he screamed. Alonzo fell over laughing.

"Go fuck yourself, Vinnie," his sister replied.

I laughed and grabbed Alonzo's Walkman, turning off "Going Back to Cali" from Biggie's new album once the movie started.

One day I skipped one of my chores and walked to Vinnie and Alonzo's place instead. Jason met us there, too. We walked to a nearby Kmart snack bar and pickpocketed someone's wallet. The first guy caught us and we ran off with nothing. Our next target was oblivious. We took the money and walked to a 7-Eleven to get Slurpees.

Once we got back to Vinnie and Alonzo's, their mom noticed we all had blue tongues.

"What were you boys doing?" their mom asked.

"Nothing," the two brothers lied.

"Robert, can you tell me?" she asked.

"We didn't do anything," I said.

"If you don't tell the truth, Robert, I'm going to call the Martínezes to see if they know what you kids were up to."

"I'm not a snitch," I said, grinning at the other boys.

She called Mrs. Martínez and was surprised to learn that I wasn't even allowed to go to their house by myself. Yet I was there most days of the week. She looked distraught when she realized that I was in more trouble than she'd anticipated.

As soon as I got home, Mrs. Martínez grabbed her car keys and told me to get in the car. We drove for a while before arriving at an elementary school playground. I began bouncing up and down in my seat from the sugar high.

"Good, you have lots of energy. Good. But we will burn it up." Mrs. Martínez's eyes narrowed.

We got out of the car and she told me to follow her. We walked across the street, away from the playground, and toward a high school. We arrived at a quarter-mile athletic track. It was July in the San Fernando Valley. The temperature was over 100 degrees.

She pointed forward. "Start running," she commanded. I stood, confused.

"Start running!" she shouted again. I took off, sprinting at first, then adjusting to a slower jog.

After six or seven laps, I stopped and began heaving. "Don't stop," Mrs. Martínez instructed. "You're going to run until your heart explodes."

I began throwing up blue Slurpee and staggered to the ground.

"Okay, that's enough." She looked around. People were staring at us. She waved to them and moved to help me up, then kissed the top of my head. We walked to the car and she drove us home in silence.

I didn't pay much attention in class. Learning to write my name, I constantly mixed up the letters, writing the *b* in my name as a *d* and sometimes writing the first letter as Я. School was just a place where I went and hung out with other kids. I'd go, make some friends, try to sit still in class, and then go to another school a few months later. I didn't really get that I was there to learn. My foster parents also didn't take much interest in whether I was studying or not. They got upset if one of my teachers called them to say I'd been involved in another fight or stolen something. When they received these calls, they'd scold me but do little else. Mrs. Martínez only punished me when I did something that personally affected her— usually skipping or messing up my chores.

I especially hated reading. One day, my second-grade teacher assigned homework. I skipped the reading and went straight to the questions, hoping to be creative enough to not have to read any- thing. One question contained a word I'd never seen before: *Citizen*. My eyes glided across the *C*, *Z*, and *N*. Sounding out the words, I figured it out: *Cousin*, I said to myself, proud that I could learn a new word on my own.

The next part of the assignment, as I read it, was, "How many cousins live in the US?" The answer must have been somewhere in the reading. I didn't want to have to go through all of it. Maybe, I thought, Mrs. Martínez would know. I wandered out of my room and into the kitchen to ask.

"Mrs. Martínez," I asked, looking down at my paper. "How many cousins live in the US?"

She looked blankly at me. "What?"

"How many cousins live in the US? It's for school."

She furrowed her brow. "What on earth? Ask your teacher."

I wanted to figure it out on my own. I thought the teacher

would tell Mrs. Martínez that I wasn't paying attention in school if I asked, and then they'd send another stupid psychologist to give me another boring test. So, I sat down and went through the reading, trying to understand what I was looking at. I slowly sounded out each letter. "Kit . . . i . . . zen," I said. What was that? I didn't know this word. I got irritated as I thought about how other kids would know this word. I didn't understand why other kids knew how to read and I didn't. It came so easily for them, when I could barely write my own name. Why did I have to learn how to read, anyway?

A few weeks later, the teacher asked the class what we all wanted to be when we grew up. I thought about it and replied that I wanted to be a scientist. I watched *Bill Nye the Science Guy* sometimes on TV and thought it was so cool.

"Okay, Robert. But you'll have to apply yourself and spend some more time on reading if you want to be a scientist like Bill Nye," the teacher said.

"Bill Nye never reads anything," I assured her.

"Scientists read all the time, silly. Just because he doesn't read on TV doesn't mean he never reads," she said.

This stunned me. It was the first useful thing I learned in school. You can't know everything about people just by looking at them— they have rich and varied lives, much of which is unseen. This revelation, plus my general embarrassment whenever the teacher called on me to read aloud, made me decide to put some effort into reading. The teacher asked if I wanted to borrow some kindergarten-level books. I agreed and quietly put them in my backpack when other kids couldn't see. I didn't want them to make fun of me for being dumb and reading books below our grade level.

I went through these books and practiced a little bit each day. On the weekends, Mrs. Martínez bothered me less when she saw me reading. This meant fewer chores. She liked to keep me busy, unless I had a book in my hands. Sometimes she'd even say things like, "That's good, Robert, reading is important." I craved these rare moments of kindness from her, so I kept at it.

"Okay, class, today we have some fifth graders who are going to be your reading buddies," said Ms. Sherman.

She explained that each of us second graders would be paired with an older kid and we would take turns reading passages of a book and talking about it. I was paired up with an older Asian kid.

"Do you want to go first, or should I go first?" he asked.

I was nervous. I hated reading aloud. "You go first," I said.

He read the first page, a simple story about a rooster. I liked hearing him read it.

"So, I think this rooster is trying to find his way back to a farm, what do you think?" he said. I blinked at him.

"Yeah, okay." I didn't know what else to say.

"Okay, your turn," he said.

I slowly read my page, tracing my finger along the words.

"So, what do you think?" the fifth grader asked.

"Think about what?"

"What does the story mean?" he asked. "Like what happened."

"I don't know. I just read it."

He gave me a confused look. "But what's happening in the story?"

I must have looked even more confused than him.

I felt embarrassed. I sounded out the words. I hadn't made any mistakes. But I wasn't *reading*.

I was slowly realizing that reading wasn't just about mouthing the sounds of letters or knowing what each word meant individually. The words taken together were meant to tell a story. I had some dim understanding of this when I would *listen* to people read at school (no one read to me at home), but it didn't really click that this was what *I* was supposed to be doing when I read.

I kept practicing on my own until reading finally made sense. I was reading a book I had practiced with before, for several days in a row, when something clicked. I suddenly understood not only each word, but also grasped the meaning of each sentence and could follow the overall story. It felt like magic. Reading the words projected coherent images and stories in my mind.

This was a milestone in my life. From then on, reading became a source of comfort for me. I began reading books all the time, and the teacher let me borrow whatever I wanted, but I still seldom paid attention in school. I read in class instead of doing whatever assignment or activity we were supposed to be doing. Reading was an escape—from my memories, from my foster families, from my feelings.

Adults forget how they processed time as children. When you're a grown-up, time flies by. As a kid, the period between the beginning of a school year in September and winter break in December feels endless. I had lived in foster homes for just shy of five years, but it felt like twenty.

If I had to reduce what I felt during these early childhood years to a single word, the only one I can think of is: dread. Dread of being caught stealing, dread of punishment, dread of suddenly being moved somewhere else, dread of one of my foster siblings being taken away. Early on, the dread was sharp—I'd see an unfamiliar car outside or a puzzled look on a foster parent's face and begin to panic. The feeling would strike suddenly and then wane. Gradually, it became blunted and ever-present. Sometimes, the sharp dread would return when I was sleeping. I'd suddenly wake up in the middle of the night and my heart would be pounding so loudly I would wonder if other people in the house could hear it. I was often sleep deprived at the Martínez house, and I couldn't wait to leave.

TV was another way to temporarily escape my current reality and spend time in another one. I'd watch at my friends' houses and loved cartoons in particular because the characters were always so upbeat even when they faced big obstacles. Mostly, I was just grateful to spend time in front of the screen and away from Mrs. Martínez.

One day Mrs. Martínez told me she wanted to show me a video. I was surprised because she had never offered to show me a video before. After watching the first minute, I was disappointed. It was a video of real-life people, not cartoons. The video starred a man, a woman, and a little girl. But then they all said, "Hi, Robert!" which startled me. I was mystified: Sometimes I wondered whether people we watched on TV also watched us, and this seemed to suggest that they did. The man bounced a beach ball on the little girl's head while the woman gave a little tour of their home. They seemed very nice. I hoped they could see through the TV how much I enjoyed watching them.

Mrs. Martínez turned to me and said impassively, "This is the Henderson family. These are going to be your new parents."

I was confused. I had never seen a video of the family before I moved to a new home.

"Why did they make this movie?" I asked.

"It's not a movie. It's just a home video they made. They want to adopt you."

"What does that mean?" I asked.

"It means they'll be your new parents. They'll be your mom and dad."

I understood instantly. So, this was how kids got permanent moms and dads! They had to be picked by them. I beamed, wondering if they were as nice in real life as they were in the video. Suddenly, I remembered the phone call I'd overheard while I was cleaning the floors and understood that Mrs. Martínez was preparing for my replacement.

As part of the adoption process, I had to undergo an evaluation by a child psychiatrist in Los Angeles. My adoptive mother later gave me a copy of the report:

> Recently, the patient has begun to get into trouble at school, and his newly aggressive behavior is also troublesome. It is not possible to predict the future for this child. He is vaguely aware of the possible changes in his circumstances and is reluctant to talk about

his thoughts or feelings about another move. I would recommend finding permanent and stable placement for Robert in a kind and supportive environment as expeditiously as possible, which will go far to mitigate against the potentially deleterious effects of his early experiences.

According to this doctor's judgment, all I needed was a permanent and stable "placement," and I'd probably be okay. It seemed, at last, that I would have it.

CHAPTER TWO

The Parent Trap

I was outside feeding the dogs when Mrs. Martínez called through the kitchen window, "We have to go to Mexico soon, and we can't take you with us." She opened the screen door to the backyard and stepped outside. "You might have to go to another foster home."

"Am I moving in with the people in the video? My new parents?"

Within a week, I went from knowing where I was going to having no idea. The sense of dread and loneliness returned. I kneeled down and petted one of the dogs as he ate, holding back tears.

"Mr. and Mrs. Henderson. And no. Well, we don't know. They're trying to speed up the adoption process. But if they can't, you'll have to go to another foster placement."

"Will the Hendersons take me later?"

"We don't know," she said. "They're coming to visit from Red Bluff. You'll get to meet them."

• • •

Mrs. Martínez wanted me to look my best for my meeting with this family that might adopt me. Most of my clothes were child-hood hand-me-downs from Mrs. Martínez's adult son. Some of the clothes were oversized. The shirts nearly came down to my knees, the sweater sleeves stretched beyond my hands, and I usu-ally had to roll up my pants. We went to Goodwill, which was exciting because it was the first time I went to a store to get clothes of my own. After Mrs. Martínez picked out some clothes that fit me properly, we went into a store that was freezing cold inside. I peered over the counter and saw a bunch of different colors in tubs.

"What kind do you want?" she asked.

"Is it candy?" I asked.

She laughed. "What? I'll just get you some vanilla. Do *not* spill any."

She ordered for both of us and handed me a cone with cold stuff inside. I saw her lick the stuff in her cone, so I did the same with mine. It was delicious. I bit into it. The icy temperature hurt my teeth. Curious, I poked my finger into it, holding it still. Then I pressed my cold finger to my cheek.

"It's so cold," I said.

Mrs. Martínez looked over at me. "Stop that!" she snapped. "You never had ice cream? You can tell the Hendersons that you had ice cream."

So, this was "ice cream." I'd seen other kids with it before. I took another bite of ice cream and part of it fell in my lap. Mrs. Martínez handed me a napkin. I was a messy eater, which she had mostly gotten used to. When I first moved in, she yelled at me because I ate too fast and used my shirt as a napkin. It was instinctual, though. In my previous foster homes, other kids sometimes took food right off our plates if we didn't eat it fast enough. Because of how I ate, my clothes were often stained, which annoyed my foster parents.

The Henderson parents looked like they did in the video. They spoke with Mrs. Martínez while I sat on the couch. After they finished talking, they took me to a nearby park without her. I played on the jungle gym while they encouraged me. At some point I stopped and asked what I was supposed to call them. "Mrs. Henderson?" I asked.

"Honey, you can just call us Mom and Dad," she replied.

"But Mrs. Martínez said you might not be my mom and dad," I said.

"Did she? Don't worry about that, Robert. Or can we call you Rob, or Robbie?" Dad said.

"I don't mind," I said, swinging on the bars. I'd nearly lost the ability to feel joy, but at this point, I felt a sense of guarded optimism. I trusted my new parents—my new mom and dad. I briefly considered whether Mrs. Martínez was being truthful when she said I might be moving to another foster home, or if it was just another one of her cruelties. But my hopes lifted when Mrs. Martínez insisted on taking a photo of me with Mr. Carlos to say good-bye.

I smiled wanly as I glared at the hyperactive parrot, grateful I'd never see him again.

· · ·

Two weeks later, my bags were packed. I was going to move in with Mom and Dad. Gerri had brought Karen, a social worker from Chico (a town in Northern California near Red Bluff), with her. Gerri explained that Karen would be flying with me to join my new family. Gerri instructed me to make sure I behaved and to do well in school. I hugged her, not understanding that this was the last time I would ever see her. She was a rock in my life, the only person who I felt cared about me. I wish I'd gotten to say a real good-bye.

"How far are we going?" I asked Karen.

"It's quite a ways, kiddo. It's on an airplane, remember." She held her hand up, making a flying motion.

"Where are we going?" I asked.

"To your new home, silly," she said.

"I think he means what town, Karen. You're going to Red Bluff," Gerri said.

"Is that in LA?" I asked.

Both of the social workers smiled. "No, sweetie, it's not in LA."

They told me the flight would be over an hour. I'd never been on an airplane before, and I was excited to see what it would be like. But shortly after takeoff, like I'd always done when traveling to a new foster home, I fell asleep.

We landed in Sacramento, and there they were at the airport. I recognized my mom and dad immediately. Dad was holding my sister, who somehow looked even smaller than she did on the video I watched.

"This is your new brother, Hannah," Mom said. "Can you say hi?"

She said hi.

"Hi, Hannah, I'm Rob."

I couldn't believe she was four years old—she looked three. Kids notice these things, mismatches between a kid's size and age, in ways that adults often don't.

Mom and Dad told me that the drive from the Sacramento airport to Red Bluff was another two hours or so. I rubbed my eyes, ready for another long trip.

My new sister, Hannah, was running in circles in the living room. "Robbie, I'm gonna show you something," she said.

We'd finally arrived in Red Bluff, to my new home. As I entered the house for the first time, I felt that familiar surge of heightened alertness; I was always a little jittery whenever I moved in with a new family. I expended a lot of nervous energy just trying to learn about my new environment for each foster placement. Usually, I wouldn't eat or sleep much for the first few days. This time it wasn't as intense, because I believed this would be the last "placement" I'd ever have. But I was still anxious about being in a different environment. I wanted to explore—to learn more about my new surroundings.

It was a three-bedroom, one-and-a-half-bath house. Mom and Dad had moved into this house from a small apartment just before the adoption, they explained, because they wanted a family home for Hannah and me.

My sister led me to my bedroom, where there were a bunch of toys on the floor.

"Oh wow!" I said. "Can we play with these?"

"These were mine. You can have them," she replied.

I picked up a yo-yo that lit up. "I've never played with one of these," I said, trying to figure out how to put the string on my finger. There was no loop tied, so I just tapped the side of the yo-yo, watching it light up.

"Mom said you never had any toys before," she said. I was surprised at how well she spoke for a four-year-old. I barely talked at all when I was four.

"Yeah. Sometimes I'd go to my friends' houses and play with their toys," I said, suddenly understanding that I wouldn't see my friends from LA anymore.

"You can play with these ones now whenever you want," she said.

"Thank you," I said. This act of kindness from my four-year-old sister is burned so deeply into my memory that I will never forget it. My foster siblings and other kids in LA could be mean. Food, toys, and adult attention were scarce resources, and so there was fierce competition. Plus, the other kids and I didn't always have a strong attachment to one another; we knew that at any moment we could be taken to another home or that a new kid would join us. Scarce resources plus environmental instability is not a recipe for prolonged kindness in young children. Still, I was often devastated when my foster siblings would have to leave or when I'd have to leave them to go to another home.

"I have a piggy bank, too. I collect change and sometimes Mom and Dad add coins, too."

We walked to her room, and she showed me a big piggy bank.

"You can have half," she said. She was definitely the nicest kid I'd ever met.

This was the strangest welcome to a new home I'd ever experienced. It was overwhelming. I went back to my bedroom and closed the door. I didn't understand what I was feeling. I couldn't quite believe that I would be living with only one family now. One family, one sister, with the same people in the same house all the time. I was used to not knowing who would be in my house from one week to the next or where *I* would be living next. I'd learned to stop thinking about the future, because I wanted to believe where I was living at the time would be where I would always be. Thinking anything else would make my heart beat really fast. Sitting on my bed in my new bedroom, I thought to myself, *No more moving.* Realizing that my sister and I would not be taken from each other filled me with unexpected joy.

For the first several months living with my new family, I'd get really intense nightmares. In these dreams, I'd wake up in my bedroom at the Martínezes' house. Suddenly, I thought the adoption had been a dream. In the nightmare, I believed that what Mrs. Martínez had told me was true, that they were moving to Mexico. She'd tell me to pack a bag for my next foster placement. Then I'd really bolt awake, my chest would be tight, and I'd take deep breaths and walk to the kitchen to get a glass of water.

Throughout my first year with my new family in 1999, I learned that Red Bluff was way different than where I'd come from. My adoptive hometown in Northern California is about 500 miles north of Los Angeles, 130 miles north of Sacramento, and smaller than either. The population of Red Bluff at that time was 13,147. It's situated in Tehama County, one of the poorest counties in the state. The median household income was $27,029[1] (the median in California at the time was $61,137[2]). Twenty-one percent of Red Bluff residents lived below the poverty line, and for those under age eighteen it was 29.6 percent. (The US child poverty rate at the time: 11 percent.) Red Bluff was mentioned once in an episode of *Sons of Anarchy* in 2009, suggesting that Charming, California (the fictional town in which the show was set), is located nearby.

Adults generally thought of Red Bluff as safe because it was relatively small and rural.[3] Familiarity bred a false sense of security. The closest "big city" was Sacramento, a two-hour drive away. But Red Bluff wasn't safe—it is consistently ranked as either the third or

1   US Census Bureau, "American Community Survey," https://www.cleargov.com /california/tehama/city/red-bluff/2017/demographics.

2   National Center for Education Statistics, "Digest of Education Statistics," https://nces .ed.gov/programs/digest/d10/tables/dt10_025.asp.

3   J. Harrop, "Does Our Crime Rate Fit Our Red Bluff Community?," *Red Bluff Daily News*, May 31, 2019.

the fourth most dangerous city in California, typically right behind Oakland. The murder rate is three times higher than the US average, and the violent crime rate in Red Bluff is more than 50 percent higher than in Los Angeles.[4]

The weather was different, too. Unlike Los Angeles, Red Bluff had "seasons." It actually rained in wintertime, and in the summer, the temperature could get as hot as 120 degrees. I learned how dark my skin could get when I played outside without a shirt on. The car rides were shorter. In LA, it took forever to get anywhere. But in Red Bluff, I'd get in the car with Mom and Dad, and we'd be on the other side of town in less than fifteen minutes. There was one Taco Bell, one McDonald's, and one Burger King. We ate out a lot more than I did with any of my foster families. The Walmart in town had a generic little snack shop inside, later replaced by another McDonald's, which we'd also eat at a lot, especially on 29 Cent Tuesdays when they sold hamburgers for 29 cents each. There was one movie theater, with a 99-cent store next to it that was later replaced by a Dollar Tree.

And Red Bluff was much whiter. My adoptive mother (whom I was happy to call Mom) was born in South Korea, but she had been adopted by a white working-class family (my grandma and grandpa) when she was two years old. Dad, who was white, grew up in a family that was even poorer than Mom's. In the LA Unified School District, my classmates were mostly Hispanic, with some Black kids, and a few white and Asian kids. In my new school, it was mostly

---

4 Neighborhood Scout, https://www.neighborhoodscout.com/ca/red-bluff/crime#data.

white, with some Hispanic kids, and a few Black and Asian kids. But the poverty wasn't different. It seemed like most of the families, just like the ones I knew in LA, were barely getting by. Adults worked at the Sierra Pacific Lumber Mill, local businesses, or the Walmart Distribution Center. The ones who went to college were teachers or worked for the county. There weren't many big chains besides Walmart—no Supercuts, for example. Mom would take me to get a haircut at a local place that charged six dollars, and she always gave one extra dollar as a tip. They had a giant sign above the counter that read "Clean hair is essential for a good haircut," which served as a reminder to squalid patrons who would sometimes visit.

Adults were always having car problems or worried about paying for gas, even though regular unleaded at the local Arco was 99 cents a gallon. Because of this, a lot of kids walked to school, and everywhere else, even though the streets weren't always safe. There were tweakers, ex-cons, homeless people, and teenagers looking to get into mischief. There was a man covered in tattoos who would speed-walk all over town, yelling to himself. The other kids and I called him Schizo Joe. We got scared when we were walking and he'd get close, and then laugh when he was far enough away. There was another guy we described as "crazy" who would wander around downtown, usually with a beer bottle in his hand. The other kids and I were afraid of him because he had "FUCK THE WORLD" tattooed on his forehead. Meth, weed, and prescription drugs—opioids, mostly—were prevalent and not always hard to get. Most kids I knew didn't live with both of their parents.

Compared to Los Angeles, Red Bluff felt both richer and poorer at the same time. My immediate circumstances had improved, but the lives of those around me were the same as or worse than the kids I'd known in LA.

I asked Mom to tell me the story of how they'd come to adopt me. She'd met Dad in the early '90s, she explained. Mom was working as a cashier at Petro, a local truck stop in Dunnigan, California (population: 897). Dad was working as a corrections officer at a prison when he and Mom got married. Mom quit her cashier job and they moved together into a fifth-wheel trailer, in a part of town that didn't even have telephone service. Mom described how she would communicate with other people—her parents, mostly—using a CB radio. Even as a child, I knew there was something odd about not having a phone and communicating with radios. All my foster homes had phones, and even in the old shows and movies on TV, people had phones. Mom said Dunnigan was, even for a small rural town, very poor.

One day at work, Dad had witnessed one of his superiors harassing a junior female corrections officer. Dad said he was conflicted because he knew the right thing to do was report him, but that there was an unspoken code at his work about not being a "rat" or a "tattletale." In the end, he reported his boss. Shortly thereafter, Dad quit his job and began working as a truck driver. He and Mom moved to a mobile home in Knights Landing, California (population: 968), which is 112 miles from Red Bluff. Mom got another cashier job, this time at Kmart, and then later became a certified nursing assistant. Then Mom had gotten pregnant with Hannah, and she and Dad decided to move to Red Bluff, which was much larger and had more job opportunities compared with the towns they had come from.

A couple years after Hannah was born, they decided they wanted a second kid but didn't want to go through another pregnancy. They met with a social worker about adoption. The social worker told them she knew of a foster child who needed a home but wouldn't show them any photographs unless they were serious about adoption. They replied that they were indeed serious and, after reading and learning more about this kid, they agreed to meet him to learn more. Then the social worker showed them a picture of me. "We knew we had to have you," Mom said.

I'd never had a father figure in my life before, so having a dad was a new experience. We'd shoot hoops at a local park and wrestle around in the living room. He told me stories about his experience in the army when he had been stationed in Korea in the late '70s. Sometimes he'd say how lucky he was to have "missed Vietnam" while holding his palm flat and ducking underneath. I didn't know what that meant and figured he just didn't want to visit Vietnam. Dad would teach me Korean words, and I thought it was funny that he knew how to speak Korean and Mom didn't, even though Dad was white and Mom was Korean. I would learn words from Dad and then tried to see if Mom knew what I was saying. She thought it was cute. They were proud of me for being able to learn the words so quickly. They were also impressed that I was doing well in school, because in the foster homes I'd been such a poor student. I'd finally gotten the stability I needed, and it was reflected in my improved grades. I surprised everyone by getting third place in my school's spelling bee, a marked difference from barely being able to read eighteen months prior. I'd grown to love reading, and I collected books that Mom and Dad would let me order from the Scholastic book catalogs my teachers handed out every few months. My favorites were *Encyclopedia Brown*, the Goosebumps series, and *The Boxcar Children*.

I liked the mysteries inside Goosebumps and Encyclopedia Brown books. I admired the way the boy detective Encyclopedia Brown used his smarts to find clues and figure out who the bad guy was. In *The Boxcar Children*, the characters were all orphaned kids who lived in an old, abandoned boxcar in the woods. I had something in common with these kids, which was why I liked the stories so much. The oldest boy was Henry, who always did the right thing and made sure to take care of the others. I thought he was the kind of big brother I would want, and the kind I should try to be. I especially liked a scene where the kids find a dump heap and pull out some teacups, an iron kettle, and spoons—which they called "treasure." The resourcefulness and curiosity of these kids inspired me. I felt alone in the world and learning about their self-sufficiency made me feel safer. If they could survive, then maybe I could, too.

There were rules at home that I had to get used to. Mom and Dad were Seventh-day Adventists, and we went to church on Saturdays. Sometimes, though, if my sister and I complained enough, they would let us skip it. But Dad was very rigid about certain rules. Once at dinner, my sister talked about what they did in first grade that day.

"We talked about our favorite word. What's everyone's favorite word?" she asked.

Dad said, "Do you want to know what my favorite word is?" He paused. "Jesus."

My sister nodded, and Mom didn't say anything.

A few days later, my sister and I were playing outside, and I said casually, "Oh my God."

Dad overheard and told me to go to my room.

I went to my room. A few minutes later, Dad walked in and said, "If you ever take the Lord's name in vain again, I will hold you two inches above the ground and give you a beating. Do you understand me?"

I nodded. "Okay, Dad." I didn't know what I'd done wrong, but I understood that he was serious. I swore all the time with other kids—*motherfucker* was still my favorite word—and wondered what Dad would do if he found out about that.

Dad was a serious man. Once I got into trouble at school for shoving a kid in the lunch line, and the principal called my parents. When I got home, Dad told me to sit at the table and gave me a pencil and paper. I had to write the sentence "I will not cause trouble" one hundred times. After writing the sentence a few times, I switched to "I won't cause trouble" because it was a little bit shorter and easier to write. When I finally finished and gave the papers to Dad, he handed them back to me and said to write one hundred sentences properly this time.

On another occasion, my teacher called them and said I hadn't turned in my science project. Dad said he didn't even know I'd had a science project. He told me to go to the living room and do one hundred push-ups. I could take breaks, he said, but I couldn't eat dinner until I had completed all one hundred. It took me most of the afternoon.

I asked why I had to do so many.

"I know it's tough, Robert. But you have to remember, I'm an ex–soldier boy," he replied.

Mom didn't like it, but she didn't stop it. One time I asked her, "Why does Dad always make me do push-ups?" She replied that Dad was worried because I'd come from foster homes. He thought I would become a serious troublemaker, and that the best way to prevent this was through strict discipline. I didn't want to make Dad upset, so from then on I made sure not to get into trouble at school and to turn in all my assignments. I wanted Dad to like me, I didn't want to do more push-ups, and I wanted to prove him wrong—to show him that I could be a good kid.

Dad later resumed working as a truck driver, so he was gone all week and came home on the weekends. One week for summer break I went with him. We drove all the way to Montana and back, stopping in different states and different truck stops like Petro along the way. I thought truck stops were cool. I liked looking at the trinkets and souvenirs of the different cities we were in. I learned that the interior of semi-trucks (not the trailers, the trucks themselves) often have bunk beds, a bathroom, and a small refrigerator. It was like a miniature motor home.

Dad also had a small portable black-and-white TV in the back of the truck, and sometimes I'd watch it if I was able to get a signal, but it usually didn't work. So, I spent most of the trip sitting in the passenger seat next to Dad. He bought me snacks and told me stories about his childhood while we listened to John Denver cassette tapes. He explained how he had grown up poor in a small rural area, somewhere in either California or Oregon (I don't remember which). He said that when he was a kid, they didn't have indoor plumbing until he started school, they'd never gone out to eat in a restaurant, and sometimes they had to go hunting or fishing for dinner. He pulled out an old black-and-white photograph of him and his family from the center console of the truck. In the photo, Dad was a teenager, and he was ripped. I asked him how he had a six-pack and he told me it was probably because he spent a lot of time outdoors working, and because they didn't always have much to eat. I asked why the man in the photograph looked different from Grandpa. He matter-of-factly explained that his birth father was an alcoholic and hurt Grandma and the others in the family. Grandma divorced him and remarried a much nicer man, whom Hannah and I knew as Grandpa.

On the way home, Dad told me how one time he had gotten into an argument over the phone with another guy. Dad invited the guy to come over to settle their disagreement. When Mom got home from work, she saw Dad and the other man fistfighting in the middle of the street. She was furious with him and threatened to leave. That's when he stopped drinking alcohol and started drinking O'Doul's instead. I asked him if he was still ripped with a six-pack when he beat this guy up. He laughed and said he was too old by that point, gesturing toward his thinning hairline. I thought it was kind of cool that he used to fight people but was happy he didn't do it anymore. He said he loved me and Mom and Hannah, and he was grateful that we all now had a better life than he'd had as a kid. I told him I was grateful that he was my dad.

• • •

In December, Mom and Dad kept asking me if I was excited that my birthday was coming up. I could tell they wanted me to be excited and say yes, so I did. But I'd never done anything for my birthday before—never had a cake or gotten any birthday presents—so in my mind I didn't have much to be excited about. On the day of, Mom and Dad said we were going to my maternal grandma and grandpa's house. They lived in a town even smaller than Red Bluff. The drive to Grandma and Grandpa's felt like an eternity, even though it was only about fifteen minutes. Time passes slowly for kids.

Grandma and Grandpa were religious—even more religious than Mom and Dad—and went to Seventh-day Adventist church every Saturday no matter what. Grandma was blind and spent a lot of time reading the Bible in braille. Sometimes I would sit with her and she would read me stories like Noah's Ark. She also told me the story of how her father had died when she was a young girl. My great-grandpa John worked at a farm, rendering animal fat. One day while he was at work, a large bucket fell and hit him in the head, killing him instantly. After losing her father at just eleven years old, my grandmother became even more devoted to her faith.

As we walked into the house to see Grandma and Grandpa for my birthday, Dad was covering my eyes with his hands. Suddenly he removed them and I saw my grandparents, along with some of Mom's extended family. In the middle of the living room was a big pile of wrapped birthday gifts.

"These are mine?" I asked.

Everyone assured me that they were mine. I said to everyone

that I never got birthday presents before, and they replied that they were making up for it now. Hot Wheels cars, finger skateboards, dinosaur books. It was overwhelming. I didn't know what to play with first. I thanked everyone many times. Then they brought out a big cake. They sang "Happy Birthday" to me, which no one had ever done before either. I had to sing it in school sometimes to other kids in class, but nobody sang it to me because my birthday was during the holiday break.

After we finished up with the cake, Mom and Dad said they had another surprise for me. We walked outside and there was a Huffy bicycle. They'd brought Hannah's bike and pulled it out of the car trunk so we could ride around together. Hannah was zipping around on her bike, and I felt self-conscious because I wasn't sure if I could ride like her. I'd practiced a little on my friends' bikes in the foster homes, but it was still hard for me to keep my balance.

I got the hang of it pretty fast. I felt the wind on my face as I pedaled harder, seeing how fast I could go. I couldn't believe I had all these toys. I wondered if I'd always get presents on my birthday now.

One night around Christmastime, my sister and I were watching *The Parent Trap*, which we had rented. Mom and Dad let us pick out some snacks, too, which they never did because candy was expensive at Blockbuster. It was the second time Hannah and I were watching the movie. The first time, we watched it as a family, and I'd kept asking how Lindsay Lohan could play two different people on the same screen. Mom and Dad said, "Movie magic, kiddo."

I was still trying to figure it out when Mom walked into the room and paused the movie. I could tell she had been crying.

"Hey, kids, Dad and I have to tell you something," she said. They sat on the couch. Hannah and I stayed on the floor. Dad looked vacant. I couldn't tell, but I thought maybe he'd been crying, too.

"We love you both so much," Mom said, while Dad nodded.

Mom went on to say that she and Dad were getting a divorce. Then she burst into tears. My sister got up and sat with them. She sat between Mom and Dad, while they wept together. My sister was five, and I'm not sure she knew what "divorce" meant. But she saw that Mom and Dad were tearing up and struggling with divulging this news to us.

I remained on the floor. I felt like the wind had been knocked out of me, but I couldn't cry. I was devastated, but I didn't know how to express it. The first couple of times I had to change families, I cried a lot. But now, nothing. The ability to feel my feelings and communicate them to others had been blunted.

This was the longest I'd ever stayed with a family—over a year. I didn't know what was going to happen to me now, but I knew that our family was about to break apart, and part of me had always been dreading a day like this. None of my other families had lasted. In the past, I'd always considered other kids who had "real" parents to be unusual. I saw them on TV, but those images did not reflect my life. My foster siblings and I were the "normal" ones. That was what I was used to, after all. That was my life. As I watched my new family cluster together, about to break apart, I thought about whether *my* life was the unusual one. And here it was changing yet again. *Adults come and they go*, I thought. *They aren't reliable. Not even Mom and Dad.*

. . .

Mom moved across town into a gloomy duplex behind a local gas station, and Dad remained in the house. Hannah and I alternated weeks with them. One week we'd stay with Mom at her house, the next we'd stay with Dad at the house we knew. During the weeks I stayed with Mom, I hung out a lot with a kid named Sean. His mom, Alice, was friends with my mom. School got out around three o'clock, and I would walk to Sean's place and hang with him until Mom came to get me at five-thirty. The house was often crowded because Sean's parents took care of some foster kids, too, some of whom were teenagers. I liked staying at Sean's, and especially staying the night on weekends, because there weren't really any rules. There were just too many kids for Alice and her husband, Jim, to keep track of what any of us were doing, or to try to stop us for very long. It was funny—I was so happy to be done with foster homes after Mom and Dad adopted me. But here I was, glad to be hanging out in another one. After the splitting of my family, it was comforting to be in a familiar environment full of noisy kids.

Alice was Sean's birth mom, but Jim was his stepdad. Sean told me he never saw his real dad after he'd left his mom when Sean was little. "He's just a sperm donor. Jim is my real dad," Sean said. I liked Jim because he had cool tattoos and stayed up late with Sean and me on the weekends to watch WWF wrestling—The Rock was our favorite. And Sean's house had a Nintendo 64. We spent hours playing Mario Kart and Goldeneye and his parents didn't mind. It was sort of like '90s-era kids' heaven. One day after school I saw Sean playing Pokémon on his new Game Boy Color.

"Dude, I wish I had a Game Boy," I said.

He handed it over to me while he logged into a Yahoo chatroom. (This was one thing Sean's parents did sometimes get strict about. They said if the kids were going to talk to strangers in chatrooms, they could never give out any personal information. Sean just rolled his eyes.) He and his stepbrother had shown me how to download music from Napster earlier that day. We listened to "Blue (Da Ba Dee)" by Eiffel 65 while I played Pokémon and Sean talked to strangers on "the web."

Mom came to pick me up. I told her how much I wanted a Game Boy. Alice told Mom that they had kept Sean's old original Game Boy, but the battery cover was missing. Mom bought it for twenty dollars. I noticed she and Dad were more willing to buy things for my sister and me since they'd split up. I thought I'd have to wait until Christmas or my birthday to get an expensive gift like this, so I was ecstatic. I had to use Scotch tape to keep the 4 AA batteries inside, but I didn't mind. Sometimes I'd switch the batteries from our TV remotes to my Game Boy so that Mom wouldn't know how much I'd been playing. Like books, games took my mind off the divorce and how I was feeling. These distractions were calming.

CHAPTER THREE

Burnout

"But why? I don't get why."

"I'm sorry, hon, it's just going to be Hannah for now," Mom replied. She'd explained that my sister was going to Dad's this week, but not me. I'd already packed my bag, which I usually enjoyed doing because it was a real duffel bag and not a black garbage bag like the ones I packed my clothes in before.

"Can I talk to Dad?" I asked.

Hannah tried to be helpful. "Maybe Robbie can just stay with us for tonight and Dad can bring him back tomorrow?"

"We'll talk more when I get back from dropping your sister off," Mom told me.

I went to my room. Twenty minutes later, Mom knocked. She explained that she and Dad were having disagreements about the adoption, about custody, and things like that. I asked if I could call Dad, and she said no.

"I don't understand why I can't just ask him why I can't come," I said. I could tell Mom was thinking about telling me something. She paused, then explained that for now, Dad was upset with her. He was mad that she left him and wanted to get revenge. She said his decision to not see me anymore was his way of hurting her.

"Why would Dad not seeing me hurt you?" I asked, trying to sound angry instead of miserable.

"Because it's hurting you, Rob." She took off her glasses and wiped her tears.

Though crestfallen that my adoptive dad abandoned me, I didn't want to hurt Mom. I didn't want to hurt. I'd long associated despair with relocation—in my mind they had become interlaced. And so, deep down, I feared that if I expressed sorrow, it would lead to a placement into yet another family. Being abandoned by my birth father when I was a baby and never knowing him was hard enough, but now, after all those foster homes, I was being discarded by a second dad. I closed my eyes and flipped the switch I had built—the one that turned off my sadness. I hugged Mom and wondered why I'd had so many moms but no dads.

It wasn't just me, though. Most of the kids I'd met either had stepdads or no dads. Even though I'd been in foster care and was adopted, my past never really came up in conversations with other kids. This was probably because the families that lived in this town were so messy that even my unusual backstory didn't raise too many eyebrows. People had heard similar stories.

Another kid I'd befriended at school was named Cristian. He

lived in a tiny apartment with his mom, who was always chain-smoking. Every time I went to hang out with him at their apartment, I saw her with a Marlboro Red (she switched to Lights later). Cristian's parents had never gotten married. He told me his dad was an alcoholic who lived in another small town in California and had spent some time in prison. Cristian also told me his dad visited once in a while and would take him to GameStop or out for ice cream. But I'd never actually seen his dad over the course of our friendship. I saw a lot of his mom's boyfriends, though. Every time I visited, it was a different man. His mom didn't have many rules, other than to keep the noise down while she watched Spanish-language soap operas in her bedroom with her boyfriend of the week.

One weekend, Cristian and I stayed up all night playing Play-Station while I told him what had happened between Dad and me and how he didn't want to see me anymore. Cristian listened and kept saying "That's so messed up" and "That's really fucked up, bro." Then Cristian and I switched to watching a movie. Halfway through, Cristian paused and started crying. I asked him if he was okay. He told me about a time a few years earlier when he was taking a nap on the couch. When he woke up, his mom's boyfriend at the time had his hands in Cristian's pants. Cristian said he was scared and had never told anyone before. I didn't know what to say. I felt my eyes getting watery and knew that if he didn't stop crying, I would soon start. I had to do something, fast.

Then I remembered his mom had a bunch of tequila bottles in the kitchen. I suggested we sneak them back to his room. He grinned and said okay. But he worried about drinking too much because of what it did to his dad. His mom told him stories about his dad drinking and hitting her. We grabbed a few bottles. We figured if we took one, his mom would see that some liquid was missing. But if we took a little bit of tequila from each bottle, she wouldn't notice.

Cristian nervously took a couple of small sips and made a face. Then I tried to impress him by taking a giant swig. The liquid burned my throat and my chest and I started coughing. This stuff was way more disgusting than the beer I'd drunk before. Cristian laughed and took a sip from another bottle. I took another big swig to impress him, coughing more. I didn't understand why adults loved this stuff so much because it tasted awful. But I felt cool that we were sneaking around and drinking it. I liked the feeling it gave me. We both felt better, not necessarily because of the buzz, though that helped, but because of the thrill of our transgression. We were nine years old.

Fights were also a reliable way to cope. At school, my fourth-grade teacher split the students into groups to build a model volcano as a science project. But instead of doing the assignment, some of the boys and I were in the corner of the room arm wrestling each other. I challenged one of the stronger boys in the grade, James, to a match. We were in a dead tie, with neither of our arms moving much. After a few minutes we both agreed to stop and switch arms. In the left-handed match, I won pretty fast. To this day, I think I was supposed to be left-handed, as my left arm is stronger and I favor it for every activity except writing. But at the schools in LA, no adults paid attention to which hand I preferred and made me use my right hand because it was easier for them.

James and I had a right-handed rematch the next day, and he won.

The other boys wanted to know who would win between me and James in an actual fight. After school, some kids told me he was walking into the bathroom. I ran in and dumped the trashcan on him while he was at the urinal. It was mostly paper towels, though there was a half-filled juice box and some of it spilled on James's shirt. He zipped up, and we got into a shoving match, then he got me into a headlock. I broke free and punched him in the forehead, hurting my hand in the process. He punched me back. Then one of the male teachers ran in and broke it up. We had to go to the principal's office. Both of us said we were just fooling around. It wasn't a real fight, we said, it was just playing. But James had a knot swelling up on his forehead, and I had a bloody nose. I winced with pain when I moved my right hand, which had bounced off his head during the fight.

Mom came and picked me up, yelling at me the whole way home about how "it's never okay to use violence." I just stared blankly out the window, not caring. I secretly wanted Mom to tell Dad, even though I didn't want to do push-ups or write sentences. I would sometimes ask my sister if Dad ever said anything about me. She always said no. Hannah would ask Dad if "Robbie can come this time." He always said no.

Mom drove us straight to the apartment complex where James and his dad lived. Mom knocked and James's dad answered the door. "My son is here to apologize to your son," Mom said.

James walked up next to his dad. I saw that his forehead knot had swollen up even more. It looked like a budding goat horn. I tried to stifle my laughter while I said I was sorry. James grinned and shook his head, then called me a "fag." His dad shot him a look, and so did Mom. James's dad then said, "Thanks for swinging by," and we left.

"Promise me, Rob, no more fights. I don't want you to get hurt. I don't want you hurting anyone else. Okay?" Mom said.

"Fine," I said, wiping my bloody nose. "I won't get into fights anymore."

My mom's cousin, whom we called Aunt B, and her kids had moved into the house next to Dad. Dad was planning to move out of his house (our old family home) soon. Mom rarely took my sister and me to visit my aunt, preferring that she come to our duplex, at least until Dad moved out. One time we did go there, though, because it was my little cousin's birthday. Aunt B and Mom set up a barbecue and snacks in the backyard, along with a birthday cake. After the celebration, the adults went back inside the house while Hannah, my cousins, and I stayed outside to play. I kept peeking through the wooden fence, wondering if I'd catch a glimpse of Dad.

I finally did. It looked like he was sweeping the patio. I walked over to the tall wooden fence. I looked around, trying to find something to stand on, to reach high enough to see him. There was a little shovel on the ground. It was small, only waist-height. I picked it up and leaned it against the fence, carefully balancing myself on top of the wobbly shovel. I was just high enough, but it was hard to remain steady.

"Hey, Dad!" I shouted.

He looked up and his eyes widened. "Oh, hey kiddo. Looks like there was a birthday party?" I couldn't tell if he was happy to see me.

"Yeah! It was fun."

"Sounds like you kids had a blast," he said.

I was having some trouble balancing on the shovel. It fell over and I dropped to the ground. I picked it back up and leaned it against the fence, but when I climbed back up, Dad was gone.

My promise to Mom to stop fighting didn't last very long.

I was already in a fight with a kid named Edgar.

During recess, some of the boys in school and I would go deep into the playground where the teachers on yard duty couldn't see us. There were lots of trees, which made it a good place to hide what we were doing. Then we'd start to beat each other up. Sometimes girls would come to watch. If we got too scuffed up, and teachers asked what happened to us, we'd say we were playing "burnout." This was a game where kids would throw rubber utility balls and sometimes "accidentally" hit each other. Even though none of us involved in these fights had made an official pact, there was an unspoken agreement that we wouldn't tattle on each other.

James and I had become friends at this point, having developed a respect for each other after arm wrestling and fighting. In the cafeteria line one day, James dared me to knock the lunch tray out of "the fat kid's" hands. His name was Edgar. We saw Edgar the day before during recess in the water fountain line. A skinny kid was drinking from the fountain, and Edgar came up behind him and held the kid's head down on the faucet to make his mouth touch the spigot, which we all thought was gross. It was funny at first, and James and I even cheered Edgar on for a few seconds, but when we saw the skinny kid crying afterward, we knew it wasn't right.

With no sympathy for Edgar, I marched up to him and kicked his tray, sending his food flying everywhere. Then I bolted. The boy was massive to begin with, and he had also been held back a couple of times. He was two years older than me and almost the same height as the teacher, but even heavier. I outran him easily, but at recess I knew he would be looking for revenge.

Our arms were locked together, and the fear surging through my body somehow prevented me from falling to the ground, where I knew Edgar would have the advantage.

Edgar was definitely the biggest kid I'd ever fought. I could see out of the corner of my eye that a girl I liked was watching. *She's probably impressed that I'm fighting this big kid*, I thought. But I knew if I moved at all, Edgar's weight would overpower me, and I'd collapse. I hoped to just stay in this arms-locked-together stalemate until the recess bell rang.

"Kick him in the balls, Rob!" James shouted. "It's okay if he's bigger than you," he said.

Then Edgar kicked *me* in the balls, stealing James's advice. I fell onto my knees, and Edgar delivered a final blow to my head. My ears rang. Then the recess bell rang. I fell over. James ran over to me while other kids circled around us. I tasted metal in my mouth, realizing one of my baby teeth was loose. Sprawled out on my back, I flicked at it with my tongue and turned my head to spit out blood. Edgar walked over and extended his arm, helping me up. This was another difference between LA and Red Bluff—fights here were more frequent, but it was also more likely that friendships formed and endured after fighting. Maybe because it was a smaller town, and everyone knew everyone else. Edgar and James helped me walk to the bathroom to clean up. A teacher on yard duty saw us and asked what happened to me. "Burnout," we said in unison.

About four months after the divorce, a middle-aged woman with short blond hair began staying the night with us a lot, especially on the weekends. Her name was Shelly, and she was generally nice to Hannah and me. Mom said that she met Shelly at a meeting, and that they had become "good friends." When we'd all gone to the grocery store together, I asked Mom if I could buy some Quik powder to make chocolate milk. I could tell she was going to say no, but Shelly had already added it to our shopping cart. Later that day, she made chocolate milk for me, adding lots of powder to make it extra chocolatey. I asked if she had kids, too. She said she had three daughters who all lived with their dad. They were teenagers, Shelly explained, but when they were little she made chocolate milk for them, too. She liked the same action movies as me and watched them with me when Mom wouldn't. I liked having her at our house. Mom seemed happier when Shelly was around.

When my tooth later fell out from my fight with Edgar, I put it under my pillow. The next morning there were two dollars there. I was pretty sure if Shelly hadn't been there, the tooth fairy wouldn't have visited that night.

I walked in and Mom and Shelly were hugging in the hallway. Mom saw that I could see them. She got a funny look on her face, and they went into Mom's room. I wondered what that was about, and figured Shelly was upset or something and Mom was cheering her up. A few days later, on Friday, Hannah left to stay with Dad. I again asked if I could go, and Mom said no but added that we were going to visit Shelly at her house in Redding for the weekend. Mom was being extra nice and took me to Blockbuster, where I rented two old James Bond movies and bought some snacks at the 99-cent store. She said I could watch the movies after dinner, while she visited with Shelly. I wondered why we were spending the night there since Redding was only thirty minutes from Red Bluff. As we approached Shelly's house, Mom parked the car and grew quiet. We sat for a few seconds, and I wondered if she was okay.

"Hon, there's something Mom has to tell you," Mom said.

I braced myself. The last time she took this kind of tone, she said Dad didn't want to see me anymore. Maybe this had something to do with the adoption. I remembered she'd mentioned on the phone with my social worker once that the divorce had complicated the custody process.

"Okay," I said. I hoped I wouldn't have to move again, but at least I'd still get to watch James Bond movies tonight.

"Mom is." She paused. Sometimes she'd talk like this, like she was telling me a story about someone else. She took a deep breath. "Mom is gay." She paused again. "And Mom loves Shelly."

This blew my nine-year-old mind. I knew what being gay was, as did most kids at school, probably from TV. And, at that point in the late '90s, it was a common insult kids hurled at one another. But

I'd never met anyone who was actually gay. Mom was married to Dad, and now she was in love with a woman?

I asked, "Do you love Tricia, too?" Tricia was another of my mom's friends who sometimes visited us.

Mom laughed and said, "No, hon. Not like I love Shelly."

"Why not?" I asked. Tricia was nice, and Mom had known her longer than Shelly.

"Well, for one, Tricia isn't gay," Mom said.

"Oh yeah." I hadn't considered that both people have to be gay for them to be in a relationship.

"Let's keep this quiet for now. I haven't told Grandma and Grandpa yet," Mom said.

"Why not?" I asked.

Mom paused, perhaps realizing this was going to be a longer conversation than she'd anticipated. She told me that Grandma and Grandpa believed that being gay was against the Bible, so they would be upset. She explained that their religion was very important to them, and when Mom was growing up, they didn't let her go anywhere from sundown Friday night to sundown Saturday night because it was the Sabbath. It was a strict Seventh-day Adventist household. Mom explained that she wasn't allowed to watch any movies or listen to music if it wasn't Christian-themed. I asked if that meant she couldn't watch James Bond movies, and she said yes. She said that it was hard for her to grow up in a small town in Oregon. My grandparents adopted her from Seoul when she was a toddler, and she was the only Asian kid in her school. She hadn't met any other Asian people until Grandma and Grandpa moved the family to California when she was in high school.

"Was it hard growing up with them?" I asked. I wondered what it would be like to not be allowed to watch movies or hang out with friends on the weekends.

"No hon, there was a lot of love in the house," Mom said. "Grandma and Grandpa were the best. They just had different ideas about things because of their faith. I wouldn't have wanted any other parents."

She patted my leg. "But things were different back then. No one was openly gay, and I was just raised to believe I was supposed to be attracted to men."

She explained that when she was in school, she'd had a crush on a female teacher but felt confused about it and never told anyone. I thought I kind of understood, because sometimes I liked my female teachers too and never told anyone. But I knew that wasn't the same thing as what Mom was telling me.

"How does all this make you feel, Rob?" Mom asked.

I shrugged, fidgeting with the Blockbuster tapes in my lap. "I don't know. I like Shelly. Does that mean she's my mom too, or my stepmom?"

"You can just call her Shelly, hon. Let's go inside; I know you're hungry."

I tried to tally in my head how many parents I'd had in my life, but I was losing track of what counted as a parent. I hoped this time, Shelly would last. But because of Mom and Dad's divorce, I had a feeling she wouldn't.

CHAPTER FOUR

No Matter Where You End Up

Months passed, and life settled down. We moved out of the duplex and into a house, where Shelly now lived with Mom, Hannah, and me. At this point, at ten years old, I was a latchkey kid—I walked to school in the mornings, and when I walked home, Mom and Shelly would still be at work. Shelly usually made dinner, and Hannah and I did the dishes. Though my environment had stabilized, the quiet disdain I felt for grown-ups lingered and flared when they tried to get me to do anything school-related. As far as I was concerned, adults were unreliable liars. With each new family, new parent, and new rejection, grief, anger, and loneliness accrued within me.

My grades were plummeting, so my teacher called Mom in for a parent-teacher conference. The teacher explained that I hadn't turned in any homework that week. Mom was livid. She and the teacher marched to my classroom desk and opened it. All three of us looked at the large stack of uncompleted assignments. Mom's eyes widened.

"What is this, Rob?" Mom asked, pointing at the unfinished schoolwork in my desk.

I shrugged. "I dunno."

"You're going to do all of these assignments when we get home and hand them in to your teacher here when you're finished."

When we got home, Mom tossed the assignments on my bed and told me to get to work.

I looked at the pile of papers.

No fucking way, I thought. After she left the room, I scooped up the pile of papers in my arms, walked outside, and dumped them into the curbside garbage bin. The weather was too nice to be doing homework anyway. I remained on the driveway for a few more seconds, seeing how long my callused bare feet could withstand the heat of the asphalt.

I grabbed some shoes and decided to walk to my friend Edgar's house. He was twelve years old now, and to me, practically an adult. He and his younger brother Enrique lived with their mom, who raised them alone. As far as I could tell, they'd never met their dad. By this point, Edgar had gotten in trouble a couple of times for stealing cars, and often got cigarettes or weed from his older cousins.

I knocked on Edgar's door.

"What's up, man."

"Yo," Edgar replied, stepping outside. He flicked a lighter. "I have one left." He pulled out a joint from behind his ear. "Let's go."

We walked to a field nearby and started smoking weed. On the ground near some bushes, I saw a pack of Camel Lights.

"Probably empty," I said, walking over and opening it. To my surprise, it was completely full.

"No way," Edgar said. "Someone must have left it? Fell out of a purse? Sweet."

We smoked the joint and as many cigarettes as we could until we started feeling sick. We joked about how the police officer who taught our DARE class would show us pictures of people on drugs. He said if we did drugs, then we would look like those people with sunken-in cheeks, bad skin, and missing teeth. But we'd been smoking weed and cigarettes for about three months now and nothing happened to us. More evidence that adults were liars.

I told Edgar about Mom discovering my unfinished assignments.

"Dude, she said I had to do all of it."

"That sucks," he replied. "So, what are you going to do?"

"I already threw it all in the trash." We high-fived and laughed.

My stomach was hurting from the cigarettes. "Let's go to Bethany's house. Maybe she's home now." Bethany was a girl in our class who we hung out with sometimes.

Buzzed from weed and nicotine, we walked to Bethany's.

I rang the doorbell.

"Dude, look." Edgar was snickering, flicking his lighter next to the eight-foot thicket by the porch. The pine needles crackled as he held the flame under them.

I tried to suppress a grin. "Are you retarded? They're going to see—"

Suddenly the door opened. It was Bethany's mom. I glanced next to me, relieved to see Edgar with his hands in his pockets.

"Hi, um, is Bethany here?" I asked.

"She's staying at her dad's this week, boys— OH MY GOD!"

The entire thicket was on fire. Pine needles were popping. The flame was spreading fast. Bethany's mom pointed us to the garden hose and called the fire department.

They arrived quickly. Fortunately, no one was hurt, and the only damage was to the shrubbery. One of the firefighters took Edgar and me aside. We insisted we didn't start the fire. He didn't believe us, but he didn't call our parents either.

"If we find you boys near any more fires," he said firmly, "we're going to contact your parents."

I ran home. Smoking a joint and a bunch of cigarettes, nearly burning down my friend's house, and pretending to be innocent was taking its toll. My stomachache was intense. I opened the garbage bin in front of our house and puked all over my unfinished homework.

Then I went inside, drank a glass of chocolate milk, and fell asleep.

I didn't get caught for the fire, but I was still getting into trouble at school. I'd disrupt class often and make a lot of jokes, which Edgar and the other kids found funny. Their laughter encouraged me to keep it up. My teacher would get irritated, and eventually he put a desk outside in the hall and told me to sit out there. He sometimes told me that I had potential, and that I could succeed if only I applied myself. But I didn't even know what that meant. I didn't know that it meant to "try harder." Even if I had, I wouldn't have done it anyway.

One day in class, the teacher told everyone that our assignment was to read (or try to memorize) a short poem, recite it in front of the class at the end of the week, and give our interpretation of what it meant. Because I enjoyed reading so much, I actually took this assignment seriously.

I chose a poem called "Twistable Turnable Man" by Shel Silverstein. It was in a book I found in the library after school. When I told the teacher, he told me to try something shorter and easier. I liked this poem a lot, though, so I chose it anyway. It began:

> He's the Twistable Turnable Squeezable Pullable
> Stretchable Foldable Man.

The poem described how the man could twist and turn and adapt to anything. I liked the way it sounded, and the way the rhyme and rhythm added to the mental image of this person who could seamlessly transform over and over. Throughout the week, I read it repeatedly and committed it to memory. The morning we were supposed to present to class, I took a big gel coloring pen from the girl sitting next to me. I held it above some kid's head and broke it in half, covering him in shiny blue ink. Everyone except the teacher laughed.

While everyone presented their poems, I sat sullenly at the desk outside and didn't get to share the poem with the class.

. . .

Mom had just finished scolding me about the gel pen incident. After she left the room, Shelly came in to talk to me. She had become a surrogate parent. Mom wasn't always forthcoming because she thought I wasn't old enough to understand everything that had happened to me. Shelly was more candid.

I asked her why Dad, whom I now called Gary, didn't want to see me anymore. Shelly explained that sometimes adults did things without understanding how their decisions affect kids. I told Shelly that I wasn't affected by anything and didn't care, but she wasn't buying it.

"A lot of this will affect you in ways you don't understand yet, Rob," Shelly said. "But you're a smart kid. Later, you'll understand."

I rolled my eyes. I didn't want to believe her.

Since Shelly entered the picture, I'd learned more about her. She'd been married to a man and had three daughters. After she had started a family, she earned a college degree by taking night classes. Her daughters were now teenagers. The middle daughter lived in Alaska somewhere with her baby. The other two lived with their father; the oldest was a single mom and the youngest had just started high school. Neither of the two eldest girls was in touch with the father of her child.

"Wait," I said when she told me this. "Does that mean you're a grandma?" I asked.

"Well, I do have two grandbabies," she replied.

"I thought grandmas were supposed to be old," I said.

"I'll take that as a compliment," she said, glancing at Mom, who was walking past in the hallway and pretending she wasn't listening in.

"Will I get to meet your kids?" I asked.

"Yes, at some point."

"Are they my sisters now?" Then I thought about my relationship to their kids. "Am I an uncle?" I asked.

Shelly smiled warmly, and said, "We're all family now."

I'd been in so many families by this point that I began to wonder how much longer this one would last.

At the request of the State of California, I started seeing a child therapist once a week. Mom explained that because of my experiences in foster care, the divorce, and all I'd been through, she and my social worker, Karen, agreed that it would be a good idea for me to talk to someone. At first, I thought it was dumb. I'd always hated talking to doctors and shrinks. Why would it help me to talk to yet another state-appointed adult? How many of these people had I talked to already? At least four or five, maybe more.

Mom then explained that the therapist's office was in Chico, a forty-five-minute drive from Red Bluff. That meant I got to leave school early every Tuesday—and suddenly I agreed it was a good idea for me to go.

The therapist introduced herself as Janet, which took some getting used to. I viewed her the same way I viewed my teachers—a nonparental authority figure—so I felt I should call her Ms. So-and-So.

She was a kind, middle-aged white lady with thick glasses. During our first session, I looked around and saw board games everywhere.

"Why do you have those?" I asked.

"For people who visit. Sometimes we play games while we talk," she replied.

"So, we can play?" I asked.

She encouraged me to pick whatever game I wanted. I chose Guess Who?, a game where each player picks a card with a person on it and then asks identifying questions before guessing who the other player has.

At first, we just played. Actually, during the first couple of sessions all I did was choose games for us to play. There was some small talk, but it wouldn't get too personal.

"What's new at school?" Janet asked during our third session.

"Just the same stuff. It's pretty boring," I'd say.

"What about Red Bluff, do you like it there?" she asked.

"It's okay. There's some crazy stuff that happens sometimes."

"Like what?"

"Like last year this cop would sometimes teach our DARE class. We thought it was pretty dumb, 'drugs are bad blah blah blah.' But he was funny, he'd tell us some stories about what happens when people are drunk. But now he's dead," I said.

"Oh dear, what happened?" Janet asked, shuffling cards for Uno.

"The teacher told us he was just, like, pumping gas into his cop car. Some dude came up behind him and shot him in the dome."

"Dome?"

"His head—the guy shot him in the head."

"What did you feel when you learned about that?" Janet asked.

"It's . . . I don't know." My eyes wandered, sneaking a glance at the clock. I wished this session would end. "It's pretty messed up, you know? People are here, and then they're gone."

Janet remained silent.

I shrugged. "The teacher told us the guy who shot him was probably on drugs, or drunk, or whatever. She told the class it was sad, or, like, tragic, that he died so young."

"That is terrible. Can you tell me a little more about what you just said, Rob, about people being here and gone?"

"I don't know why I said that." I had a hunch about where she might go with this. I didn't want to have that conversation.

Whenever she asked me anything too personal, I'd either ignore her or give short answers, and she wouldn't push.

After a few sessions, I felt more comfortable opening up. I told her about the fights I'd gotten into in foster homes and at school in Red Bluff. She nodded and said there were many reasons why kids fight. But a possible reason in my case was that I moved a lot. Boys can be competitive, Janet explained, and sometimes when there is a newcomer, they want to test him. She said kids in poor families, and of course, foster kids, are more likely to move around and change schools a lot. This increases the odds of fights breaking out because boys constantly feel the need to reestablish the pecking order. At schools where everyone already knows everyone else, fights are less frequent.

One day, she asked me how I was getting along at home.

"It's fine, but I'm still confused about something."

"Okay, what is it?" she asked.

"I don't know. I don't understand people. Gary was my dad.

Then he stopped talking to me. Mom was married to him, and now she's with Shelly. She liked guys, now she likes girls. None of it makes sense to me."

Janet said it was understandable that I was confused, and that adults get confused about things, too. She asked how I felt that Mom was gay.

"I don't mind. Shelly is pretty nice. She's a better cook than Mom and makes good food. Mom burns everything. Anyway, I get why girls would like girls, but don't get how boys can like boys. That's also confusing," I said.

"Why?" Janet asked.

"Because boys are gross."

"Are the boys you know gross?"

"Yeah, I mean some of them. Girls aren't as gross. There's a boy in my class who farts all the time. We call him the 'stinky cheese man.'"

Janet laughed. "Where is that name from?"

"It's a character from a book my teacher read to us in class: *The Stinky Cheese Man and Other Fairly Stupid Tales*."

Janet raised her eyebrows. "Interesting choice. What about the books your teacher assigns you, do you like them?"

"Yeah, some. I like the books I choose on my own more. The librarian at school is really nice. She taught me how to check out books. She said I could take up to ten! I can't even fit ten in my backpack. So, I usually get like four or five."

"You know, I've noticed my grandchildren's backpacks keep getting heavier. That can't be good for kids' backs. How is school going overall?"

"It's pretty good. Mom and Shelly make sure I'm doing home-work now. I wish I didn't have to do it, though. Mom said she could handle it if I got a C-minus but would be mad if I got lower than that."

"I think you're capable of a lot higher than that, Rob. What about your friends, do they enjoy school?"

"Not really. My friend Jeremy down the street says his mom and stepdad give him a dollar for every good grade on his report cards, but I don't believe him. I go to their house sometimes, and they don't even have a real couch. It was just plastic patio chairs and stuff. The TV and VCR were sitting on the floor, plus his stepdad drinks a lot."

Janet nodded. "What about sports, do you play any sports with your friends?"

"We play basketball and football. I keep asking if I can take Muay Thai classes. There's a new gym that opened up in Red Bluff. I walked by it once and saw people hitting punching bags."

I thought if I said this to Janet, then maybe she'd talk to Mom about it. I was about to tell her about the fire incident with Edgar, too, but then our time was up.

At eleven years old, I hated when Mom would treat me like I was a little kid. It was Saturday and I wanted to go stay the night at my friend's house. It was a little after ten o'clock. Mom said she didn't want me wandering around late at night but also didn't want to drive. Finally, when I promised her I'd call her when I got to John's house, she relented and let me go on my own.

Before leaving, I grabbed a Dr. Thunder soda from the fridge to drink on the way. I walked along the Antelope Boulevard Bridge over the Sacramento River. Up ahead, I saw a guy on a bicycle in the middle of the road, riding around in circles and trying to pop wheelies. He had a long goatee and tattoos across his arms and shoulders. He tried again to lift his handlebars and fell over on his bike. I glanced at him as I was walking by.

"You got a problem?" he asked, getting up and brushing himself off.

This guy was clearly high on something. His eyes were blood-shot and he looked stressed out. Now I was, too.

"No," I said, heart racing in my chest. It was strange, I felt both terrified and *alive*. Even though I was scared, I enjoyed something about the rush. Maybe the fact that it temporarily distracted me from everything else.

He rode his bike in front of me to cut me off as I was walking, then said, "Don't be talking shit to no motherfuckers around here!"

"Yeah, okay," I mumbled.

He got off his bicycle, and suddenly I remembered something Shelly had told me: in Red Bluff, grown men on bicycles usually had had their licenses taken away for committing crimes, because otherwise they'd be driving cars. Seeing this guy made me think she was probably right.

He stepped up to me. "Did you say something: yes or no?"

"What?" I stammered. "No, I didn't."

He looked down at my Dr. Thunder can and slapped it out of my hand. I quickly stepped back to avoid getting splashed.

"Best not be talking shit." He got back on his bike and rode away.

I was afraid I'd see this guy again. When I told my friend John about it, he said, "If I was there I would have kicked his ass."

"Yeah, I should have."

"Actually, you should have pushed his ass over that bridge," John said.

"Yeah, and then dropped his bike on him, too." I laughed, trying to act tough.

My middle school was pretty far from home, about a forty-five-minute walk. At least once a week I stopped by the local library in town and went straight to the biography section. I'd flip through books about the lives of guys I'd heard of, usually athletes. I watched a lot of WWF wrestling with my friend Sean, so when I came across a book called *The Rock Says . . .* by Dwayne "The Rock" Johnson, I sat down on the floor and read half the book before going to the librarian to check it out. Mom and Shelly got mad because I didn't get home until late in the evening, after dinner had already started. When I explained that I lost track of time because I was reading a book by The Rock, they were still irritated, but I overheard Shelly tell Mom in the kitchen it wasn't the worst excuse, and Mom seemed to agree.

I'd also been reading biographies of boxers and martial artists like Muhammad Ali, Rocky Marciano, and Bruce Lee. I rented the Martin Scorsese movie *Raging Bull* starring Robert De Niro and watched it multiple times. Then I went to the library to read the book it was based on, by the mid-twentieth-century boxer Jake LaMotta. These guys lived brutal lives—LaMotta grew up in the Bronx, and his dad forced him to fight other children in the neighborhood, and adults tossed their loose change at them while they brawled. His dad would then take the coins for himself and leave nothing for his son. Reading these stories inspired me and made me a little more grateful that my life wasn't as bad as what some of them had gone through. Reading these books and watching TV shows like *The Fresh Prince of Bel-Air* or movies like *8 Mile*, I discovered idols who were funny, confident, tough, and athletic.

I kept asking to enroll in the new boxing gym that had opened downtown. Mom and Shelly agreed it was a good idea, but said I had to pay for part of the monthly fee and for the equipment (like gloves, shin guards, and a mouthpiece). I mowed the lawn and did yardwork at our house for an allowance, pulling weeds, raking leaves, and cleaning the gutters. I didn't mind—I was used to doing chores after living with the Martínez family. I did yardwork for some of Mom and Shelly's friends. I spent several days shirtless with no sunblock digging ditches to help install a sprinkler system for one of the neighbors. I developed blisters all over and had to take Tylenol to relieve enough pain for me to sleep. I spent a couple nights at Cristian's house and drank tequila while there to numb the pain.

The work paid off. I started going to Muay Thai classes five days a week for the summer, and sometimes on Saturdays when the coach would open the gym on weekends. I became obsessed with fitness and learning how to fight, but Mom and Shelly warned that if I got into any real fights, they wouldn't let me go anymore. That was fine with me. For the first few months, the coach simply drilled new students on proper form and technique. Then we moved on to practice on punching bags and focus mitts. Later, he paired us up and let us spar with each other. The gloves, mouthguards, and headgear didn't actually cushion the force of the blows as much as I expected. The first time I got punched stunned me—it felt like any of the real punches I'd taken. The instructor explained that box-ing gloves were actually invented to protect the hands of the per-son throwing punches more than the person receiving them. That added up, based on how badly I hurt my hand on James's forehead when I fought him in the bathroom back in fourth grade.

The instructor also stressed that if he found out we were start-ing trouble, he'd kick us out of class. Echoing Mom and Shelly, he said we could punch each other in the gym but weren't supposed to punch anyone outside of it. Around this time, I read a book by Chuck Norris—I want to say it was *The Secret Power Within: Zen Solutions to Real Problems*, but I'm not entirely sure. He describes sitting in a bar and someone coming up to him, insulting him, and challenging him to a fight. Norris declines. Later, someone asks him why he didn't take the guy apart, and Norris replies that he didn't feel the need to prove himself to anyone. For me, this was a new and appealing idea—being so strong that you don't feel the need to prove it. But, of course, he was Chuck Norris. He'd already estab-lished a reputation of being tough; most guys don't have that luxury.

This had become my new routine: I'd wake up, go to school, go home, do homework, feed and walk our three dogs—every time Hannah and I saw a small dog looking for a home, we wanted to keep it. Mom and Shelly drew the limit at three. Anyway, for most evenings during the week, I'd go to boxing class, then come home for dinner, and read a little before bed. I asked Mom and Shelly if I could get a punching bag, and they said I'd have to earn my own money to buy one. So, I spent some time doing chores, trying to save up. That December, though, they surprised me with a high-quality Everlast punching bag for Christmas. I'd punch that thing every night after dinner. I didn't wear wraps or gloves, so I grew calluses across my knuckles. My mood always lifted after spending twenty or thirty minutes hitting the bag.

Mom asked me how things were going with Janet. I said they were fine.

"Your grades are good, hon. You've been staying out of trouble, too. I'm really proud of you. If you want, we can see about not visiting Janet anymore, but it's up to you," Mom said.

I liked getting out of school early for our sessions, and after I talked to Janet, I felt better. But I always got nervous on the long car ride there. Thinking about upcoming appointments made my heart race. I didn't understand at the time, but the prospect of vulnerability, of revealing my fears and uncertainties, was terrifying. The *idea* of letting my guard down was scarier than actually doing so, at least within the context of therapy. It was sort of like hard workouts at the gym: I hated the feeling before, but usually felt better after. But with a gym routine you can see visible progress. This wasn't necessarily true with my sessions with Janet, and it made my choice clear.

"I don't feel like I need to see her anymore," I said.

Sean's mom and stepdad were going through a bitter separation, and he was always asking me to stay over on the weekends or asking if he could stay the night at my house. We were in his basement one Saturday night, close to midnight, playing Mario Kart and smoking weed. His older foster brother always had a supply for us. Sometimes we'd have to buy it from him, and sometimes he'd give it to us for free if he smoked with us. One time, when I was twelve and Sean was thirteen, his foster brother asked if we wanted to smoke some crystal with him, but the smell of meth was so bad—a combination of burnt plastic and body odor and urine—that I said no.

Sean took a long pull from the bong. I asked him if he knew why his parents had split up. Sean knew what I had gone through with the divorce in my family and said his situation was different. I took a hit off the bong, seeing how long I could hold it before I started coughing.

Then Sean explained that after Mom and Shelly had revealed that they were gay to his mom, Alice, Mom and Shelly then introduced Alice to a bunch of their friends. Alice hit it off with one of the women and decided to leave Sean's stepdad, Jim, for her. Then Jim decided to move out, and Alice's new partner began staying the night a lot. Later, Alice asked Jim if he could still pay the bills for the house and offered to have threesomes with him if he did. I started laughing.

"Are you serious?" I asked.

"Not bullshitting you, man." Sean laughed too. "This is what's happening. She told him he could even stay in the house, just in a different bedroom, but they could have threesomes once a week if he kept paying rent and shit," Sean said.

I doubled over laughing again. "So, is he going to?" I asked. "I mean, your mom is kinda hot."

"Shut the fuck up." Sean threw a Nintendo controller at me.

I managed to duck just in time, thanking my boxing lessons for my sharpened reflexes. Then I felt a stinging pain on my ear as Sean threw a second controller at me. It missed, but the cord whipped across my earlobe. I was about to find something to throw back when Sean's sister came down.

"Is there any weed left?" she asked.

Sean's older sister was fifteen, and I thought she was very pretty. I had no idea she smoked. She was dating a good-looking guy named Justin who had recently gotten his driver's license. We made jokes sometimes because he looked kind of like Justin Timberlake.

"No," Sean said. "Go away."

"We're having more fun upstairs anyway," she said, referring to herself and some of the older foster kids living with them. We heard them playing "What's Luv?" by Fat Joe in the room above us.

Sean and I walked upstairs after her, curious to see what she meant. As soon as I opened the door I was immediately alarmed. One of Sean's foster sisters had her hands wrapped around Justin's throat, pressing the bottoms of her palms on the sides of his neck on the carotid arteries. Justin turned red and slowly fell to the ground, unconscious. Then he woke up a few seconds later with a goofy smile on his face.

"The choking game," Sean's sister explained to us. Sean nodded knowingly. "Who's next?" she asked us.

I didn't mind the prospect of Sean's sister putting her hands on me, so I volunteered. She told me to first take really fast and shallow breaths for about a minute.

"Why?" I asked.

"It makes you light-headed, it helps to get a better buzz."

I took a few quick breaths and confidently said that I was ready, but really, I was worried about being choked out. Sean's sister smiled and said I'd be fine. She pressed her hands on my neck. I looked into her eyes, hearing Ashanti sing the chorus from the CD player, and went numb. Suddenly I awoke on the sofa.

"What the fuck was that?" I asked. My body tingled. I felt light and euphoric. "I blacked out?"

"You did," she said.

I shook my head. I felt like I'd just time traveled. "But it's not actually choking. I could still breathe," I said.

They explained that the "choking" was really just to slow breathing down, to reduce oxygen to the brain. It wasn't meant to cut off air completely.

I didn't quite prefer it to weed, but it was still a new kind of high, which I liked. Sean's sister taught me that I could even do it to myself, if I wanted. We played the choking game every few weeks, and I taught my friends Cristian and John how to do it, too. None of our parents ever found out we were doing this.

That year, I'd go into the backyard and read a book if the weather was nice. Then Mom and Shelly would come home and cook dinner while my sister and I set the table. We'd eat dinner together, and Mom and Shelly would ask, "How was school today?" or, "What did you learn in school today?" As a twelve-year-old, I'd usually give sarcastic responses at first, but I'd also try to think of something I actually learned. I always had second and third helpings, because I was trying to gain some muscle. Mom and Shelly got me a weightlifting set for my thirteenth birthday, and I used it every day. I was trying to get fit for boxing and didn't mind that girls seemed to notice results, too. In math class a girl had put her hand on my chest and said, "Wow." I said thanks, wishing I could respond in kind.

On Wednesdays we'd have family board game nights. I jokingly called them "bored game" nights. While the four of us played Monopoly, Shelly would take it as an opportunity to tell my sister and me about the importance of education. I rolled my eyes every single time.

At this point, I had internalized that college was only for really bright kids, like my friend Richard, who had gotten straight As since the fourth grade. He always did homework and turned every assignment in on time. This dude did the extra-credit assignments even though he never needed to. Richard would tell us he was doing them "just in case." *In case of what?* I'd wonder. *That* is the kind of person who is supposed to go to college—not me. Most of the kids in my school were not bound for college, anyway. I enjoyed reading, and I liked school sometimes. But having to pay money to keep going to school as an adult was not something I was interested in. I never said any of this aloud because I knew Mom and Shelly really wanted me to go. I would just nod during the game, noticing that Mom, Hannah, and I were more concerned with holding on to cash, while Shelly bought up every property she could. She seemed to know a lot about money and would often take Mom to the casino with her.

After playing board games, we watched TV together as a family, usually *American Idol* or *Friends*. Shelly would fall asleep first, then

Mom. Hannah and I would stifle our laughter when we heard them snoring and would turn the volume down while we kept watching.

After one night of "bored games" and TV, I eavesdropped on Mom and Shelly as they were getting ready for bed.

"I made a lot of mistakes," Shelly said. "Rob and Hannah don't know how good they have it."

Listening in wasn't that difficult. Their bedroom was right next to mine, the walls were thin, and they probably thought I was sleeping because it was after eleven o'clock on a school night.

"That was just weird, Shelly," Mom said.

Listening closer, I gathered that they had visited Shelly's old house, where her ex-husband and two daughters still lived. I'd been curious about Shelly's kids, and the fact that she, just like Mom, had a husband before coming out as gay.

"We just walked in," Mom said in an aggravated tone, "picked up your mail, never said hello to anyone, and left. Your daughters were there, and they didn't say anything to you."

"That's just how we are right now," Shelly said. She explained that things hadn't been the same since she left them a few years ago. She and her ex were on good terms, but her relationship with her daughters was tense. I figured this must be why I hadn't met them in the four years since she and Mom got together. I wondered if Hannah could also hear this conversation. Her room wasn't much farther away than mine.

"You have grandkids," Mom said, the volume of her voice slightly rising. "And none of us has ever met them."

"You will," Shelly replied.

I wondered when that might be.

One night a few months later, the three of us (Hannah was with her dad) were eating dinner together when the phone rang and Shelly picked it up. After listening for a few seconds, she leapt up and raced to her and Mom's bedroom and slammed the door. Mom followed after her. I sat alone, eating and wondering what was going on. Mom came out and told me we were going to the hospital, but she wouldn't explain why. I helped her quickly put the leftover food in the fridge—we couldn't afford to let it spoil—and we got in the car and left.

It was a school night, so I figured whatever this was, it must be serious. Still, I was annoyed that no one was telling me what was happening. I turned on my Walkman that I'd gotten for my birthday and listened to *Get Rich or Die Tryin'* by 50 Cent. One of my classmates had burned the CD and sold it to me for five bucks.

As soon as we stepped foot in the hospital, Shelly started speed-walking. Mom and I trailed closely behind.

"When is someone going to explain what's going on?" I asked.

"We'll tell you later," Mom said.

In the waiting room, I sat in one of the chairs. I listened to my music and looked around. A young woman with dark blond hair, lots of makeup, and a small tattoo on her right arm joined Mom and Shelly, who were standing and pacing nervously. The woman had a toddler with her, and Shelly gave a big smile to the little girl, picking her up and hugging her. I looked at the woman with her kid, and at Mom. Both made awkward small talk. Suddenly I realized: this woman was Shelly's daughter. They had the same hair color and facial features and were about the same height.

Hours passed, and during that time Shelly officially introduced me to her daughter, Katrina, whose kid was asleep in one of the waiting room chairs. I got up to take a long walk around the hospital and stop by the vending machines, where I got a Snickers and a Coke for myself, and a coffee for Mom, who looked exhausted.

I was about twenty feet from the waiting room on my way back when I saw a young-looking guy, maybe seventeen or eighteen years old, slowly approach Mom and Shelly. He had big arms and a backward visor on his head. Shelly got up from her chair abruptly and shoved her finger into the guy's face and started yelling at him.

"You fucking idiot!" she yelled. "How could you be so stupid?"

I stopped and tried to listen. Embarrassed, Mom steered Shelly and this guy outside to continue their altercation. I continued walking and gave Mom the coffee.

"Who's that guy?" I asked.

Mom took a deep breath. "Shelly's youngest daughter had a serious . . . incident. We're here to visit her. That's her daughter's boyfriend. Or ex-boyfriend, or something." She glanced outside.

Mom took another breath. "Janine—Shelly's youngest daughter—had a miscarriage."

I'd heard of this before; one of the eighth graders at school had had a miscarriage and had to take time off from school.

Mom continued, "They found Janine in their bathroom and the floor was all covered in blood. They rushed her here."

"Is she going to be okay?" I asked.

"So far they say she will be," Mom said. "Don't worry about school tomorrow. It's going to be a long night."

Mom fell asleep a few minutes later. I put my candy bar and soda on the table. Katrina looked over and asked if she could have them to give to her daughter. I said sure. She unwrapped the Snickers, and I asked if her kid was skipping school tomorrow, too.

"Natalie? Oh no," Katrina said. "She's still too young. I'm the one who is supposed to be in school."

"What grade are you in?" I asked.

"I'm not sure, actually. I'm supposed to be a senior, but I guess if I went back, I'd technically be a junior to finish up my classes from the year before." She poured some Coke in a sippy cup and handed it to Natalie.

"Thanks again," she said.

So, this is Shelly's family, I thought. *At least they have their mom now, and their dad is still around.* I thought her daughters were lucky.

"So how much did you find?" Katrina asked.

"Uh, hang on." I put all the coins on the table and counted them up again. "Ninety-three cents."

"Okay, I have two dollars and some change; this should be enough," Katrina replied.

Katrina and her three-year-old, Natalie, had moved in with us shortly after Shelly's other daughter Janine had been hospitalized. Katrina and Shelly had been estranged, but at the hospital they reconnected. I overheard Katrina describe to Shelly how her ex had put a gun to her head and said he wasn't going to send money for Natalie anymore. Shelly decided she'd be staying with us now.

Katrina had an old car and sometimes gave me a ride when I needed to go somewhere. We were usually strapped for cash, and it was tough to get enough together for gas. I'd search between sofa cushions or collect some soda cans to turn in at the recycling center. Sometimes I'd gather up to seven or eight bucks, but often I'd have less than a dollar. We were embarrassed about how little we had when we went to the gas station. So, what we'd do is buy something cheap, like a Slim Jim or a can of root beer, and ask the gas station clerk to put the rest on the pump. Then, we thought, it would look like we were just topping off before a long trip.

Katrina pulled into the Arco. I went inside with a little over three dollars, mostly in change, and did our thing with a small soda.

Katrina dropped me off at Muay Thai class.

"Thanks, I'll see if I can get a ride home after," I said.

The coach knew I couldn't always afford the monthly fee, but he gave me a break, saying it was because I'd grown up in LA, just like him. But really it was because I gave it my best in the gym. Sometimes he gave me a steep discount, and other times he'd let me make it up by helping to clean up the gym or assist with teaching classes. I taught the children's class and the novice adult classes, where I enjoyed repeating the lessons I learned from the coach ("Don't block punches with your head"). I also visited my coach's house to do yardwork sometimes on the weekends—cutting grass, digging up old tree stumps, raking leaves. I had grown to enjoy it because I thought of it as a good workout.

I met a lot of people at the boxing gym—including an elderly guidance counselor named Joe who worked at the main high school in town. He saw how hard I worked at the gym and how I would stay after to help clean up. Our coach sometimes paired us up to spar, and I was surprised by how hard he could hit for an old man. After classes, Joe and I talked about Arnold Schwarzenegger movies ("the Governator" was campaigning for election at this point), and Joe would tell me stories about how he was in the army before attending college.

I asked if the army made him tough, and he said it probably helped. I asked if he had to do a lot of push-ups, and he said they'd do knuckle push-ups on gravel. I looked at the calluses on my knuckles and figured I could probably handle that if I had to.

One evening after class, Old Joe stayed late, too, helping me sweep up the floors and wipe down the equipment. I was going to ask the coach for a ride home, but Joe said he could give me a lift. That's when he noticed the books I'd brought with me.

"What are you reading there?" Joe asked as I picked up my backpack.

"*Tao of Jeet Kune Do* by Bruce Lee," I said. "I watched a movie about him on TV a few months ago."

"Bruce Lee had a fascinating way of thinking about things," he replied.

We talked about Lee's idea of "being like water," which we both thought meant to be formless and flexible both mentally and physically. The idea, we thought, was to be prepared for anything.

"That's great that you're reading about him," Old Joe said. "When do you start high school?" he asked.

"Next school year," I responded. "So, this fall."

"Any plans for what you want to do after?" he asked. "I know you're young, but you'll have to think about grades and other considerations, depending on what you'd like to do."

"I don't really know. College sounds hard, and I know we don't have the money for it."

Old Joe nodded while he drove. "Well, there are scholarships and other options. Again, depending on grades and so forth."

I hated talking about college. "Maybe the military," I said. "But I haven't thought much about it."

"The military can be a good option for young men; the wars in Iraq and Afghanistan notwithstanding. I have a feeling, Rob, you're going to do well no matter where you end up," Old Joe said.

No one had ever said anything like this to me before. Old Joe saw the effort I'd put in at the gym. He knew I couldn't afford the fees but worked to stay enrolled in classes. I'd heard from teachers that I could do well if I applied myself, but no one had said that *no matter what*, I'd be okay. It made me feel something I rarely felt before: pride. His praise felt earned.

"It wasn't his place to tell them," Mom said.

I overheard Shelly and Mom having a heated conversation about Hannah's dad, Gary. Mom had been thinking about how to tell Grandma and Grandpa about her relationship with Shelly. Mom was stressed about this because she wasn't sure how they would react. But then the choice about when and how to tell them vanished because Gary had written them a letter instead. In the letter, he told them that it was Mom's choice to leave him, and that she had entered a relationship with a woman. Mom was furious, but also said she was slightly relieved because she had been dreading breaking the news herself.

Weeks later, Mom, Shelly, Hannah, and I all visited my grandparents' house together. The first few minutes after we arrived, there was a peculiar silence as we sat around the living room. Everyone was polite and spoke quietly.

Grandma and Grandpa then told Mom that they disagreed with her lifestyle but would always love her. They said that Shelly was now part of the family. I looked at Shelly and Mom, and both were teary-eyed. My mom's brothers—my uncles, who I usually saw only once a year for the holidays—were there, too, and said something similar. "If our sister loves you, then we love you, too," they said. "Just like with Rob here. She picked him, though we're not entirely sure why," one of my uncles teased. I was grateful someone made a joke to lift the mood, and then tried to take him to the ground to wrestle, but he was too strong from his years working as a logger. I could barely move him. Mom laughed and then cried for a while after that. Shelly cried, too, which I'd never seen her do.

I was about to finish eighth grade. Meanwhile, Shelly had gotten a promotion in her job at an assisted-living facility for the developmentally disabled, and we moved into a bigger house. We needed the extra space because we had more people living with us now. Janine had gotten pregnant again by the same guy Shelly had yelled at after her miscarriage. At sixteen years old, she gave birth to a daughter. By this point, Shelly's other daughter, Katrina, had moved out. So now Janine and her baby were living in the house with me, Mom, Shelly, and Hannah.

A few months later, Mom's cousin, Aunt B, along with her young daughter, moved in with us, too. Aunt B was having some trouble with her husband, who drank a lot and broke things. She said she had been able to deal with it until he started shouting insults at their daughter. Mom once explained to me that Aunt B's father was a logger and had been killed in a logging accident when a large limb had snapped and fallen on his neck. Aunt B was devastated, and ever since then had had difficulties with drinking and choosing men.

When she lived with us, Aunt B would sit on the front porch, smoking cigarettes and cracking wise about people in the neighborhood or what she'd recently watched on television.

I sat with her one evening before family dinner.

"How's life, Rob?" she asked.

"It's good, I guess."

"Getting excited for graduation?" My middle school was holding a small graduation ceremony.

"No, I don't have my cap and gown yet," I said.

"Well, why not?" Aunt B took a long drag from her cigarette.

"They cost fifteen bucks. I don't want to ask for it. Maybe I can skip the ceremony." Money was tight, and I knew having extra people living with us wasn't helping things.

"No, you're going to that ceremony, kiddo. Your mom won't shut up about how well you've been doing in school. Meanwhile, I'm over here giving everyone a headache."

She pulled out her purse and handed me the cash. "This'll make me square with your mom, I think." She lit another cigarette.

"Thanks, Aunt B," I said. This was a huge relief. I didn't want to have to make up a reason to my friends about why I couldn't go to the ceremony.

"Can I have a cigarette, too?" I asked.

"I just gave you fifteen bucks. Go get your own."

We laughed together. Aunt B coughed and then said, "Okay then. Let's get some dinner."

I was outside shooting hoops one summer day between eighth grade and high school, happy about how my life had improved. Under the advice of Old Joe, I'd taken some initiative. A few months earlier, I was walking home from school and saw a bunch of guys outside of a neighbor's house doing construction. Some of them were carrying Sheetrock, tools, and other equipment. I saw that their trucks were dirty from all the dust around. I asked if I could wash their cars for six dollars each. They looked at each other and shrugged, "Why not." I did a good enough job that some of them hired me later to stack wood for the upcoming winter. I also raked leaves, cleaned gutters, and helped them haul heaps of garbage and old appliances to the local landfill. I made a few hundred bucks that summer. I started to understand that there were reliable connections between good choices and good outcomes and bad choices and bad outcomes. It had taken a long time for me to internalize these connections because outcomes were so often delayed.

Mom and Shelly bought some lumber from these guys when they learned that heating a house with firewood was less expensive than central heating. They wanted me to wake up at five-thirty every morning to build a fire so that the house would be warm by the time Mom and Shelly got up to get ready for work at seven.

At first, I argued with them about my new chore. Shelly sat next to me and replied that she and Mom worked all day to pay the bills, and it was the least I could do as "the man of the house." I couldn't argue with that. I'd always thought of chores as something imposed on me, like a punishment or something. Now, I became aware that I had an important role in the family and household. Shelly told me I was getting older, and that it was time for me to take some more responsibility. She treated me like an adult, which I found both gratifying and annoying. I did this all winter, when temperatures would dip into the low thirties—frosty weather for Californians.

So, I'd wake up bleary-eyed and think to myself that my relationship with fire sure had changed since the episode with Edgar a few years ago. One time I got up at half past five, barely conscious, and built a fire. Then I walked into the bathroom, thinking about what school assignments I had due that day, and I realized it was Saturday. I groaned as I brushed my teeth, then put out the fire and went back to bed.

With the money I'd made, I paid the coach the debt I owed him for boxing lessons and still had some cash left over to buy a portable outdoor basketball hoop from Walmart. I set it up in the driveway.

I dribbled away.

The house was empty—Mom and Shelly had gone somewhere

with their friends that afternoon, and Hannah was at her dad's. Aunt B and Shelly's daughters were out, too. Mom and Shelly had invited me to tag along with them, but I said no way. I loved being home alone. It was tranquil, the opposite of chaos. I basked in the calm of the afternoon, shooting hoops and drinking lots of iced tea Shelly had made the day before.

When the phone rang inside, I ignored it, figuring whoever it was could just leave a message on the machine. But it kept ringing and wouldn't stop. I walked into the kitchen and wiped my forehead while I picked up the phone.

"Hello," I said.

"Rob." It was Mom. It sounded like she was stifling laughter. "Shelly was in an accident."

"What?" I asked. "Then why are you laughing?"

"Listen, hon," she said.

I could tell she was having trouble breathing, then I realized she was crying, not laughing.

Mom paused and then said: "Shelly was shot."

CHAPTER FIVE

Little Boy

Shortly after Mom had told me she was gay, I wondered what my friends and their parents would think. It was a different era—Britney Spears kissing Madonna was the edgiest thing on television, and kids regularly used *gay* as a synonym for *bad*. In the mid-2000s, more than half of all Americans reported that they believed same-sex marriage shouldn't be legal; by 2020, it dropped to 31 percent.[1] And Red Bluff, a rural, blue-collar town, was not exactly the most welcoming environment for gay couples.

Cristian—the friend who I'd drink tequila with while his chain-smoking mom was sequestered in her bedroom—was the first one I'd told. He was the most open-minded and curious of all the kids I hung out with. And his mom was the nicest (or, in any case, was the most

---

1   "LGBTQ+ Rights," Gallup, https://news.gallup.com/poll/1651/gay-lesbian-rights.aspx.

mentally checked out and least likely to care), so I felt like I could trust them first.

After I explained that Mom was gay, Cristian replied, "You're lucky, you know."

"Lucky . . . like winning the lottery? I mean, no one else you know has gay parents," I said, trying to figure out if he was joking or not.

"That's not true, there's that chubby kid a few blocks down. His mom lives with a woman, and some kids are saying she's probably a lesbo," Cristian said.

"Oh yeah, I remember seeing them all together at Burger King. Okay, so what's lucky about it?" I replied.

"Your mom is with a girl. Or a woman, or whatever. She's not going to bring random guys around. That's lucky," Cristian said.

I knew what he meant but didn't know how to respond. So, I just said, "Yeah. Shelly has been really cool."

Not that we always got along. Shelly and Mom sometimes tried to find "male role models" or "father figures" for me—a male co-worker, or the husband of one of their friends, or the brother of so-and-so. I hated this and resisted any discussion of it. I was a stubborn kid and didn't want adults designating yet another unreliable quasi-parent for me. I'd had enough of that.

Still, Mom's and Shelly's instincts were right—I did want a father figure. I just preferred to choose for myself who it would be. I'd constructed makeshift role models from fragments of pop culture and television and books. These distant idols were reliable—there was no risk of them disappearing from my life.

. . .

A couple hours after the phone call, one of Mom's friends picked me up to take me to the hospital. Mom was already at the emergency room. As her friend explained to me, Mom was in no condition to drive.

On the journey to the hospital, Mom's friend explained what happened.

Shelly and Mom had met up with several of their friends at an outdoor shooting range. They'd gone once before; this was their second time. One of their friends was firing her weapon, and it suddenly jammed. As she tried to figure out what was wrong, she carelessly moved the pistol around. Suddenly, the gun fired. Shelly was standing fifteen feet away, talking to a man and his young son. The bullet went straight into her lower back. Had Shelly not been standing there, the bullet would likely have killed the boy.

When we got to the hospital, I saw that Mom was still in tears. I hugged her while she explained that Shelly was in surgery. Some of their friends were in the waiting room, too. I asked why they wanted to learn how to shoot guns. They replied that sometimes women can be vulnerable, so they were learning how to protect themselves. For some reason, that made me think about boxing classes, and how we have to purposely put ourselves in danger to learn how to protect ourselves. I was thinking and overthinking, trying to keep my mind occupied.

Shelly's daughters had arrived a bit later and brought my sister with them. Hannah and I were sitting on opposite sides of Mom in the waiting room, holding her hand and giving her tissues. Mom then whispered to us that she hadn't prayed since she lived with Grandma and Grandpa as a kid, but she asked us to pray with her that Shelly would be okay. We said a quiet prayer together. It reminded me of when we'd visit my grandparents' house and Grandma would pray before dinner. That had always comforted me. Mom promised God that if Shelly lived, she would start going to church again.

Hours had passed. The doctor told Mom and me that we could see Shelly later, but that for now only her daughters could go inside the room to visit her. I asked why, and Mom glanced at me. The doctor looked at both of us and said that only family could go inside.

"Aren't we family?" I asked.

"Yes, but not legally," Mom said.

We walked back to the waiting room. I was fuming. I knew that Shelly's daughters were related to her by blood and that was why they could go inside to visit her. *But Mom and Hannah are not my blood relatives*, I thought.

Would I get to visit them if something happened? Would anyone visit me if something happened to me? I refused to accept this stupid rule about "family."

When Mom had finally fallen asleep, I got up and quietly walked into Shelly's room. I immediately wished I hadn't. Shelly was unconscious, with tubes in her arms and down her throat. I couldn't believe this had happened to her. Yesterday she was totally fine, and now she was on the edge of death. How was this happening? I was terrified that Shelly wouldn't survive. I felt great affection for her. I had been rejected by other parental figures, yet Shelly chose to care for me. My heart was pounding in my chest, my throat was closing, and I felt like I couldn't breathe. Still, I refused to let myself cry. I was at war with myself, trying not to feel what my body was feeling.

Sometimes actions and outcomes are linked, I thought. But sometimes, shit just happens.

Two months had passed since Shelly was discharged from the hospital with spinal cord damage. I alternated between feeling numb and distraught after the shooting, and I felt this need to prove to the world, and to myself, that I hadn't been affected by what had happened.

At school, I got into an argument with a kid named Jared. I'd never gotten along with him. In middle school, he called a Black kid the N-word and the kid responded by punching Jared in the face. His favorite band was Insane Clown Posse and he talked about girls and sex nonstop even though he'd never had a girlfriend. We were arguing about something unimportant and I was trying to find a way to get him pissed off enough to fight me. I looked at Jared's jersey.

"What does the fourteen stand for? The number of dicks you sat on?" I said.

He immediately got in my face and grabbed my shirt. After shoving each other and exchanging headlocks, I punched him three times, and he fell to the ground. I went to help him up, extending my hand, when his friend ran over and kicked my hand away. I was startled by how much it stung, until I saw that my attacker was wearing steel-toed boots.

Throughout the week, my index finger had become swollen and immobile. I didn't tell anyone except my friends because I didn't want to get in trouble for fighting. I concealed my hand by gingerly putting it into the pocket of my hoodie or covering it with my other hand. I didn't do any of my schoolwork for a couple of weeks because I couldn't write anything. I didn't even realize my finger was broken at first. My habit of disengaging from emotional pain had blunted my ability to feel physical pain. I sometimes pressed my inflamed purple finger against hard surfaces and discovered that, to some degree, I enjoyed the sensation. It forced me to concentrate on one acute feeling and ignore everything else.

Weeks later, my finger healed on its own. The rest of me remained unwell.

Well into my first year of high school, I was still reeling from seeing Shelly on the verge of death. I never told anyone I'd snuck into the hospital room to see her. Within a day or so, we learned that she would live. But it was unclear whether she would be able to regain full use of her legs. She had to attend physical therapy for the next several months. To get around, she used a walker with tennis balls on the bottom, like Grandpa did. It was hard for me to see her like this. To me, she'd always been a steady and reliable figure.

Mom would later say that after Shelly got shot, "Everything changed." There was a shift in the emotional configuration of our house. Of course, we all felt stressed and uncertain about Shelly's injury and recovery process. But bills were also accumulating because

Mom took time off work to help care for Shelly while she recovered, and Shelly was obviously unable to work. Anxiety over money and responsibilities permeated the house. On top of all this, Mom and Shelly were frustrated by their interactions with the shooter and her insurance company. As a result of the contentious discussions concerning money, their friendship with the shooter had grown cold. Shelly was trying to recover, and Mom was trying her best to help her, and both were doing their best to keep the family financially afloat. Gradually, the routines that were so crucial for me in middle school had dissipated.

Shelly had typically been the one to cook, so family dinners stopped. We started using the microwave a lot, and Mom supplemented frozen meals with Top Ramen, Shasta sodas, and toaster pastries (generic Pop-Tarts from Walmart). I drank soda and ate snacks, sometimes because I was hungry, sometimes out of boredom, and sometimes to distract myself from my feelings. Hannah was spending more and more time at her dad's. I missed her, but I didn't blame her. I figured she was trying to get away from the family turmoil in the aftermath of the shooting.

At school, I tried to remember what Old Joe and others had told me about how up until now, my grades had been a "trial run," and that my academic performance in high school was what really counted. But my grades took a nosedive.

I just couldn't bring myself to exert the effort required to excel in school. I was absolutely devastated and didn't know how to express this to anyone. I didn't even know exactly what it was that I was feeling. I was in the midst of adolescence, when the body delivers a massive dose of hormones. A messed-up childhood, family tragedy, distracted parents, and puberty. This potent cocktail guaranteed that I would talk to no one about what I was feeling and find other ways to cope instead.

In the middle of my freshman year, Shelly and I talked a little about what had happened. I asked how she was doing. She was in a recliner in the living room.

"I'm going to be okay, Rob," she said, muting the TV. "I just thank God it was me and not you."

"What do you mean—why would you say that?" I asked.

"Your mom and I wanted you to come with us that day, but you wanted to be on your own," she said.

"I forgot about that," I said quietly. In the foster homes, I'd always wanted to have a family and stay close with them, but now, ironically, being separated had kept me safe. "They told me you were standing in front of a little boy, and that he would have been killed if you weren't standing there. You saved that kid."

I stayed with her for a little while longer. When I noticed she'd fallen asleep, I walked outside to buy cigarettes and weed from my neighbor.

My neighbor was this tall dude with glasses who lived nearby. I met him at the school bus stop during my first week of high school.

"You must be a freshman, right?" he asked.

"Yeah man," I said. "How about you?"

"I'm a sophomore."

He looked a little old for a sophomore. I was about to ask if he'd been held back but figured it was none of my business. I later learned he wasn't a student at all. He'd dropped out and would hang out at high-school bus stops looking for prospective customers. I looked at the headphones around his neck and saw the outline of a portable CD player in the pocket of his hoodie. "What are you listening to?" I asked him.

"Nelly," he said. He pulled out a cigarette. *Smoking at the bus stop?* I thought. This guy must be hard-core.

"You want one?" He pointed his pack to me.

"I'm good," I said, looking around. "Can I get one later?"

"I can get you whatever you need." He told me where he lived and when I could drop by.

The kids in the neighborhood called him Julius, even though it wasn't his real name. I asked him if it was his middle name and he said no; he got the name because he'd had a seizure as a kid, and one of his friends called him Julius Seizure. It then got shortened to Julius. I went to his place every so often to get cigarettes, weed, and sometimes booze. Occasionally, Julius gave me some hydrocodone (generic Vicodin) or Triple C cold medicine hoping I'd come back and buy some more. A few years later, California enacted laws restricting sales of certain kinds of cold medicine to minors because they were so widely abused to get high.

One day I was walking from school to a nearby park before Muay Thai class. Once I left the view of the school so that teachers couldn't see me, I pulled out a joint and started smoking.

"Yo, is that you, Rob? Wait up, man!"

I glanced over my shoulder and saw Tyler, a kid from one of my classes. With everything going on in my life, I didn't want new friends and definitely didn't feel like talking to Tyler today.

"Rob!" he kept calling. He ran and caught up next to me.

"Hey man," he said.

"Hey," I replied blankly. "What's up?"

"Not much, bro. Can I share that?" Tyler asked. "I'll pay you back tomorrow."

Tyler was a tough kid who spent a lot of time in the high school weight room. He looked sort of like a young, muscular Alec Baldwin. I didn't know if I could trust him to actually pay me back. I had plenty of weed though, and figured he might be a future contact to get more later.

We finished the joint off.

He took out a pocketknife and cut a hole into an empty Rockstar can to use it as a pipe. I pulled out some more weed I'd bought that morning from my neighbor.

We sat at a picnic table in a local park, took a few hits, and talked for a while. First about school and girls, and later about more personal stuff. I gave him vague answers about my family life, and I appreciated that he didn't seem to notice how guarded I was. That school year, we were in the same circle of friends.

Tyler had never met his dad, who had been arrested many times, mostly for drug-related offenses, and was now in jail for stabbing someone. His mom was a drug addict, and he hadn't seen her in years. He lived with his grandma, whom he sometimes called Mom, on the outskirts of Red Bluff, which was basically the middle of nowhere. One night when he stayed over, I showed him a clip from an old Chris Rock stand-up special where he said, "If a kid calls his grandma 'mommy,' and his mama 'Pam,' he's going to jail." Tyler thought this was hilarious.

One of my other good friends, John, and his brother Tom lived with their dad, who had been divorced five times. Their mom lived in Sacramento. She left their dad after learning that he'd been cheating on her with multiple women.

Cristian, at this point, still lived with his mom. He had lost all contact with his dad, who had recently been arrested again.

Antonio was our only friend who lived with both of his birth parents. His dad was a middle-school teacher, and they lived in a nice house in town. They had a spacious living room with high ceilings, a large kitchen, and an in-ground swimming pool in their backyard. Antonio played football for the school and was generally well liked. His parents were not so involved in his life, though. He never had to check in with them or anything when he'd hang out with us, and his grades were as bad as ours even though his dad was a teacher. There were rumors that his dad was cheating on his mom, but we never knew for sure.

Once I was walking to a party with Antonio and a girl he'd been seeing for a few days. Along the way we ran into some of her friends. One of them pulled out a baggie of cocaine and asked if we wanted to do "a gummie." I asked what that was. She licked her finger, put it in the bag, and then rubbed it along her gums with her fingertip, like people do when they forget their toothbrush.

Not long after that, I was hanging out with one of these girls, Sarah, at her place. We were both sophomores by this point. Her mom usually had random guys over, sometimes more than one at a time—just like my birth mother had done. Sarah told me that ever since she was a little girl, her mom had been like that. We were chilling on the couch watching *Lost* when she pulled out a bag of meth. She asked if I wanted to try. I'd always been grossed out by the stench. Once again I said no thanks and rolled a joint while she smoked.

My friends and I were impressed when Cristian told us he got a job at a local sandwich shop. This was really something to us. Even though we got into mischief, we still wanted to be seen as mature. Being called "immature" was a big insult. Maturity, for us, meant something like being able to drive, having access to drugs and beer, and having a job. It meant you weren't just a kid anymore. Maturity meant having the means and the freedom to get into trouble. It meant not having to ask permission to do anything—it almost meant the same thing as "cool." That was our adolescence: precocity followed by arrested development. Fifteen-year-olds acting like they were twenty-one, and twenty-one-year-olds acting like they were fifteen.

Seeing Cristian get a job was motivating. I wanted to get one too so I could save up for a car. Cristian told me he got a job by just going to different places and asking for an application. Then he went into the businesses every week to "check in." After a few weeks, the sandwich shop interviewed him and then offered him the job. *That's it?* I thought. I could do that. I told Mom and Shelly my plan, and they supported it. They added, though, that I'd have to keep my grades up if I got a job. Fortunately, they were too distracted to keep track of that.

By this point, I'd been hiding my report cards from Mom and Shelly. We were visiting my grandparents when I realized my first sophomore report card was likely to arrive in the mail that day. I called Cristian and asked him to steal it from our mailbox. He walked all the way across town to fish my report card out and handed it over the next time I saw him.

I opened it and looked at my grades. Cs and Ds. I was pleasantly surprised that I wasn't failing anything. I walked into the kitchen and rummaged through the drawers, digging out some old documents with Mom's signature on them. I went back to my room and practiced copying her handwriting. After a few tries, I forged Mom's signature on the report card to "acknowledge" that she had seen that I was in danger of failing, then I returned it to the school. These were the good old days, just a few years before parents could look up their kids' grades online.

I spent more time figuring out how to do just enough to pass classes than simply doing the assignments. I'd get an A on a test, look at the different weighted percentages for each type of assignment, and then try to figure out how much homework I'd be able to skip to still maintain a C-minus in the class.

There was a girl who sat in front of me in math class. We competed on the tests sometimes to see who could score higher. She earned a better score half the time, and I'd outscore on the other half. But at the end of the semester, she got an A in the class, and I got a C, because she did all the homework, and I did none. I would read the textbook and practice doing the math exercises. But I had no interest in getting a good grade—I simply wanted to pass the class.

I reverted to the same habits as my ten-year-old self. I slept during class, and my teachers sent me to sit outside or sent me off to sit in another class. Still, some teachers were surprised when they'd ask the class a question and I'd give the right answer. Once my history teacher asked me, "How did you know that?" because he'd asked a question from a chapter we hadn't yet read. I told him I'd read the textbook already, which was true. He told me to stay after class, and I figured he was going to chew me out for being a smartass.

After class, he asked me if what I had said about reading the textbook was true. When I said it was, he told me I had potential but was "letting my bad habits get the better of me." I knew what he meant, but I told him that I didn't see the point in trying harder.

"And what about your future?" he asked.

"Look, it's not like I'm going to college," I said.

"That is not written in stone, Rob. That is a choice you are making," he replied.

"Yeah, and that's fine," I said, walking out.

I did feel a little bad about this—he was a decent teacher. A few weeks later, one of my classmates asked him if being a teacher was hard work. He told us how his family had come to the US from Mexico and how he worked at a lumber mill until he was in his late twenties. Then he decided to go to college and become a teacher.

"This isn't 'work,'" our teacher told us. "I'm in an air-conditioned building, sipping coffee and reading books with you guys."

This was the first time I'd learned that the word *work* has different meanings depending on one's perspective. I also learned that it was possible to go to college much later in life. It held the possibility that maybe, someday, I could go, too.

. . .

One thing I didn't like was that my friends were in different classes than me. The high school had a "tracking" policy, meaning kids were placed on different academic paths based on grades and test scores. The school placed me in geometry, while my friends were in high school math. I went to biology, and they went to general science. Kids made a distinction between the "retard" classes, and the "prep" classes. My school registration forms had a little *p* next to each class, indicating that they were "preparatory" courses. By default, kids called the other classes the "retard" ones. I was placed into my classes on the strength of my grades and scores in middle school—back before Shelly had been shot, when I'd been performing well.

When Mom and Shelly saw this, they were pleased. They thought this meant I was succeeding. But gradually, my grades deteriorated. I was in the strange position of sharing classes with kids who got straight As and were college-bound when I was not. I was doing just enough to stay afloat because I thought if I failed anything, the school wouldn't let me graduate. Later, I discovered that if I'd done just a little worse, they would have moved me into the "retard" classes. Getting C-minuses kept me from being where I wanted to be—in the classes with my friends. There were periods when I considered whether it was even worth it to remain in school. But some part of me enjoyed learning, though I would not have acknowledged it. I definitely enjoyed being around my friends—in some ways I felt closer to them than my own family, not uncommon for teenagers. In fact, if they had all gotten kicked out of school, I suspect I would have tried to do so as well, simply so I could be around them more.

At first, it was isolating to be in the "prep" classes as someone who was not part of any of these kids' social groups. Over time, I got along well enough that I made friends with some of them. I found my place as a class clown.

Once, in English, a kid asked our teacher about the difference between "hung" and "hanged" and I announced, "Hung is when you have a huge cock!" while unfolding my arm and dropping it down on the desk. "You know where to go," the teacher said, pointing in the direction of the principal. In one English class, there was a really smart kid named Hugo I got along with. His parents were from Mexico and had a lot of money. At least, that was the impression I got because Hugo always wore nice clothes and his parents were paying for his older brother to go to college. We'd visit the high school weight room together after school to work out and talk about class readings and girls and sports.

Hugo was a better influence on me than I was on him. We later had another class together. One day our teacher bent down over his desk to grab something, but then dropped the object and had to bend even farther. I handed Hugo a rubber band and dared him to hit the teacher's ass with it. Hugo grabbed it, took aim, and snapped it right on target. Our teacher immediately jumped up and saw that the entire row of students, including me, had buried our heads in our arms trying to stifle our laughter. He demanded to know who did it. Nobody said a word, so he sent the entire row of eight students to the principal's office. The principal individually spoke with each of us. He said that if we didn't tell him who had snapped the rubber band, then he would suspend all of us. But if we told him the truth, he would spare us. A real-life prisoner's dilemma. Hugo and I were relieved when no one ratted us out, and no one was suspended.

I'd somehow gotten through my biology class with a B-minus, and was subsequently placed into chemistry for my sophomore year. Chemistry was tough, even tougher than the advanced English class I'd taken. I neglected my assignments and slept through class. When my teacher, Mr. Nichols, handed out our first progress reports, I saw that, for the first time, I was actually failing a class. To pass, I'd have to put forth some actual effort. I'd have to study for the tests and commit to doing the assignments in a structured way, not just haphazardly. *No way*, I thought. *Not happening.*

My teacher Mr. Nichols said he would never travel farther south than Chico, which I found strange. I asked him why, and he replied that this part of California was "safe and cohesive" and suggested that bigger cities were dangerous. I was skeptical, because the Red Bluff I knew did not seem that safe. Later, I learned that Red Bluff is one of the most dangerous cities in California.[2]

Tyler was a little older than the rest of us and the first to get his driver's license. At sixteen, he could already grow a full beard. Meanwhile, me and the other guys were shaving even when we didn't have to.

---

2 "Red Bluff and Redding Top the List of Most Dangerous Cities in California," Action News Now, September 13, 2019.

It was Thursday, and I was out in the school parking lot with Tyler next to the car his uncle loaned him. He leaned over to me and quietly said, "I want a three-day weekend."

"What are you talking about?" I asked.

He pulled out a small chain from his car and wrapped it around his knuckles. He walked over to another kid a few parking spaces down who was leaning against his car with a couple of his friends.

The kid saw Tyler and me and spread his arms out. "What's up, man? You and your boyfriend got a problem?"

Tyler walked right up to this kid and punched him on the side of the head. The kid crumpled to the ground. A small crowd formed around us. A few kids started yelling, "Fight! Fight!" but when they saw what had happened, they stopped.

The kid tried to get up and fell down again, rubbing his ear. Blood was dripping out. I'd never seen anybody bleed from their ear before. I didn't even feel bad for the kid. Tyler was my friend, and all I thought was that he threw a solid punch. Some girls alerted a teacher nearby, who contacted the school nurse. Tyler didn't secure his three-day weekend. He got a full week's suspension instead.

During the week Tyler was suspended, he invited me to break into an office building with him. I brought Edgar and his brother Enrique, and we all met up in the middle of the night. Tyler grabbed a brick and broke one of the windows. We climbed into the building and began to destroy it. I saw a fire extinguisher in a glass case fixed to the wall. I broke the glass, grabbed the nozzle, and sprayed everywhere. Edgar took it from me and sprayed some more. We breathed in the chemicals, which tasted like salt. Enrique threw chairs and vases across the room. Tyler took a few swigs of vodka and then shattered the bottle on the floor. I thought about the fire extinguisher cabinet, "In case of emergency, break glass."

I filled out applications for Taco Bell, Grocery Outlet, and a few other places. Then every week I visited each business, like Cristian suggested, asking if they'd had a chance to look at my application. Eventually, I landed a job at a local Italian restaurant as a busboy and dishwasher. This job sucked about as much as you would expect. Still, it was better than all the manual-labor jobs I'd done before because it was indoors.

And I liked my coworkers. Most were in their early twenties, some in their thirties. My manager, Jim, was a small guy with a mustache who was in his forties. During my interview with him, he explained that he had been in prison but that the owner of the restaurant thought he deserved a second chance and hired him to manage the restaurant. Jim was very loyal to the owner because of this. He worked harder than anyone I'd ever met to ensure that the restaurant operated smoothly.

Jim's commitment rubbed off on me. I approached tables after guests left, collected dirty dishes, and wiped the tables and seats down. It was simple, mindless work, but it was surprisingly difficult to keep up on busy nights. Only one dishwasher was ever on shift and sometimes we'd have sixty patrons dining in on a Friday night. I had a cart with large rubber containers I'd bring out to the tables and devised a system for placing each type of dish (plates, pizza pans, etc.) in each rubber container to minimize the number of trips I'd have to make. I remembered in the book *Down and Out in Paris and*

London, George Orwell said working as a cook in a busy restaurant was like racing to sort a deck of cards against the clock—the task is easy, but the time constraints make it hard. Being a dishwasher and busboy was no different.

When work slowed down, I'd daydream about the future. I'd see patrons who were "rich," meaning they drove a car less than five years old, and think how someday I'd drive a nice car like them, too. Maybe I would also have a big house. Actually no, I didn't care much about living in a big house, but I knew Mom and Shelly would like that. So, I'd buy one for them, and I would just have a place big enough to fit some weights and other gym equipment, with a garage for my car. How I planned on making all this money, I had no idea. But I liked thinking about it. That was where my mind was: the immediate present or the distant future without a bridge in between, but never the past. I didn't like thinking about the past.

On breaks, all my conversations with coworkers eventually turned to the topic of money, or lack of it. We would fantasize about what we would do if we suddenly struck it rich (a few co-workers played the lottery): vacations, cars, a house by the beach. I was making minimum wage, which was then $6.75 an hour. Jim and the owner noticed how efficiently I worked and gave me three raises within the first two months. I was earning more than some of the pizza makers.

Even though the job wasn't the best, I liked that it gave me a reason to not be at home. Mom and Shelly hadn't been getting along, and I could sense the negativity in the house. I volunteered for every extra shift and worked on both Saturdays and Sundays. I liked that I was making my own money, and I especially liked getting tips. When I'd bus the tables, I'd collect the tips left by patrons and stuff them into my apron. Then, at the end of the shift, I'd pull out these dollar bills from my apron, soaking wet from an evening of washing dishes, and split them with my coworkers.

With this job, I was able to pay for driver's-ed classes to get my license. And beyond that, I still had my sights set on a car.

Between school, the job, and screwing around with my friends, I felt like I never had enough time, and something had to be sacrificed. I chose school.

Which meant I needed to get out of this stupid chemistry class.

At lunch with my friend John, I asked him, "Dude, what class are you taking for a science credit this semester?"

"It's called like 'nutritional science' or something. It's easy as fuck," he said.

"Is there homework? What do you guys actually do?"

"We copy definitions of words from the textbook. We sometimes have to answer some questions at the end of the chapters. Then on Fridays we get to cook," he said. "Last week we made some pasta thing."

This was blowing my mind. "You are literally copying words from a book and cooking. That's the class?" I raised my eyebrows.

"Yeah," he said, laughing. "It's stupid. I have an A, and I don't do shit."

I visited my high school advisor's office and explained that I wanted to switch out of chemistry. He tried to talk me out of it, saying that it would throw me off my "academic trajectory." I told him that was fine, and he gave me a form.

I was also reading a lot of books during this time, and I was drawn mostly to memoirs by people who had lived tough lives. I read *Black Boy* by Richard Wright, *This Boy's Life* by Tobias Wolff, and *Daughter of Joy*, about a Chinese woman who worked as a prostitute in San Francisco during the Gold Rush. I found these books in the school library, which I'd browse alone before or after school. Whenever I felt down, it was soothing to read about others who had experienced hardship and found ways to rise above it. It seemed like whenever something good happened in my life, something bad was right around the corner. Then I'd read a few pages of a book, and I'd remember I was not alone. If, instead, I'd read stories (or scrolled images) of people living wonderful lives without any setbacks, it might have just led me to feel sorry for myself.

As far as I knew, I was the only one among my friends who regularly read books on my own. Although I didn't exactly hide my reading habit, I didn't advertise it either. I didn't want anyone to accuse me of being smart, because that would mean I would have to acknowledge that I wasn't living up to my potential. I wanted to keep expectations low, both from others and from myself.

More than a year after her injury, Shelly had mostly recuperated and regained use of her legs. Not completely, though—she would have to use a walking stick sometimes, and a wheelchair for long distances.

Seeing how she carried herself with determination throughout her recovery was both painful and moving. I saw how devoted Mom was to Shelly as she helped her. Even though they would argue and yell, they unfailingly tried to reassure Hannah and me that everything would be okay. I rarely believed them, but I wanted to. I loved them for saying it.

At last, Shelly had received a large insurance settlement from the shooting. She and Mom never mentioned the specific amount. I figured it was a few hundred thousand dollars, given what they bought: a new truck for Shelly, a Ford Mustang for Mom, and a motorboat they kept docked at a marina at Shasta Lake. In Red Bluff, having a new boat and a new Ford Mustang was really something. Mom let me drive it as practice for my driver's-ed classes. Out of the corner of my eye, I could see how nervous she was during our practice sessions. I tried to be as careful as possible, hoping that after I got my license, she would let me drive it by myself.

For Christmas, Mom and Shelly gave Hannah and me wrapped gifts that turned out to be prepaid Motorola cell phones. These types of phones had become common around this time in 2005 among my classmates and friends. Months earlier, I'd asked Mom and Shelly about getting one. As I opened the box, they explained that I would be responsible for any fees to load minutes onto my phone, and that it would cost ten cents to send and receive text messages. I nodded and glanced at the wheelchair in the corner of the living room that Shelly sometimes had to use. Yeah, we had this financial windfall, money was no longer a problem, and we had these neat trinkets. But the cost was the total emotional upheaval of the family. I looked down at my new phone, happy that I had it and wishing I didn't.

Mom and Shelly also bought three houses in Red Bluff. One was for us to move into and two were investments to "flip." They had agreed that the family should move into another home as a way to "start over." But they strongly disagreed about what to do with the rest of the insurance settlement.

Shelly was more of a risk taker—she enjoyed visiting casinos, and whenever we played Monopoly during "bored game" nights, she always tried to buy up as much property as she could. Shelly was adamant that they should invest in real estate, but Mom was more cautious and thought they should put the money into savings. Shelly explained to Mom how safe the real estate market was and how they could easily double or triple their initial investment. Mom was skeptical but had heard that many Californians were striking it rich by buying up houses. The new gold rush.

Our new home was by far the nicest I'd ever lived in—it was a two-story house, which I'd always associated with rich people. It had a spacious kitchen, a laundry room bigger than any bedroom I'd ever had before, and bathrooms both upstairs and downstairs. The house also had an in-ground swimming pool in the backyard. Some of my classmates from school had aboveground pools, but everybody knew that wasn't the same as having a real pool. When I first entered the backyard, I gazed at the crystal-clear blue water. I inhaled the chlorine smell and my mind flashed back to when I nearly drowned at the Martínez house all those years ago, but then I stopped myself—I didn't want to dwell on those memories for too long. Instead, I thought of how great it would be to have a pool party here with my friends.

Mom and Shelly expected to make a lot of money by selling the other two homes they'd bought. These houses required some upkeep, and I wanted to help out, so I'd stop by both homes every week to rake the leaves and mow the lawns. Shelly explained that both houses would likely be sold within two or three months at the most, and I didn't mind doing the extra work for that amount of time.

But three months passed, and there were no buyers.

Mom was livid. "Tell me how you got these," she said. She was holding a pack of Marlboro Reds.

"I found them on the ground on the way home from school," I replied. I wasn't going to tell her where I really got them.

Earlier that day I had been hanging out by my locker with my friend Edgar.

"Yo, dude," he said. "That's the fucking vice principal over there. He's coming right towards us. Can you put these in your locker or what, man?" Edgar was holding two gym bags filled with weed, pills, cigarettes, and God knows what else. He was sweating bullets, paranoid that people could sense that he was carrying contraband. But his flop sweat and darting eyes weren't just nerves. He looked high on something.

"Yeah, man, whatever," I said. I took his bags and put them in my locker. They were heavier than I expected. I was about to ask what was in them but stopped myself. Instead, I asked, "Why do you have all this shit, anyway?"

"It's for my brother Enrique. They need him to deliver it," Edgar replied. Enrique had been trying to join a gang.

I didn't feel great about having this in my locker, but figured if I needed a contact for any of this stuff later, I could hit these guys up. Maybe I'd get a discount or get something for free since I was doing a favor here for Enrique and Edgar. Later that day I met up with Enrique to give him the bags. He said thanks and stuffed a pack of Marlboros into the side of my backpack.

After school I went to work. On my break, I went outside to join my coworkers for a smoke. They knew I was underage, but nobody cared. Sometimes one of the pizza makers bought my friends and me booze and didn't even charge us extra. That same guy asked if he could get a smoke, and I told him where my backpack was.

After work, I walked home. When I stepped into the house, Mom immediately saw the pack of cigarettes sticking out of my backpack pocket. My coworker must not have pushed the pack all the way down, and I hadn't bothered to check.

We argued for a while. Mom and Shelly told me how stupid I was to be smoking. I tried to explain that it wasn't that big of a deal, but I understood why they were upset.

"Look, I know smoking is bad," I said. "I know a lot of stuff is bad. I just don't care."

They grounded me and took my phone. *I'll have to be more careful*, I thought. I couldn't hang out with my friends while I was grounded, so in the meantime, I asked for more hours at work.

In addition to grounding me, Mom and Shelly enlisted me to

help spruce up the houses more because they still didn't have any potential buyers.

The next day, we visited Target to get house paint and other supplies. I'd been quiet for most of the afternoon, trying not to say anything else that might get me into more trouble. The night before, I was listening to the radio show *Loveline*, and one of the cohosts, Dr. Drew Pinsky, explained that statistically, each time a person gets pulled over by a police officer for drinking and driving, there are at least eighty other instances that the person decided to drink and drive but didn't get caught. I thought about how many times I'd done something that would infuriate Mom and Shelly, and yet this incident with the cigarettes was one of the few times I'd gotten caught. I wondered what they would think if they really knew what I'd been up to and felt glad to have been caught only for this relatively minor infraction.

While we were at Target, Shelly had been having back pain and decided to use one of the store's electric wheelchairs.

I was looking at some clothes, about twenty yards away from Shelly, when I saw her sitting in her wheelchair, leaning over to touch a bookshelf. As Shelly pressed forward on the shelf, we realized it was actually *two* shelves, one stacked on top of the other. The top shelf fell over. Suddenly, I heard a loud *thud!* as the shelf toppled and a corner slammed into Shelly's head. Shelly jumped up from her chair. Mom ran toward her to see if she was okay.

She wasn't. Blood began to spurt from her scalp like a sprinkler. Droplets spread around the store's glossy flooring. People around us stared, unsure what to do. Mom was frozen, shocked at what was happening. My sister had a hand over her mouth, and I could tell she was scared. I was scared. I looked around and grabbed some nearby towels off a rack and ran over to hand them to Mom. She held them against Shelly's head. The white towels quickly turned to red while store employees rushed to call an ambulance.

We waited at the emergency room while the doctors examined Shelly. Mom and Hannah were silent, but I was pretty sure they were thinking what I was: *What the fuck just happened and why would something so awful happen to Shelly so soon after she had been shot?* It felt, for me, like further evidence that the world was fundamentally unstable, and that giving any thought to my future was senseless. Mom was strangely silent, and I was surprised that she made no mention of prayer or God. I tried and failed to stop thinking about that blood spraying everywhere. I couldn't get that horrifying image out of my mind.

A few minutes later, Mom said that she wished she'd had a camera to take photos of what had happened for insurance purposes.

"Mom, your phone has a camera," my sister said, pointing at Mom's flip phone.

"Oh, you're right," Mom said. "The pictures come out all blurry though."

The doctors gave Shelly a few staples in her scalp, an ice pack, and some painkillers, and told us she would be fine. Apparently, minor head injuries can cause a lot of bleeding, and can appear more serious than they really are.

. . .

For my friends and me, it seemed like half our waking hours were spent trying to find booze or weed or God knows what else. For the girls we knew, their mission to get drunk or high was seldom as hard to accomplish. There was no shortage of predatory twenty-three-year-old guys on motorcycles who were more than happy to supply drugs and alcohol to a fifteen-year-old girl.

For groups of girls aimlessly walking around, "fun" would find them in the form of a guy who had graduated high school five years earlier and rode a beat-up dirt bike. At the time, that made sense to me. If some twenty-three-year-old woman had pulled up to my friends and me and offered us some booze to come chill with her, we would have leapt at the opportunity. But that doesn't happen for boys. We had to go out ourselves and find the "fun." It was an endless quest, and our conversations went something like:

"What about Sean's cousin? He's twenty-one. Maybe he'll hook us up?"

"Nah, every time we give him cash to buy us beer, he takes like half the case for himself. Fucker is a thief."

"What about the guy from Cristian's work? We bought weed from him in the parking lot before."

"Nah, he's on probation or something. Too sketched out to sell to minors right now."

"What if we just waited by Circle K and offered to give someone money to buy for us?"

"Dude, I've heard that cops go undercover and try to bust kids for buying booze like that all the time. My aunt calls it 'entrapment.'"

"Rob, what about your neighbor Julius? He's hooked us up before."

"He got his stuff from his stepdad, but they got into a fight. Last time I saw him, his arms were all cut up and shit. He told me his stepdad threw him through a glass door."

"Well, shit."

Months later, I walked home from work and saw an unfamiliar car parked in front of my house. I still detested the sight of strange vehicles in the driveway—holdover feelings from my experiences in foster care, when an unknown car often signaled a surprise visit by a social worker coming to take me to another home.

The car was a 1992 Ford Escort. Mom was washing it.

"What's this?" I asked. "Don't tell me you're planning to trade in the Mustang for this clunker."

"Careful," Mom said. "Don't let Shelly hear you say that."

"Okay, why are you washing this car?" I asked.

"I was hoping it would be ready when you got here," Mom said.

I realized then that the car was for me. Thrilled, I thanked Mom and walked inside the house to thank Shelly. They explained that they'd negotiated a good price for the car, and that I'd have to pay for the insurance, the gas, any repairs it might need, and so on.

This was a given; it had never crossed my mind to ask them for financial help with car expenses. I'd saved up most of my earnings over the last few months at my job.

As soon as Mom handed me the keys, I went to pick up Tyler and John, and we took a long ride. Both of them were already driving by this point, so it wasn't that big a deal to them. But for me it was the freest I'd felt in a long time.

Tyler, sitting in the passenger's seat, pulled out a plastic squeeze bottle from his backpack.

"What is that?" I asked.

"Vodka," he said. "Don't worry, guys, I brought enough for the class." He took a swig, twisted the cap back on, and handed it to me.

"No fucking way, dude. I literally just got this car," I said, snatching the bottle and tossing it into the backseat with John. "Keep this back there."

I thanked Mom and Shelly again for the car when I got home that night, and they reminded me to be careful when driving. Hannah announced she would be old enough to get her license in a few years, and asked if she could practice driving my car.

"Yeah, whenever you want," I replied, tossing her the keys.

Mom glared at us. "Absolutely not," she said. "Give me those keys now."

"They're joking," Shelly said.

Mom rolled her eyes, and we all laughed. Shelly cooked, and during family dinner we sat around the table, and I told them how much I liked my car. Even though the mood was pleasant, Mom still looked worried. I reassured her that of course I wouldn't let Hannah take my car out, but her expression remained unchanged.

"I would lie awake in bed at night for months, because I knew this day would come," Mom said.

We were sitting in the living room of the biggest house I had ever lived in, and I learned that it had been a temporary dream.

Eight months had passed, and the two houses Mom and Shelly had intended to flip had still not sold. Shelly and Mom had run out of money. The year 2005 was the right time to invest in houses in California, they said. But not 2006. They explained that all our homes were being foreclosed, and that we had to leave Red Bluff.

CHAPTER SIX

Stray Dogs

"I knew we'd find some good stuff in this neighborhood," said the new owner of our family sofa.

I glared at him as I helped lift it into the bed of his truck at the end of our driveway. He handed me the cash, which I gave to Mom. Ten months earlier, we'd moved into a dream house, and now, with my final year of high school about to begin, it was nearly empty. We were having a massive yard sale—the biggest I'd ever seen—with furnishings from each of the three houses Mom and Shelly had mortgaged.

They explained their new plan to Hannah and me: we would relocate to the Bay Area because there were more job opportunities. This made sense, but I also had the feeling that they wanted to leave Red Bluff to escape the ignominy both of the shooting incident and their ruinous investments in real estate. Mom and Shelly were clearly ready to relocate; they had already found a mobile home in a trailer park in a low-income neighborhood in San Jose. Because they wouldn't have space in their cramped mobile unit, and because they needed the money, Mom and Shelly sold everything: the boat, one of the cars, the flat-screen TV (a hot-ticket item in 2006), and the furniture. I spent a few days helping with the yard sale, lifting the heavy items, and watching the material goods of our life being exchanged for cash.

On the final day, I walked through the house. I felt a sense of vertigo as I registered its emptiness. I walked through the backyard and looked at the sprinkler system I had helped install the summer prior, spending several days digging ditches in the scorching heat to lay PVC pipe around the edge of the fence. I looked up at the window of my bedroom on the second floor and wondered what my new room in San Jose would be like. Thinking about the prospect of another move, I realized then that I was not going to leave Red Bluff. I wasn't going with Mom and Shelly.

"Where would you stay, hon?" Mom asked.

"John's dad says it would be okay if I lived with them," I replied.

I had my arguments ready, mostly focusing on the fact that I only had one year left of high school, and that my friend John's house would be a suitable and safe place for me. John's dad was a retired cop and military veteran, and he had already granted me permission to stay with them. He was impressed that I'd recently talked my manager at the restaurant into giving John a job as a pizza maker. He also knew that I had recently urged John to ask a girl from school out, and now they were dating. So, John's dad considered me a positive influence. A low bar, given our friend group.

The year before, I was sleeping over at John's house, and we decided to go out looking for something fun to do. Sometimes John, his brother Tom, and I would go to the train tracks behind Walmart and play "chicken." When we heard a train approaching, we'd stand on the tracks. Whoever jumped off the tracks first was the "loser." Sometimes the loser would have to cough up more money for beer or buy everyone Taco Bell.

Shortly after John got his license, we took his truck on the freeway.

"Hell yeah," John said, suddenly swerving the truck onto the dirt on the side of the I-5.

"Dude, what are you doing?" I asked, looking around from the passenger's seat.

"Look, man." He pointed to the enormous mounds of dirt around us. "Dirt jumps."

"Let's do it," I said.

The truck was an old Dodge. I don't recall the model, but it did have four-wheel drive. John gunned it off a dirt jump but we didn't get much air.

"That was pathetic," John said. "We need more speed."

John was determined to get all four wheels off the ground no matter what. After a few more false starts, we finally found the right dirt mound and got enough speed to launch into the air. I rolled down the window and looked down at the ground as we achieved liftoff. My stomach dropped, and I quickly gripped the side handle above the window as we descended. We gave no thought to the danger of what we were doing or whether people driving by on the freeway would see us. We focused solely on the thrill.

John and Tom, in their aim to get their dad to agree to let me stay, reminded him that I rarely got into serious trouble at school. A more honest statement would have been that I was simply caught less often. When I hung out at their house, John's dad would sometimes say, "If you don't open your mouth, then no one will know you're stupid." John and I had learned on our own that, similarly, if you don't get caught, then no one will know you're a troublemaker.

After a long conversation with John's dad, Mom agreed I could stay with his family. Shelly and Mom said they believed I was better off in a familiar environment. They also alluded to how small the trailer park in San Jose was, which may have also played a role in their willingness to let me stay in Red Bluff.

"To be honest, Rob," Shelly said, "it might be better for you to live with some guys."

She and Mom had never gotten over my rejecting their offers each time they broached the idea of finding a "father figure" for me. I was just glad to hear them agree with the plan.

I asked my sister what she was going to do. She was irritated that I even asked and said that of course she was staying with her dad here in Red Bluff. I was relieved, because that meant I could keep an eye on her as she started high school.

I asked her how she felt about Mom and Shelly moving to San Jose. She shrugged.

"They can do whatever they want," she said. "I'm staying."

Even though he had a background in law enforcement, John's dad was an extremely laissez-faire parent. He worked all the time in his private investigator job and had recently been divorced for the fifth time. From my perspective, he was more of a buddy than a father figure—there was a kind of "don't ask, don't tell" policy in the house. We could do whatever we wanted, as long as he wasn't made too aware of it. John and Tom told me I was lucky because their stepmom had just left, and she would not have let me stay with them for a whole year. Plus, their stepbrother had moved out, which freed up a room in the house for me. I asked John and Tom if they missed their stepfamily, and they said no, describing how each time their dad got remarried, they never got too attached to any of their new family members because they didn't expect it to last long. I knew what that was like.

For our final year of high school, John and I took an auto-shop class for first period. We genuinely intended to learn more about cars, but it didn't pan out. Because we usually stayed up all night playing basketball, drinking, playing video games, or figuring out ways to get into trouble, we got to class totally exhausted. The classroom was in a separate campus building, attached to a large repair shop. We typically spent the first few minutes of class answering questions from the textbook and the rest of class in the shop working on cars. One morning I drove my car onto one of the car lifts in the shop, and John raised it up. I was in the driver's seat and reclined all the way back. I sipped fruit punch–flavored Gatorade (with vodka mixed in) and fell asleep for the entire period.

John took his car on the lifts, too, and we both just slept through class. This became a routine. The teacher eventually caught on to what we were doing and told us to knock it off. Fortunately, he never learned about the drinking.

If you leave a group of seventeen-year-old boys alone long enough, something will usually happen.

John and I tricked Tyler, my friend who lived with his grandmother, into thinking his car had been stolen. John purposely left something in Tyler's car so he could nonchalantly borrow his car keys to retrieve it. He then handed the keys to me to make a copy at a local key shop. Three days later, John and I took the copied key and parked Tyler's car across town. When Tyler discovered that his car was not where he'd parked it, he began fuming and shouting, "Someone stole my car!" John and I barely contained our laughter, giving the game away. Tyler couldn't believe the lengths we went to in order to pull off this little prank.

But sometimes our pranks were more extreme. A few weeks after the car prank, we did something more gratuitously stupid.

"Where's Max?" I asked, looking through John's fridge for another Keystone Light. Maybe my sixth or seventh one that day.

"He's sleeping in his room. He has work tomorrow," John replied.

Max was one of our friends who had moved in with us a few days ago because his dad and stepmom kicked him out.

"How can we mess with him?" I asked, sipping my beer.

"I have fireworks." Tom opened his backpack to show us.

I started going through the kitchen cabinets, searching for the biggest container. I pulled out a Crock-Pot.

"Shh." We carefully opened the door and heard Max snoring. John had the Crock-Pot full of fireworks. The plan was to light the fireworks, then lock Max inside his room. Tom had a set of bungee cords ready so that as soon as John and I stepped out, he could secure the door shut from the outside.

We lit the fireworks and, in the excitement, forgot to put the Crock-Pot lid on.

"Yoo, what the hell!" Max yelled.

John and I were giddy, running out of the room. Tom attached the bungee hook to keep the door shut.

"THIS IS BULLSHIT!!" Max frantically tried to open the door.

The three of us were on the ground laughing. Max eventually managed to open the door. He had burns on his arms, and he was holding a pistol with the safety off.

He never aimed the gun at any of us. Nothing more eventful happened that night. He just wanted us to know he was angry and could have killed us if he wanted. We genuinely felt bad for Max and bought him Taco Bell—his favorite food—to make up for it.

This is how my friends and I treated each other. There were plenty of other examples of stupidity. Taking baseball bats to taillights in parking lots. Driving around town shooting pedestrians and bicyclists with Airsoft or paintball guns. Somehow, we had all created a situation where the coolest person was the one who had most recently done the most dangerous thing. Before this fireworks incident, Max held the top spot because he had won a fight against some other kid at a party the weekend before. He'd had his turn at the top, but we couldn't let him stay for long. Now it was his turn to be humiliated.

Our diets were generally a disaster—SpaghettiOs, cold pizza, Pepsi, and cheap beer. Taco Bell, Arby's, Burger King, and Chef Boyardee were staples. There was also this amazing local burger joint called Bud's Jolly Kone, but we didn't visit too often because it was a little pricier than other fast food. Occasionally, we would visit a fancy restaurant with cloth napkins like Olive Garden or the Cheesecake Factory. We'd go to Subway if we felt like eating "healthy," which wasn't too often. We bought a deep fryer and would go weeks eating only deep-fried chicken strips, jalapeno poppers, and shoestring French fries or potato wedges.

The cold pizza came from work—sometimes the manager would give John and me free food at the end of the night, which we took home for a late dinner.

Despite the free pizzas, I wanted to quit my job at the restaurant. I had grown weary of washing dishes, to the point where the smell of tomato sauce made my stomach turn. I associated it with dirty dishes and half-eaten plates of pasta. The only time something exciting happened was when I was washing dishes, heard some glasses shatter, and looked out into the dining area. Two guys I knew from my high school were in a fistfight, and my manager broke it up and told them to leave or he'd call the cops.

A few weeks after moving in with John, I interviewed for a new job at a grocery store. They hired me, saying I could start in three weeks. I was so relieved—stocking shelves and bagging groceries were not the most glamorous tasks, but they beat scrubbing dishes and trying to get the smell of onions and garlic out of my fingernails.

I was a little nervous about telling my manager at the restaurant that I got a new job at a grocery store. I'd always gotten along well with Jim, and good-byes weren't easy for me. So, I was surprised at how well he took it.

"This is very good, Rob, very good," Jim said. "I know no one wants to be sweating their ass off in a steaming hot dish room. This is what you want in life. You want each job you get to be better than the job you had before."

Was there really such a big difference between washing dishes and bagging groceries? The reality was that I'd just moved from one menial, low-paying job to another. But thanks to Jim, I felt I was advancing in the world. I wanted that feeling again.

Between the end of my old job and the start of the new, my sister called.

She explained that a few days before, Mom and Shelly had suddenly arrived at her dad's house. They told Hannah to pack up her stuff, announcing that she was moving with them to San Jose. My sister said she had no forewarning of this, and that Mom, Shelly, and her dad had arranged it without asking her. Mom helped her pack a couple of suitcases, and off they went. Mom told Hannah they had already enrolled her in a school in San Jose.

Hannah was in disbelief. She generally preferred living with Mom, but she had not agreed to move to San Jose. She wanted to stay in Red Bluff and was clearly livid that she had not been given a choice. I knew Mom wanted her to live with them, so I wasn't entirely surprised. But Hannah then went on to say something that did surprise me.

"Rob, I've barely seen Mom this whole week," she said. "She's always over at her friend's house, and Shelly is always at a casino. I go to school, I come home, and I hardly ever see either of them."

"That's weird," I said. "But I doubt it has anything to do with you." It dawned on me that if anything, that situation must have been the same or even worse *before* Hannah moved in with them.

"Have you tried calling or texting Mom?" I asked.

"I text her all the time. She gets home pretty late, and we talk for a little bit, and then she goes to bed," Hannah replied. "I hate it here. I miss our old house—I miss Red Bluff."

"Okay. Maybe things will get better. I don't know," I said. "Do you want me to come visit?"

"Yeah," she said. "I was actually thinking about running away. Just like getting on a bus or something back to Red Bluff."

"Don't do that. I'll be there this weekend."

That week, I was at a party with my friends, and we were sitting around a fire. Someone was playing "Forgot About Dre" out of his car. He got out of the driver's seat and walked toward us, pulling out a pipe. It was crank.

A girl sitting next to me said, "Oh my God, be careful. That stuff gave me a heart attack a few months ago."

Earlier in the day, we figured we could invite a few people over to the middle of the woods on our friend Nick's parents' property. The house was in the middle of nowhere, so we thought we could have some beers, maybe set up a couple tents, and camp out for the night. Nick repeatedly stressed that his parents *could not* find out about what we were doing. They were still in the house.

Initially, we invited only about ten people to camp out. But then they texted all their friends, who texted more people, and so on. Pretty soon we were having to direct traffic away from his house so his parents wouldn't see what was happening. By ten that night, more than sixty people arrived, hearing that there was going to be a bonfire. Nick was freaking out, sure his parents were going to see a line of cars all along the property. Somehow, though, they didn't notice anything.

We kept redirecting people farther away, half a mile or so from his house, deep into the woods. Some guys started building a campfire.

"No! Don't do that, do not do that!" Nick shouted. He began pacing back and forth with his hands on his head. "My stepdad is going to kill us. He's definitely going to kill me."

The guys built a huge fire, ignoring Nick. I looked up and saw the smoke climbing up toward the sky. I pointed this out to Nick, and he replied that if his parents glanced out the window and saw smoke, then they would definitely call the cops or the fire department. I opened a beer, figuring that if we were going to get into serious trouble soon, we might as well enjoy the party while it lasted.

About two hours later, we were all sitting around the campfire.

"Wait, really?" I asked the girl next to me, circling back to her story. I didn't believe that people our age could have heart attacks.

"Yeah, so I smoked some crystal and had to go to the emergency room," she said.

"No, Kate, that is not what happened," her friend sitting nearby said. "You bought it from some guy, but it was a bad batch. He told us later that his dealer wanted to like poison him or something. So, the dealer gave him a batch that was supposed to kill him. But then the guy thought something was fishy about it, so he just sold it to people instead of smoking it. Kate bought some from him. But it wasn't really a heart attack, she just had trouble breathing."

"Sounds horrible," I said, feeling the effects of the alcohol kicking in.

We played a few rounds of beer pong and flip cup, and I became progressively more impaired. Tom asked if we could drive home before Nick's parents figured out what was going on.

"I might be too smashed," I slurred. "Probably not the best idea."

"Dude, it's not like we can stay at Nick's. And we can't just camp out here. We don't have tents or anything, I forgot to bring one," Tom replied. "I'm not sleeping in dirt! Let's get the fuck out of here."

"Yeah, okay," I said.

I staggered over to my car and turned on the ignition while Tom got into the passenger's seat.

My vision was blurry. "Dude," I said, "I'm going to crash this thing. We are fucked." I slowly drove through the woods, trying to find the main road.

"We'll be okay," Tom said. He kept grabbing the steering wheel, trying to keep it steady while I began to doze off.

"I'm tired, might need a nap on the way." I reclined my seat all the way back. "Why don't we just sleep in the car?" I asked.

"Robert, what the fuck!" was the last thing I heard.

Suddenly I woke up and I was sitting in the back of John's car. John was driving, Tom was in the passenger's seat.

"Where are we?" I asked.

They explained that I'd fallen asleep, and Tom had pulled the car over and called John to pick us up.

"We're going to Jack in the Box," John said. "We haven't eaten since lunch."

I fell asleep again, sprawled across the backseat, and came to in the drive-thru while John was ordering.

He pulled forward to the pick-up window. I was about to vomit. I panicked, trying to figure out how to unlock and open the door, but in my current state I couldn't solve the puzzle. I climbed between John and Tom in the front seat and lay across John's lap. My right elbow pressed against the steering wheel, accidentally honking the horn.

"Rob, what the hell are you doing?" John said, laughing.

The Jack in the Box employee opened his window to hand us the food. I grabbed the bag from him and threw it behind me. After making eye contact with the employee, I leaned forward out of the car and puked up about twelve beers. I glanced blearily to my left and saw the driver in the car behind us, then looked down at the giant puddle as the car backed up and drove away.

The weekend was approaching, and I needed money to see my sister in San Jose. I was between jobs, and the money from my dishwashing job went to car insurance, gas, and John's dad for rent. I poorly budgeted anything left over. I bought booze, fast food, new clothes, whatever I felt like. Without a short-term, concrete goal to save for (like a car), I just blew my money without a second thought. At this point, the future didn't yet feel real to me, so, why save for another day?

I arrived at school and met up with Tyler in the high school parking lot. He explained that his grandma was really sick.

"Like, seriously bad. First, it was just a cough, but now she has pneumonia or something," Tyler said.

"How old is she?" I asked.

"Hell if I know. Seventy-something. My grandpa was almost seventy when he died. I was in like fifth grade," he replied.

"That sucks, man, I hope she gets better."

"Eh, whatever. I don't give a shit. Kinda hoping it happens."

"What the hell. Are you serious?"

"I don't know. Maybe."

Since we were talking about family issues, I told him about how my sister had unexpectedly called me and how she wanted me to visit her.

"The problem is," I said, "I don't really have enough to make the eight-hour round trip. Gas isn't cheap."

Tyler reached into his pocket and pulled out a wad of cash. "Not sure how much is there, but it should be enough," he said.

He got into his car and drove away. I didn't know where he was headed, but clearly not class.

I unfolded the bills Tyler gave me. Twenty-eight bucks—more than enough.

The following day, though, I received yet another unexpected call. Then I had to give Tyler his money back.

I'd just finished my first day of work. I came to like this new job because of my manager, a guy named Mike. He was in his thirties, but had a PlayStation 3 and wore Heelys, which were black sneakers with a small retractable wheel installed in the outsole. Mike would glide up and down the aisles asking grocery shoppers if he could help them find anything, and to check on me and the other new employees.

Right away, I noticed the prices here were significantly higher than at the store Mom and Shelly would visit across town.

Just before my shift ended, I asked, "Hey, Mike, why would anyone shop here? You can get a lot of the same stuff at FoodMaxx for like half the price."

"That's true, bro, but who shops here?" Mike asked.

"Uh, I saw one of my teachers here when I started my shift."

"Right. Our shoppers are white-collar people who don't mind spending a little more to feel classy."

I was thinking about this idea when my phone started vibrating. I pulled it out and saw five missed calls from Mom and Shelly. My shift was over, so I thanked Mike and walked out into the parking lot. I sat on the hood of my car and called them back.

Shelly immediately picked up and said, "Rob, I'm not abandoning you."

She wasn't making sense. She was sobbing and kept saying that she would always love me and that she would never abandon me.

I had no idea what was going on. But I knew something awful was about to happen.

Mom took the phone from Shelly. "Hon, can you hear me?"

"Yes." I masked my fear with as much bravado as I could muster. "What's happening? Is Hannah okay?" I asked.

"Your sister is fine. Look, hon." Mom paused. "Shelly and I have been having some . . . disagreements. Ever since we moved to San Jose. But we both want you to know that we love you and Hannah both very much."

"Okay, what does that mean—you guys are splitting up?" I asked.

"We don't know what's going to happen yet. We just want you to know we love you and your sister," Mom said.

I hung up, wondering if they were really going to separate. I lit a cigarette and read a text from my sister. She said that she hadn't seen Mom or Shelly at home for a week, that Mom was driving her back to live with her dad in Red Bluff, and that she couldn't wait to leave San Jose.

If Mom decided Hannah should live with her dad, that means Mom and Shelly are definitely splitting up.

I had never before heard Shelly cry like that, not even when she was recovering from her injury. I had a feeling they thought having Hannah move in would help repair their relationship, but all it did was give her a front-row seat to watch it dissolve. I couldn't believe they were separating. After everything that had happened, my family was coming apart again. Even though I no longer lived with them, just knowing Mom and Shelly were together gave me a sense of security. Now, that was gone.

I sat in the parking lot smoking for a long time after that.

It was getting late—almost eleven o'clock. I opened the trunk of my car and glanced at the disarray of books I'd picked up from the library that morning. I grabbed my aluminum baseball bat that was next to them.

For as long as I could remember, I felt a constant undercurrent of throbbing rage, along with anxiety and shame (which I sometimes mistook for rage) for being abandoned, for being unwanted. But I was incapable of understanding it or communicating it. I was so overwhelmed by emotions I didn't understand that I acted impulsively just to prove to myself and others that I wasn't weak. I'd once read that when an animal gets hurt, they know they are vulnerable and that predators will target them, so they are prone to lash out at the slightest sign of danger.

I gripped the bat and smashed the taillights of a nearby car in the parking lot. I was still wearing my work clothes and realized that someone might notice. I grabbed a gym shirt from my car, still soaked in sweat from an earlier weight-lifting session, and changed.

I walked to another car in the parking lot across the street, where I thought I'd be less recognizable. It took two careful swings to shatter its windshield. I was careful because I'd seen a kid from school try to break a windshield once and the bat bounced off the car, rebounding and hitting him in the face.

I saw someone walking by. I considered whether to flee the scene or try to intimidate the person into silence. Flight or fight. I was relieved to see it was just an elderly man.

"I wonder what your parents would say if they saw you doing that," he said softly.

"I wonder if I care," I sneered.

Driving home that night, I stopped at a red light at a four-way intersection, and a gray SUV pulled up next to me.

"Hey!" the driver yelled. "You need to slow the fuck down. You blew through a stop sign back there."

"Who gives a shit!" I shouted back. "It's late. There aren't any cars around, moron."

I flipped him off and drove away.

Even though Antonio was my only friend who lived with his biological mom and dad, they were mostly checked out and didn't seem to care much about his homework or grades. As long as he did well enough to stay on the football team, his parents seemed to be happy. He was the tallest and most athletic of our friend group and played on the high school team with Tom. He stayed over at our place a lot, and we'd play basketball and video games. John and I had bought some boxing gloves, so we'd go into the backyard and hold boxing sessions with guys from our high school.

We were in the backyard when Antonio explained to us that his football coach thought he might be good enough to be recruited to play football in college, maybe at Sacramento State. My other friends and I had always thought that Antonio would be the most likely of us to actually go to college. But he had recently failed one of his classes and had to make it up by going to a class during spring break.

"That's just a two-week class, right?" I asked. "Should be easy."

"Yeah, man, but I have to get like a B or B-plus I think to keep my GPA high enough," Antonio said.

Antonio attended for the first few days, but the second week he stopped going. Instead, he'd either hang out with his girlfriend or with us.

He was staying over that week with Tom, John, and me at our place.

We were hanging out in John's room watching *The Departed* when Tom suddenly asked where Antonio was.

"Where did he go?" Tom sounded nervous.

"Probably went to the bathroom or to talk to his girlfriend or something," I suggested.

"Bullshit!" Tom shouted, and ran down the hallway.

John and I laughed as we heard Tom pounding on his bedroom door.

"Antonio," Tom said, "open this fucking door!"

John and I looked at each other, wondering why Antonio had locked himself inside Tom's bedroom.

"Hey, Antonio, is everything okay?" I shouted.

"Fuck off, guys, I'm almost done," Antonio replied.

John laughed. "He's jerking off in there."

"No!" Tom cried, and kicked his door open.

Antonio frantically pulled up his gym shorts. We walked in. I glanced at the TV, seeing that he was playing a DVD of some *American Pie* sequel. John and I walked out, laughing, while Tom and Antonio yelled at each other.

"Why the fuck were you jacking off in my room? Why not the bathroom?" Tom shouted.

"I can't play a DVD in the bathroom, Tom," Antonio said. "Use your head, think about it."

"Promise you won't jack off in my room again," Tom said. "Or I'll jack off all over your sheets the next time I stay over."

"Goddammit, Tom!" Antonio stood up and punched the wall. We grew silent when we saw that he had left a big hole.

"Dude, are you serious," John said. "Our dad is going to be pissed."

"Oh shit oh shit oh shit," Antonio said. "I'm supposed to be in school right now. He can't tell my parents about this."

Antonio and Tom left the room, while John and I continued watching the movie. Twenty minutes later Antonio handed me a hammer.

"I found this in the garage, Rob."

"Okay," I said. "Are you gonna smash another hole in the wall?"

"I need you to do me a favor," he said, trying to get me to take the hammer. "I want you to use this to break my toe."

I started laughing. "Are you high? What the hell is going on today?"

"No, man, look, I have a plan," Antonio explained. "I'm going to say Tom and I got into an argument, and I got so mad I kicked the coffee table and broke my toe, and then, because of the pain, I punched a hole in the wall."

John paused the movie and said, "That is by far the dumbest thing I've ever heard. You and Tom are straight-up retarded, but I still figured you guys would come up with a better story than that. I want to break your toe just for being stupid. Rob, give me the hammer."

"Guys, my parents think I'm in school right now," Antonio said. "They sort of know I haven't gone every day, but if they find out I was here and punched a hole in your wall, they will lose it."

I shook my head. We heard a car pull up and Tom ran to the window. "Fuck, guys, my dad's here." We saw that he was sitting in his truck in the driveway.

"Why's he just sitting there?" I asked.

"He probably heard us!" Tom said.

"What are you talking about?" I asked.

"Sometimes Dad says he has microphones installed around the house because he's never home but wants to make sure we're not doing anything stupid. I can never tell if he's joking or not. He probably heard us!" Tom said, pacing and panicking.

Antonio gripped the hammer and looked at his foot. "It's not too late. If he didn't actually hear us. It's not too late. I could do this myself," he said, trying to amp himself up.

John egged him on, "Do it, pussy."

Then his dad walked into the house.

"Okay okay, we're sorry!" Tom blurted out.

"Sorry for what?" his dad asked.

"Shut up!" Antonio said. "We don't know what he knows!"

Tom broke down and told the whole story. Antonio stood next to him, hanging his head in shame. John and I burst into laughter every few seconds.

At first, their dad looked serious, but slowly smiled, then started chuckling. "I agree with John and Rob, then. You two are the biggest idiots in California. You're going to help me patch up that wall."

Antonio opened his report card a few weeks later, hoping he'd somehow earned a B. He got a C, was kicked off the football team, and never went to college.

My new job required employees to wear solid black shoes. Fortunately, there was a Payless right next to the grocery store. I bought the cheapest size 11s from the clearance rack for $19.99. These turned out to be wildly uncomfortable. It wasn't just that I had to bag items—the store also had "carry-out service," meaning we walked customers' groceries to their cars for them. The job also required stocking shelves, sweeping and mopping, cleaning spills, and collecting carts around the parking lot in the scorching hundred-degree weather. These cheap shoes became gooey in the heat and provided little support. I mentioned this to John's dad.

"Well, I have some Dr. Scholl's inserts in a pair of boots I don't wear anymore," he replied. "You could pull them out, see if they help."

I thanked him and pulled out the boot soles. They were for a size 13, so I had to carefully cut around the edges to get them to fit into my shoes. They helped a little; my feet hurt less at the end of long shifts.

In the meantime, Tyler and I had been thinking about what we wanted to do after high school.

We were in the school parking lot again. "I've been thinking about it for a while, bro. It's not like I'm going to college," Tyler said. He explained to me that he'd made an appointment to visit the air force recruiting office downtown.

"One time I told my mom's friend that I was thinking about joining the military," I replied. "She was like, 'That's stupid! We're in the middle of two wars—do you want to get your ass shot off?'"

Tyler laughed. "Whatever. People get shot here, too. Did you hear about Enrique?"

"What about him?" I asked.

"Dude. You don't know? Edgar's brother got shot."

"What the fuck—are you serious?"

"Yeah, he was like trying to join a gang or something. He had to do deliveries and shit for them. For part of the initiation, he had to play Russian roulette and, well, yeah."

I shook my head in disbelief. I knew Enrique was trying to join a gang last year but hadn't heard that he'd been shot. I'd known him and Edgar since grade school. Enrique used to part his hair on the side and get good grades. He even tucked his shirt in. I rarely talked to Edgar anymore but saw him around school sometimes. He was naturally a big kid but I'd noticed he'd recently put on a lot more weight. I wondered whether that was because of what happened to his brother.

I tagged along with Tyler to the recruiter, who gave him a bunch of brochures and helped him schedule a time to take some kind of standardized exam for the military.

The recruiter turned to me and said, "So how about you? You could join Tyler here to take the test on the same day together. There's no obligation or anything, but you'll learn which jobs you qualify for."

I flipped through a pamphlet, looking at the images of service members in their dress blues. I thought they looked sharp. I didn't see myself like that.

"I'm not interested," I replied.

John's dad was telling me about his experiences in the air force and how it had helped him. "It might be a good choice for you. Has Tyler said what branch he's joining?"

"No. He's been talking to the army and air force."

"Well, he can come talk to me if he wants."

John's dad wasn't the only one who supported the idea of enlisting. I'd told my history teacher, whom I liked as far as teachers went, that I sometimes thought about the military. On his computer, he pulled up an old photograph of himself wearing an air force flight suit.

"Are you thinking about community college? That's where a lot of kids in this class tend to go," my history teacher said.

I'd noticed the difference between the two history classes he taught. Really, this difference existed for every subject at school. There was one class for kids going to four-year colleges and one for the kids going to community college or not continuing their education at all. By this point, my grades had dropped low enough that I was no longer in the "prep" classes.

"I don't know," I told my teacher. "I don't like school."

"You might later. Not many kids are reading books from the library instead of doing their homework. The military might be a good option for you in the meantime."

By this point, after never knowing my birth father and being rejected by my adoptive father, some part of me was seeking guidance from an older male. Between John's dad and my teacher, I began to take the idea of enlisting seriously.

In addition to visiting the school library, I spent several days a week in the campus weight room instead of going to class. I figured that if enlisting was a real possibility, then I should be strong. Tyler and I ditched our classes and worked out. We also signed up for a local gym and challenged each other to lift more than the other guy. It was a competition. Bench press, squats, snatch and clean, incline bench. We'd go to the clearance rack at the local GNC to buy their cheapest creatine and whey protein powder. After a few months, I gained around twenty pounds of muscle, plus a little fat too because of how I ate at John's place.

One day I texted Tyler, asking why he wasn't at the gym at our usual time, and asked him if he'd taken that test to join the military. He responded by asking me to come over to his house. He and his grandma lived out in the middle of nowhere, on the outskirts of town near the Sacramento River—endless trees, grass, and dirt roads.

"So, how'd the test go, man?" I asked.

"Didn't go. Not going to," he replied.

"What—why not?"

Tyler glared at me. His eyes were bloodshot.

"She died. My grandma is fucking dead," Tyler said.

"Damn." I paused for a few seconds, unsure how to respond. So, I just said, "I'm sorry, man." Tyler's grandma had been sick for months. We both hoped she would get better, despite Tyler's twisted jokes about hoping she'd die. I figured that was just his way of dealing with the possibility that she wouldn't be around much longer. "What about your uncle, are you moving in with him?"

"Who the fuck knows. Who fucking cares."

I was about to ask Tyler if his mom or dad had said anything but thought better of it. As far as I knew, he hadn't talked to either of them in years.

Tyler went into the house and came out with a bottle of Captain Morgan rum and a two-liter bottle of Shasta Cola. We blasted songs by the Offspring while we sat outside on an old wooden picnic table and got drunk. I texted John, who replied that he would join us soon.

I looked warily at the cliff about fifteen feet away from us. I walked over and peered down. The view was covered by tree branches and thick shrubbery, so I couldn't tell how far down it went.

Tyler, to avoid talking about how he was feeling about his grandma, was telling me about his job at the local car wash, and how they were going to give him a raise. In the distance, we saw a group of stray dogs, their fur covered in grime, their tails wagging. They paced toward us. Tyler stood up, and all but one of the dogs took off running. Tyler leaned down to the one who remained, petting it. Then he stood up and kicked it, and the dog yelped in pain. I ran over and shoved Tyler away.

"What the hell is your problem?" I asked.

"Fuck off." He grabbed the rum bottle, took two quick swigs, and started coughing.

I felt bad for him. I thought of how I felt when I learned Shelly had been shot and figured Tyler must be feeling something like that. Maybe worse, because his grandma had actually died.

We looked over at the dog sniffing around the edge of the cliff.

All of a sudden, Tyler ran over and kicked it again. It felt like time stopped as I watched that dog launch into the air and then plummet down the cliff. I ran over and looked down. I couldn't see what happened through the thickets of branches, but I had serious doubts it survived that drop.

"What the fuck . . ." I said, in disbelief.

"It's . . . a fucking . . . dog," Tyler said slowly. "My grandma just died, and you're more upset about a dog."

Enraged, I grabbed him by the shirt and pulled him close. "Fuck you," I said. "It should be you down there." I pointed toward the cliff.

John pulled up in his truck just then, and shouted, "Yo, is everything okay?"

I got in my car and drove away.

Did he really just kick a fucking dog off a fucking cliff? I sped through the highway. I'd always known Tyler was crazier than the rest of us. A couple years before, we were hanging out in a large old shed next to

Tyler's house with John and Cristian. Tyler spotted a bird fluttering around the tall shelves near the ceiling. He closed the door so that the bird couldn't escape. Then he grabbed a rake and started chasing the bird around. John reluctantly joined him while Cristian and I sat silently.

After twenty minutes or so, they wore the bird out from the chase. Tyler sat quietly in a dark corner of the shed. The bird landed next to him. Tyler snatched the bird and ran outside.

"What should we do with it?" Tyler asked. He suggested getting some of his grandma's hairspray and a lighter to make a flamethrower.

Cristian glanced at me. Neither of us was okay with this. John looked interested, but I had a feeling he could be talked out of it.

"We're not doing anything with it," I said. "You caught it," I nodded, acknowledging that I found this impressive. "But let's just let it go."

"Are you serious? Fuck that. We're scorching this thing, right, Cristian? John?"

Cristian shook his head and walked away.

John said, "Eh, I don't know, man. If these guys aren't down, then maybe not."

"Lame," Tyler said as he threw the bird into the air. It flew away.

I thought about this as I drove down Highway 36. Then a car zoomed up behind me.

I gripped my rearview mirror, worried that it might be a cop—I was definitely drunk. I saw that it was just a gray SUV driven by a chubby-looking guy wearing sunglasses. I was pretty sure this was the same guy who yelled at me at the four-way intersection a couple weeks back. Whatever. I kept driving.

The guy started flashing his headlights, then his high beams at me. He pressed on his horn. *What the fuck is this guy's problem?* I thought. I pulled off to the side of the road, and he pulled up next to me.

"Yo, you need to slow down, motherfucker. I remember you from before. You're the kid who blew through that stop sign by Walmart. You're gonna kill someone out here, driving like that."

"Fuck off," I said.

He looked down at the backseat of my car and saw my work clothes.

"You work there? I can get you fired—I know the owner there," he said.

I was afraid. Afraid of losing my job. Scared this guy was going to call the cops. Afraid that Mom and Shelly would find out that I'd been drinking and driving.

"Go fuck yourself," I said.

He opened his door. "The fuck did you say? How old are you anyway?"

"Old enough to beat your fat ass." I stepped out, too.

We got into a shoving match while he kept saying he would get me fired and I kept saying I didn't give a fuck.

This guy was plump, so his shoves were more effective than mine. Plus, my balance wasn't especially good since I'd been drinking all day. He pushed me to the ground. Enraged, I got up and punched him in the face, which turned him around a little, but he stayed on his feet. He tackled me. I could hear cars whizzing past as we rolled around like two idiots in the dried-out grass on the side of the road.

While he was still on the ground, I managed to get on my feet before him and land a few kicks on his head. His nose started bleeding. I was wearing shorts—blood splattered across my legs. As I stopped to catch my breath, he staggered to his car. He opened the driver's-side door, holding it to steady himself.

I walked over, gripped his door, and slammed it against him as hard as I could.

I thought about Tyler and that stupid fucking dog. I slammed the door against this guy six or seven more times until he finally buckled and screamed at me to stop.

I looked in his car and noticed there was a little stuffed giraffe and toy cars scattered on the floor.

"Dude, you have kids and you're getting into fights on the side of the road?" I asked.

"Fuck you," he replied. "Don't talk about my fucking kids."

I walked back to my car and watched him drive away.

The thrill of the moment dissipated, and my anxiety resurfaced. Rum and cheap cola gurgled in my stomach. I leaned against my car and threw up on the side of the highway. As I wiped my mouth, I considered what I'd just done: raced through the street drunk out of my mind, called some guy fat because I was angry at him for telling me to slow down, and then beat the shit out of him on the side of the road.

For the rest of the week, I waited in dread. Every time I saw my manager at work, I thought that he knew what had happened. But nothing came of it. Eventually, a coworker mentioned that someone had called to complain that one of the store employees had been speeding.

I felt my phone vibrating. It was a text from Shelly, saying she was visiting Red Bluff soon and asked if Hannah and I would have lunch with her.

At lunch, Shelly tried to put on a brave face. Mom had officially entered a new relationship with a woman she had met in San Jose, and they had recently moved in together. This was the woman Hannah had told me about—the one Mom was always visiting when Hannah had briefly lived in San Jose.

Seeing Shelly without Mom made it more real for me that they were truly separated. For Shelly, the wounds from the separation were still fresh. I thought how strange it was that this had all happened because of a freak accident four years ago. The shooting led to the insurance windfall, which led to the housing investments, which led to foreclosures, which led to Mom and Shelly moving to San Jose, which was where Mom had met her new partner.

After lunch, Shelly drove Hannah and me to meet Mom, who was also in town. On the way, Shelly picked up two of her friends. We said good-bye to Shelly and her friends and met up with Mom and her new partner at the movie theater.

Mom and her partner, along with Hannah and I, were standing in line to get tickets. Suddenly we heard yelling in the parking lot.

I turned my head. Shelly was running toward us, clearly enraged, shouting, "How could you do this to me? HOW THE FUCK COULD YOU DO THIS?"

Shelly's friends ran toward her and held her back. Mom and her partner walked into the theater quickly. Hannah froze, unsure what to do.

I walked to Shelly.

"I'm sorry you're going through this," I said. My voice broke up.

She looked up at me. "I just miss your mom, Rob. I'm sorry. Go. Tell your sister I'm sorry about this."

I embraced Shelly as she shook with rage and anguish, familiar feelings I often tried to block. It dawned on me that adults feel emotional pain, too. I thought about how even though I was technically bordering on adulthood, I wouldn't suddenly become invulnerable. Maybe I'd just gotten better at ignoring it or hiding my feelings. *Maybe all adults get better at this.* They could appear perfectly fine, even when experiencing internal agony.

Walking into the theater, I thought about how after graduation, I wouldn't have the option to "go back home" to Mom and Shelly, because I had never lived in San Jose, and because they lived apart now anyway.

My mind flashed back to that military recruiter I talked to.

CHAPTER SEVEN

What's Expected of You

I wanted to build a new life.

Throughout my final year of high school, I thought a lot about my friends and where we were all going. Cristian and John said they were going to turn it all around in community college—they both planned to get good grades and then transfer to a four-year college. When they told me this plan, I thought about how we were C-minus students at best, and now that we were nearly adults, we would soon have more freedom. The marginal adult oversight we currently had would soon be nonexistent. Which meant we would go from a little bit of friction to none at all when we felt the urge to ditch class and do something reckless. Gradually, I realized the path I was on had nothing but a tragic ending and came to believe that the military was my only lifeline. It was an environment that would present maximal friction if I felt the urge to do something stupid. And it didn't hurt that enlisting would also provide a decent income. As I write this, I'm reminded of a quote from George Orwell: "The thought of not being poor made me very patriotic."

But I was nervous about enlisting.

A few years before, Aunt B's son had graduated high school. He subsequently moved to Sacramento and started selling drugs for a local gang. He got into an altercation with a rival gang and wound up in the hospital. He realized he was not on a good path and decided to join the military. The whole family was proud. Then at basic training, he punched one of the other recruits, tried to fight the drill instructor, and was then kicked out. After that, he moved in with Aunt B and spent most of his days drinking on her couch. Aunt B begged him to get a job to no avail.

I wasn't entirely sure the military was the right option for me, but I knew the path I was currently on was definitely the wrong one. Enlisting seemed like a smart choice.

But I wasn't smart about how I went about it. I met with the air force recruiter and scheduled a date to take the ASVAB, the Armed Services Vocational Aptitude Battery, which is a standardized test similar to the SAT required for potential recruits. It tests math ability and reading comprehension, among other skills. This was the same test Tyler blew off when his grandma died. The night before the exam, I stayed up most of the night with John and Tom playing Xbox 360 and getting drunk on Four Loko. I knew that the test was scheduled for 10:30 in the morning, two hours later than when school started. I also knew the test was a valid excuse not to go to class. So, with the extra two hours, plus an alibi, I didn't even think to get a good night's rest.

The following morning, I woke up bleary-eyed. I checked the clock and registered that I had just enough time to drive to the testing center. On the way there, I chugged a big can of Rockstar energy drink. I didn't know what to expect with this test but figured a large dose of caffeine would help.

As I wrote my full name on the Scantron and awaited further instructions from the test proctor, I thought about how I'd grown up. I thought about the many families I'd lived with, and what was left of my current family arrangement. I looked down at my last name: Henderson. I'd seen enough movies to know that everyone in the military would call me primarily by this name. This sparked a sense of resentment—why did I get named after someone who wanted nothing to do with me? Upon further reflection, though, I realized that my whole life I'd been called the name of another guy—Robert—who had also abandoned me.

Until this point, my life had been a series of adults making decisions for me: foster parents, doctors, therapists, and social workers. I'd never had a say in the adoption, divorces, and separations. Now, here I was, finally making my own decision about how my life would unfold, and I showed up hungover, exhausted, and hungry. That's how much thought I gave to my future. Still, when thoughts about my past entered my mind, I felt more determined than ever. I gripped my number 2 pencil and gave it my best effort.

Two weeks later, I met with my recruiter to review my exam results.

"This is a great score, you qualify for every job," he said.

He showed me some charts, explaining how my results could be converted into SAT scores. I noticed that my SAT score, according to the charts, would have been the same as my straight-A classmate, Richard, who was heading off to college. A knot formed in my stomach as I considered what that meant: I might have gotten better grades if I'd tried harder. But as things stood, I had a 2.2 GPA and was about to graduate in the bottom third of my high school class. I lied to myself that I didn't care that I hadn't done well. It was too late. *Maybe someday I'll give school another try.*

I graduated in June and was scheduled to ship out for basic training in August. I was still underage and still buying cigarettes from older coworkers because I wasn't old enough to buy them at the gas station. Seventeen-year-olds can enlist, but they require consent from a parent or guardian. When my recruiter gave me the form, I briefly considered forging Mom's signature, but I wanted to ask how she felt about my decision.

Mom expressed some concern, but not as much as I'd anticipated.

"Where else am I going to go?" I asked her.

She conceded, "I know you're going to go off to God knows where when you're an adult anyway." She had long sensed my desire to escape and perhaps implicitly understood that I was either going to enlist or run away.

I arrived at Lackland Air Force Base, Texas, for basic training. This was before new recruits were allowed to use their cell phones, so my recruiter suggested that I take some quarters to use for the outdoor pay phones. The situation sort of reminded me of jail scenes on TV.

During the first week, everyone got one phone call. I had about ninety seconds to call Mom, hope she answered, tell her my mailing address, and hang up. Fortunately, she answered right away. All the while the instructors were pacing back and forth behind us telling us to hurry the hell up.

Throughout training, when it was safe, the other guys and I would laugh at how crazy the simulated stress was. I had only one tense moment where I was genuinely unsure what to do. The instructor for our "flight" (an air force military unit, roughly equivalent to a platoon) rewarded us after a particularly successful week of training by letting us write a letter to our families. I wrote a letter to my mom and sister, and, on my way to deliver the envelope to the mailbox outside, a different instructor stopped me. I recognized him as an instructor from another military unit in a different part of the squadron.

"Where the hell do you think you're going, Trainee Henderson?" he barked, looking at my name on my uniform.

"Sir, Trainee Henderson reports as ordered," I responded. "Sir, I'm on my way to the mailbox."

He snatched the envelope from my hands. "If you bring this anywhere near that mailbox, I will make sure you lose the capacity to write anything ever again, do you understand?"

"Yes, sir."

He handed the letter back to me. As he returned to his unit, I stood silently and considered my options. On the one hand, my instructor gave permission to mail the letter. On the other hand, I didn't want this other instructor to murder me—or, more realistically, discipline me or possibly throw me out of the military. Was he serious about the letter, or was this a silly mind game? It was important to me to tell Mom and Hannah that I was okay. They'd sent me several letters, so I figured I should try to send them this one, especially since I might not have another chance. Between my desire to contact my family and my inclination for risk-taking, the choice was clear. I waited until the instructor could no longer see me and made a beeline to the mailbox.

My favorite part of training was the camaraderie. I especially enjoyed drill and marching. The synchronized movement with others, moving as a single element, instilled a feeling of belonging. Everyone dressed the same, was held to the same expectations, and was treated on merit. I also enjoyed the physical training, obstacle courses, classes on military history and structure, and combat arms training. Considering what a poor student I'd been in high school, I was surprised at how much I was enjoying this experience. The psychologist Joyce Benenson has written that, often, when a young male has been overlooked by his parents, he "will gravitate to the ubiquitous male peer-militaristic world. He will then join this world as a child soldier, a gang member, mercenary, member of a militia, or, if he is lucky, a well-resourced military unit."[1]

According to this logic, I was lucky.

Still, I didn't enjoy the tedious requirements for bed-making, rolling and folding our clothes *just* right, and ensuring there was *never* any dust or dirt visible in our living quarters.

The guy in the bunk above me had a dad who was in the navy.

---

1 J. F. Benenson, *Warriors and Worriers: The Survival of the Sexes* (New York: Oxford University Press, 2014).

He explained that the reason for all this attention to detail is that it was all part of a test.

"If they can't trust you to make a bed perfectly, how can they trust you to carry a weapon or repair multimillion-dollar equipment?"

Contrary to my belief, I learned that the military is not just a destination for poor or working-class kids who join because their options are limited. The others weren't like me—most of the guys spoke of their excitement at the prospect of seeing their parents at the boot camp graduation ceremony. Many of them had been raised by two parents and seemed to be on good terms with their families. Also surprising to me, around half the guys were older than eighteen, having spent some time working or studying before deciding to enlist. The oldest was twenty-seven and had a bachelor's degree. At age seventeen, I was the youngest of the fifty-five members of my flight, suggesting that I was in more of a hurry to leave home than most of them.

Following basic training, each new member was assigned to attend "tech school," where we obtained additional training for our specific military occupations. I traveled to Keesler Air Force Base in Mississippi. Tech school was a slightly less prison-like existence than boot camp. We still had to wake up at 5:45 a.m., we still had regular uniform inspections, and we had to march everywhere. From the hours of 0545 to 1900 (5:45 a.m. to 7:00 p.m.), we were either in class, doing assignments, doing physical training, or practicing drill. The system was designed to keep us too busy and too exhausted to get into trouble. I looked forward to checking my mailbox on Fridays, where I would collect the latest DVDs I'd ordered from

Netflix to watch during the evenings and weekends. I watched a lot of episodes of *The Office* during this period.

My occupation was highly technical and required follow-on training at Sheppard Air Force Base in Texas. All this training and moving led me to reflect on what I might do after the military. One of my new instructors provided some guidance. He was a quiet man and looked young for his rank. One Friday afternoon he asked the class if we had any questions about military life.

I asked him, "If you could do it all over again, would you still have enlisted?"

The instructor paused for a few seconds and then replied, "There are some misunderstandings, I think, about what the military can do. You should keep your expectations in line with reality. If you view the military as a job, you will be miserable. It's not a job, it's a lot more than that. As long as you wear that uniform, it is your entire existence. The demands of this 'job' will loom large in just about every decision you make in what you think of as your 'personal life.' If you view the military as a club, you're also going to have a hard time. It's not some special affiliation you get to brag about—that mind-set will hold you back. And if you're easily offended, you're going to be miserable, too. You need a thick skin. But if you see the military as a system to obtain as much experience, training, and knowledge as possible in order to advance in your life, then you'll be fine. Understand that the air force is going to ask a lot from you. Just remember that you can get a lot in return from it, as well."

I meditated on this as I traveled to my first assigned duty station in Washington State, about forty miles from Seattle.

* * *

I began my official duties at McChord Air Force Base as an elec-
tronic warfare technician. I didn't have any special reason why I
chose this occupation. When I reviewed what specialties were available with my recruiter, I simply selected the one that sounded the
coolest to my seventeen-year-old mind. I hadn't yet formed a clear
sense of myself and my interests, or a guiding principle for what
I wanted for my future. I made the central choice of my life—
enlisting—primarily to get away from my past. Now, as usual, I was
focused on the present and had little sense of the future.

I performed service checks on missile warning systems and
other countermeasure devices installed on aircraft. These systems
are intended to deter or jam projectiles seeking to destroy the air-
planes. In practice, this meant regularly testing the equipment on
board.

Here is a typical task. After pilots returned from a mission in
Iraq or Afghanistan, I would walk 360 degrees around the aircraft and aim a special device at it that imitated the signals of a
heat-seeking missile. Another technician in the flight deck (cock-
pit) would report to me via radio whether the radar installed in the
airplane registered the signal, which indicated that the system was
working as intended. My counterpart would then test whether the
system responded to the "incoming missile" by emitting another
signal that matched the heat signature of the airplane. This signal
would divert the "missile" in another direction, thus preserving
the aircraft. Every jet required these maintenance checks every
ninety days. There were plenty of other tasks, too, like replacing

old devices with new ones or uploading new software onto the existing systems.

Many military jobs are similar to civilian nine-to-fives, except longer and more unpredictable. I always tried to be the first one to arrive at work and the last one to leave. Grateful to have found a new path in life surrounded by driven people, I threw myself into the job. New members were given fifteen months to complete their training requirements to be fully qualified to work without oversight; I completed them in six months. In addition to on-the-job training, we had to take a systems knowledge exam, and I obtained the highest score in my cohort.

As a kid, I was weighed down by instability and hopelessness. The military helped to unlock my potential, because it provided a structured environment, a sharp contrast to the drama and disorder of my youth. I was surrounded by supportive people who wanted me to succeed. In this new environment, I gradually came to realize that my childhood was anomalous, and I didn't have to let it define the rest of my life. I'd been liberated from the mistakes of my past. I believed that the external comportment I had cultivated would allow me to control my internal demons and productively channel my restless energy.

I would probably have committed at least one felony had I not been locked in the military throughout these years. For behaviors and habits to be stable and predictable, one's environment needs to be stable and predictable. I didn't have discipline, mentorship, healthy camaraderie, and so on back home, but I had them now. My new, highly rigid environmental constraints kept me out of trouble.

But there was something else, too: time. In a very real way, simply being confined to a schedule steered me away from misconduct. Military life consists of physical training (PT), room inspections, uniform inspections, and mandatory tasks outside of standard work hours. Every aspect of existence is tightly regulated, and this is especially true for new recruits. Your life isn't really yours. No institution is more aware of the latent impulsivity and stupidity in young people, especially young men, than the military. It has evolved into an environment in which it is very hard to do something reckless, because the consequences of failing to meet standards are both clear and severe. Major infractions like not showing up for work or failing a random drug test result in literal jail time.

I learned that so much of success depends not on what people do, but what they don't do. It's about avoiding rash and reckless actions that will land us in trouble. The military presses the "fast forward" button on the worst, most aggressive, and impulsive years of a young man's life—the time when a guy is most likely to do something catastrophically stupid. Studies have found that a man's likelihood of committing a crime peaks at age nineteen, and then gradually declines throughout his twenties.[2] This has led some psychologists to describe their larger appetite for violence, risk-taking, and competitiveness as "the young male syndrome."[3]

For me, the military presented a clear juxtaposition with ordinary civilian life, where a misguided teenager can gain plenty of

2   E. P. Shulman, L. D. Steinberg, and A. R. Piquero, "The Age–Crime Curve in Adolescence and Early Adulthood Is Not Due to Age Differences in Economic Status," *Journal of Youth and Adolescence* 42 (2013): 848–860.

3   M. Wilson and M. Daly, "Competitiveness, Risk Taking, and Violence: The Young Male Syndrome," *Ethology and Sociobiology* 6 (1985): 59–73.

ground on the path to self-destruction before slamming headfirst into a wall of consequences. You can commit a lot of crimes before finally getting caught. You can do a lot of drugs before they start to take over your life. You can have a lot of hookups before confronting the consequences of pregnancy. For many young people, the gap between impulsive and unwise decisions and the consequences of those decisions is large. In the military, there is almost no gap at all.

Even if a young man learns absolutely nothing during a military enlistment, that's still four to six years he spent simply staying out of trouble and letting his brain develop; the same guy at twenty-four is rarely as reckless and impulsive as he was at eighteen. The reason my life didn't go off the rails is because I was *just* self-aware enough to decide to have my choices stripped from me.

But I still found ways to bend the rules.

I lived on the second floor of a building on base. Life in military quarters is not particularly exciting. We were required to live within them until we reached a certain rank, typically achieved after about three years, at which point we could choose our own place to live off-base. This is by design, so that young members could be easily supervised and prevented from misbehaving. We had to take our meals at the dining facility (we called it the "D-FAC"). I was amazed the first time I visited for breakfast and saw real Pop-Tarts. It's a small thing, but at my high school Pop-Tarts were a prized commodity. Mom and Shelly would buy the Great Value generic ones from Walmart. But now I could get name-brand snacks in all-you-can-eat quantities. No one else seemed fazed by it.

One day I'd just finished PT when I heard some music blaring in the room next to me. It was a new song, "LAX Files" by the Game. I recognized that music because I knew the Game was from LA. I walked out onto the balcony to smoke—I was now eighteen and could, at last, legally pay for the risk of lung cancer. Technically, we were supposed to smoke at the "designated tobacco use area," colloquially called a "smoke pit," but the more careless guys (like me) didn't bother. I saw a guy standing out on the balcony, too, right in front of the room playing the loud music. Also a smoker, he lit a cigarette, and I asked if that was his music.

"Yeah, man, I love the Game," he said.

"He's from LA," I replied.

"Yep, Cali. Me, too." He introduced himself with his last name, Curtis, and I told him my last name, too.

"I read that Texas and California are overrepresented in the military. Those two states account for a ton of enlistments," I said.

"Yeah, makes sense, they're big states, bro."

"How did you end up joining?" I asked. It was one of the more common questions newbies asked to get to know one another.

Curtis paused, looking sheepish. "Ah, fuck it, I'll just tell you. I played baseball at UC Santa Barbara. My coach found us doing coke in the locker room after practice. Some other stuff happened too, but that was really the main thing. I dropped out, did some other dumb shit. I worked at a golf course and usually got high on the job—weed, not coke. Anyway, my mom and dad were like 'You can't keep doing this.'" Curtis wagged his finger in the air and raised his pitch, sounding like a cartoon character. "'You have to go back to college! Or join the military! Or something! No more smoking dope and fucking around at the golf course!'"

I laughed. "So, you joined because of your parents?"

"Sort of. I think they were joking about the military because my mom almost lost it when I told them I'd enlisted. My dad thought it was chill, though. I just didn't want to disappoint them anymore."

This is a great story, was my first thought. I saw some parallels in how we ended up enlisting to correct the course of our lives. *This guy's parents are together*, was my second. In fact, I noticed, more often than not, the parents of my coworkers were married, which was a sharp contrast to the people I grew up with.

The song switched to "Day 'n' Night" by Kid Cudi.

"Yeah, makes sense," I replied. "Are you glad you enlisted?"

"I don't know, man. I'm twenty-one, so there are people my age who outrank me now, you know? You're younger than me, most likely."

"I turned eighteen in tech school," I said.

"I mean, I was a fucking slacker in college. If I'd given college and baseball even half the effort I gave in boot camp and tech school, I never would have had to enlist in the first place."

That applied to my situation in high school, too. Still, I was glad to have enlisted. I liked that I was physically, if not mentally, separated from my past.

Curtis and I continued to make small talk about the ways our lives were the same and different. Later that evening, Curtis bought some beer for us and we introduced ourselves to some other guys in our building.

Before I joined, I'd heard that the military basically becomes your parent. I found this to be true. They teach you about finance and budgeting, and supervisors would lead new guys away from doing stupid things like blowing their savings on a brand-new sports car. Instead, they'd say to buy a sensible car. Some of the guys didn't listen, though. New members made about thirteen hundred bucks a month. It wasn't much, but it was more than I'd ever made before.

While military life was demanding, my efforts paid off. Many people say that to do something difficult and worthwhile, they need to be "motivated." Or that the reason they are not sticking to their goals is because they "lack motivation." But the military taught me that people don't need motivation; they need self-discipline. Motivation is just a feeling. Self-discipline is: "I'm going to do this regardless of how I feel." Seldom do people relish doing something hard. Often, what divides successful from unsuccessful people is doing what you don't feel motivated to do. Back in basic training, our instructor announced that there are only two reasons new recruits don't fulfill their duties: "Either you don't know what's expected of you, or you don't care to do it. That's it."

One day my supervisor informed me that he had something serious to tell me. I wasn't sure what it was about—maybe he'd heard that I'd been drinking in the dorms with Curtis and some of the other guys?

"Shut the door, Henderson."

"Yes, sir." I closed the door and waited.

"We're going to request that you be given an early promotion," he said.

He described the "below the zone" early promotion program, intended only for the top 15 percent of new airmen. Only high performers are eligible, he explained. Other applicants were being considered, he said, but he believed I would be a competitive candidate.

"How old are you, Airman Henderson?"

"I'll be twenty soon."

"That's pretty damn young. Most people are at least drinking age before they reach E-4. Look, this promotion means you would carry more responsibilities," my supervisor said. "I think you can handle it. What do you think?"

"I think so, sir," I said. Actually, I was not sure that I thought so, but I could tell he had confidence in me, which bolstered my own. I knew I was excelling at the job but still couldn't believe I was being considered for this.

"More responsibilities mean more money, too," he said.

"I actually looked at the updated pay charts recently; I think it would be almost two hundred dollars more a month."

"Just don't do some stupid shit like buy a Mustang off the lot like some of these morons."

"I was thinking a Dodge Viper," I joked.

"Haha," he replied dryly. "Now go do some work."

Weeks later, our squadron commander approved my application, and I was promoted six months ahead of schedule.

My promotion allowed me to move off-base and get a house with Curtis and a couple other guys, too, so four of us split the rent in a large two-story house. Curtis's parents came up to Washington to help us move into our new place. His parents rented a truck, which was helpful to move the furniture we'd bought for the living room. I'd been around friends who had more "normal" family lives than the one I had. But being around Curtis and his family crystallized something that I had always sensed but never quite realized: my life up to this point had been something of an obstacle course. I thought about how well I'd done in middle school, and how poorly I'd done in high school. There were a few reasons for this—instability, anger at how messed up my life had been, wanting to impress my friends, and the ease of doing something fun rather than something difficult, especially when no one had expected anything of me.

After we moved everything in, his parents went back to their hotel room, and Curtis and I hung out in the kitchen and cracked open a few beers.

"Your parents seem nice, man," I said.

"They're all right," he replied. "My dad used to be a real asshole, but he's mellowed out since I enlisted. You know how it is."

"We should get a beer pong table for the backyard," I said, trying to sidestep any discussion of my family.

"Hell, yeah. And a flat-screen." He nodded toward the living room, where our other roommate, Dominguez, was playing Guitar Hero. "Sweet Child O' Mine" by Guns N' Roses blared through the speakers of the 32-inch Panasonic tube TV that we bought for twenty bucks from the previous tenants.

Curtis and, later, Dom always kept our house supplied with booze. It was basically a sadder version of a frat house. We had parties every couple weeks, but it was mostly a bunch of dudes we knew from work getting drunk, playing beer pong and video games. Practically monastic for those of us under the age of twenty-one.

Curtis, though, was the oldest of the housemates and soon began dating a girl he'd met at a bar.

She invited Curtis, Dom, and me to a Halloween party in Tacoma. The house was packed with around thirty people, with another forty or so outside. While Curtis talked to his girlfriend, I walked into the backyard and saw a DJ standing on a small stage. "Forever" by Drake was playing.

He grabbed a microphone and said, "Okay, who wants to be Tased?" and he pulled out a Taser.

I looked at a guy standing next to me. "Is this guy serious?" I asked.

"Yeah, I think so," he replied.

A guy in a red Tapout shirt and wearing a Batman mask and cape raised his hand and said, "Tase me! Tase me!"

The guy on stage then said, "Okay, we have a taker. Who wants to Tase him?"

A girl walked over and took the Taser from him. She aimed it right at Batman and fired. It was kind of like that scene from the *Hangover* movie. The Taser hit him right in the chest and he fell over twitching. His friends circled around him, helping him up. The girl dropped the Taser, laughing, and disappeared into the crowd.

About an hour later, Batman challenged Curtis to a game of beer pong—Curtis and Dominguez on one side, Batman and his friend on the other. The trash talk started out good-natured, but Batman's remarks were growing increasingly snide as Curtis got closer to winning. After a few rounds, Curtis landed his ball in the other side's cup, securing victory.

Batman then said, "Bet you had a lot of practice with those dainty little fingers."

Curtis got in his face. "What's your fucking problem?"

Trying to defuse the situation, I put my hand on Curtis's shoulder and whispered, "This guy literally volunteered to get Tased. I don't think it's a great idea to get into a fight with him."

"Okay, we should get going anyway," Curtis said.

"'Okay, we should get going anyway,'" Batman mocked him.

Against my better judgment, I made a stupid joke: "Is that Taser still around? Might be time to use it again."

Batman shoved me. I responded by hitting him in his right eye. He stepped backward onto his cape, stumbled over a chair, and fell straight through a glass coffee table.

I was in that interim stage where I was mature enough to give Curtis good advice but not wise enough to take it myself. I was still an impulsive, insecure kid and wanted to be tough at someone else's expense.

"Okay!" Curtis announced as Batman rolled in broken glass. "Time to get out of here!"

"Of course, he tripped over his cape," Dominguez said. "I knew that Christian Bale movie was bullshit." We'd just watched *The Dark Knight* on Blu-ray a few days prior.

As we walked outside, I heard Curtis whispering to his girlfriend how sorry he was and that he'd cover the cost of the table.

"I'll pay for it," I said. "Sorry about what happened back there."

"It's all good. If you hadn't knocked that dude out, I would have," he replied.

The military asked that I put myself in the service of something higher than myself. I had a seriousness of purpose that I lacked before and experienced a new feeling about who I was and who I could be in life. But it didn't fundamentally "transform" me. It just provided conditions that prevented me from acting out the way I had as a kid.

Enlisting provided a stable setting that allowed me to mature enough to start reflecting on my life and what I had gone through. I still held some residual anxiety and rage from my upbringing. Despite the complete change in my circumstances, *I* had not completely changed. There was a lingering sense that something wasn't right—I was still running from something.

The military improved my life in a lot of ways. But I was still who I was and a product of where I came from. I sought ways to stifle any sense of emotional feeling within me. Having my wisdom teeth pulled provided a great opportunity to do that. The doctors prescribed far more Norco pills than I needed for recovery. I enjoyed them so much that when I heard that the same meds were prescribed for corrective eye surgery a year later, I immediately put my name on the list for the procedure. I told myself it was because I hated wearing contact lenses.

Upon recovery from the procedure, I made plans to visit California for my sister's seventeenth birthday.

• • •

In Red Bluff during the summertime, young people take inflatable inner tubes and floating rafts out on the Sacramento River. So, for Hannah's birthday, we arranged to go floating and reserved an extra tube for a portable speaker and a cooler full of drinks. We invited a few of her friends to join us, and I invited Tom, who was currently unemployed and taking one class at a nearby community college.

As we floated along the Sacramento River, Hannah repeatedly said to everyone, "Okay, let's just make sure we get back by four o'clock, because I have to pick up my boyfriend at a bus stop near Chico." This was a forty-five-minute drive from Red Bluff.

The third time she made this announcement, I set my beer can down and said, "Why is he taking a bus? This dude doesn't have a car?"

While not unheard-of, it wasn't especially common for young people in Red Bluff and Chico to take buses. I knew Hannah's boyfriend worked part-time at a coffee shop and figured he must have his own means of transportation.

"He can't drive right now—he was just visiting his friend for a few days in Yuba City and took a bus."

Can't drive? I sensed my sister wasn't being entirely forthcoming, but I brushed the thought aside and opened another beer.

As we approached four o'clock, Hannah's friend reached into the ice chest and, in the process, accidentally knocked Tom's car keys in the river. As soon as the keys hit the water, I saw the look of shock on Tom's face. The current was strong and the river was deep—in other words, there was no getting those keys back. Tom was drunk, and we spent more than an hour with him in a parking lot by the river before finding a solution to get him another set of keys. In the meantime, Hannah was stressing about the fact that we would be at least an hour late to pick up her boyfriend.

Hannah and I got in her car, and she sped toward Chico. Tom, who wouldn't get his new set of keys until the following day, tagged along with us.

"Oh my God, he's going to be so upset. I hope he's okay," my sister said.

"What's the big deal—can't he just call a taxi?" I asked.

Hannah gave me the side eye.

"What?" I asked. "This guy doesn't seem like a winner, Hannah. Mom told me that when she took you guys to dinner with her and her friends at the Sierra Nevada Brewery, you asked if your boyfriend could get a beer. Then he kept ordering more, and Mom paid for like five beers?"

Hannah remained silent.

Tom had been drinking and cracking jokes in the backseat. "Beers at Sierra Nevada aren't cheap. Your mom paid like fifty bucks for him to get a buzz. Here I am, buzzed on like ten bucks' worth of Natty."

"Shut up, Tom," I said.

"There are so many losers around here," he replied. "Trust me, I know. I feel bad for your sister, Rob. She's not gonna find Prince Charming making nine bucks an hour in Red Bluff."

"So that's the issue then," I suggested. "He can't afford a car, so he takes the bus?"

"No!" Hannah said. "Fine. If you really must know. He wasn't at his friend's in Yuba City." She took a breath, and said, "He was in jail, just for a few days."

Tom leaned between us, looked right at me, and blurted, "Well, that escalated quickly!" I glared at him, but then we both started laughing.

"Why was he in jail?" I asked, concerned about this guy my sister was dating.

"He was driving," Hannah said, "and we got pulled over because one of his taillights was out. The cops gave him a Breathalyzer. He'd only had a few drinks, but it wasn't his first DUI. They told him he could either pay a fine or spend a few days in jail."

"Jesus Christ. You're dating inmates now." Then, after a pause, "Okay, let's see if he's all right, then." I knew my sister could do better. But I also considered Tom's comment, about the crop of guys available to choose from. Her boyfriend wasn't in college, barely employed, likely had a drinking problem, and had no plans for his future.

Five months later, I was relieved when my sister declared that she'd split with him.

Shortly after my sister had told me about her recent breakup, John called me. He still lived in Red Bluff and had recently moved into an apartment with Cristian.

"What's up, man?" I asked.

We caught up for a few minutes, and he told me he'd been enrolled in classes at a nearby community college.

"What's the plan, when do you transfer?"

"I failed my last class, so I have to retake it. I missed too many lectures and couldn't catch up on the reading, but that's okay, I'll make it up next semester."

This was a common line. Community college creates a holding pattern, where people can take and retake classes for years with some pie-in-the-sky dream of transferring to a four-year college. Seventy percent of community college students in California never complete their programs.[4]

"Listen," John said. "Tyler's in serious trouble."

"What happened?" I was concerned, but not surprised. Ever since Tyler kicked that dog off a cliff back in high school, I'd figured his life would eventually go off the rails.

"Tyler was drunk on his motorcycle with one of his dealer friends on the back—on their way back from delivering drugs. He was completely hammered, speeding on the 505 when the cops tried to pull him over. He led them on a chase for a few minutes before swerving and crashing. He got scraped up pretty bad, but the other guy cracked his skull."

"Jesus. So, Tyler's okay and the other guy is . . . what?" Tyler had had multiple run-ins with the cops and had spent more than one night in the drunk tank.

---

4   G. Chen, "New Study: 70% of California Community College Students Fail," *Community College Review*, September 3, 2020, https://www.communitycollegereview.com/blog/new-study-70-of-california-community-college-students-fail.

"Tyler seems fine. But the other guy was in a coma for a while, not sure what the situation is now. Anyway, dude, Tyler is going to San Quentin. Fucking state prison."

I paused, trying to process this. I hadn't talked to Tyler much since high school, but I'd long assumed this was the path he was on. It was the one I was on before I left, too. If you replayed the circumstances of my early life repeatedly, nine times out of ten I suspect I would've wound up in prison, too.

In 2012, I was assigned to deploy to Al Udeid Air Base, Qatar, with a team of other guys in my unit. Our itinerary: fly out of Washington State, overnight layover in Baltimore, then a flight to Qatar, where we would be stationed for the next four to six months. On the way to the airport, I stopped by a bookstore and picked up a copy of *How the Mind Works* by the Harvard psychologist Steven Pinker. The title caught my eye, and I thought *Hey, how does the mind work, actually?*

When I wasn't working or screwing around with Curtis and Dom, I'd be in my bedroom reading. I'd read *Man's Search for Meaning* by Viktor Frankl, and was moved by his observation that although his fellow prisoners in a Nazi concentration camp were in the worst environment imaginable, they responded to it in radically different ways. Some were primarily self-centered in their quest for survival, while others became selfless and sacrificed for others at great risk to themselves. I also read *The Autobiography of Malcolm X* and, though my situation was drastically different from the author's, his anger at society resonated with me.

But this book about the mind was different. I flipped through it on the flight to Baltimore and found that it referenced *Calvin and Hobbes*. I loved these comics as a kid, and, in one amusing passage, Pinker describes a scene from the comic in which Hobbes, Calvin's pet tiger, mocks humans for having no fangs, no claws, no fur, and poor reflexes. And yet, the book explained, it is humans who control the fate of tigers rather than vice versa. This is because of our brainpower, which evolved just like every other trait. "Human evolution," Pinker wrote, "is the original revenge of the nerds." This helped awaken my interest in studying human nature.

In another memorable passage, Professor Pinker describes how across cultures and time, people strive for "a ghostly substance called authority, cachet, dignity, dominance, eminence, esteem, face, position, preeminence, prestige, rank, regard, repute, respect, standing, stature, or status." I thought about how happy I was to make my family proud when I'd enlisted. Now I was learning that this pleasure had its origins in the fundamental human longing for acceptance.

How the Mind Works was the only book I brought with me overseas. This was also the era of easy torrenting (online file sharing), so I knew I wouldn't be bored. My coworkers warned me that during deployment, the only things you could do when you weren't on duty were either work out, read books, or watch movies. To prepare, I downloaded the entire series of *The Sopranos* to my bulky Sony laptop. The episodes had those sketchy pirated labels like "TheSopranosS01E01.DVDRip.avi." After a long shift, I'd go straight to the gym to lift with my coworkers or go for a run. Then, after a shower, I'd either read books or watch an episode of *The*

Sopranos. This show confirmed a message I'd seen in other shows—college was an important ingredient of success.

Early in the series, Carmela Soprano issues a thinly veiled threat to their neighbor, Jeannie Cusamano. Carmela's aim was to pressure Jeannie into getting her sister, a Georgetown alumna, to write a letter of recommendation for Carmela's daughter, Meadow, for Georgetown University. Neither Carmela nor her husband, Tony, graduated from college, and neither had a strong network of college-educated friends and family. This one neighborly connection with Jeannie is Carmela's only "in" to the inaccessible world of prestigious colleges she desperately wants for her daughter so that she can escape their criminal family. Later, Meadow gets into Columbia University, and Carmela and Tony beam when one of their friends compliments them upon learning about this news.

I found it odd that even for this crime family, it was crucial that their daughter get into a good college. Tony Soprano wanted to fit in with the affluent doctors and lawyers in his neighborhood. But they treated him as a curiosity, cracking jokes and asking him about John Gotti during their golf outings.

I watched this show closely, feeling more conflicted than ever about college and my future. I was beginning to find my military job unfulfilling, yet also felt unprepared for college.

We referred affectionately to Al Udeid as "the Deid" (pronounced "deed"). As in, "I'm doing 'the Deid' for the next six months." The base looked like what you'd expect. Lots of sand, warm and arid weather, large tents and makeshift buildings. It was constantly windy, which blasted sand and dust everywhere. On particularly windy days, we had to wear face coverings to prevent sand particles from entering our lungs. Somehow, no matter how thoroughly I showered and how well I cleaned my living quarters, there was always sand in my bedsheets.

In the middle of a long night shift, I walked to the smoke pit, the designated area for tobacco users. Smoking, chewing tobacco, snus, coffee, and energy drinks were deployment fuel for the sleep-deprived. I'd been smoking regularly ever since my dishwashing job. It was a mental vacation from tedious labor. It broke up a workday into manageable chunks. *So I've smoked four cigarettes; when I have six left, that means I'll be off.* I'd just finished up repairing a jet full of caskets draped in American flags. Casualties of war.

A senior NCO was at the pit, too, smoking and gazing at the sun rising over the flight line. He looked over at me.

"Henderson, what's your plan?"

"Uh, just to finish this cigarette and get back to work," I replied.

"No. What is your long-term plan—what are you doing with your life?" he asked.

"Oh, I'm not sure. Maybe college?"

"Yeah, that's what everyone says," he replied.

"What do you mean?" I asked.

"Look, a lot of people say they're going to separate and think they're going to live that sweet college life, get a degree, get a high-paying job, live happily ever after."

"I do hear that a lot—you don't think it's a good plan?" I wasn't sure where he was going with this and thought maybe he was going to try to talk me into reenlisting.

"Nothing's wrong with it, obviously. Problem is, it's just talk." He made the "yapping" gesture with his hand. "I've been around long enough to see it. Kid your age gets out, fucks around in community college or some online college for a year or two, and never graduates. To be honest, I'd prefer you get the degree and come back as an officer. You could run a squadron someday."

I didn't know how to respond to this. Every so often my co-workers would make these kinds of remarks, and the comments embarrassed me. My roommates would crack jokes about me being smart—poking fun about my exam scores, early promotions, the stacks of books in my bedroom. I always viewed them as jokes—I didn't want to be thought of as smart. I didn't see myself in that way. Some part of me rebelled against that image, because if it was true—if I was "smart"—then I might have to raise my sights for my life. I didn't have any long-term goals and I didn't want them. I didn't want to think about where my life was going. For the time being, despite my growing dissatisfaction with my job, I liked that the military made all my choices for me, and I could just cruise through each day on autopilot.

After I returned stateside from my deployment, I went on leave to visit California. I met up with Tyler and Tom at a bar in Vallejo. Tyler had served twelve months of his eighteen-month sentence in San Quentin. He was released early and now on parole. The passenger from his motorcycle accident had survived. By this point, Tyler had been out for nearly a year. We spent a few minutes joking around when he asked me about the military.

I told him a little about it and he replied, "Basic training does actually sound kind of like prison."

"So, we both had to 'do time,' didn't we?" I said.

Tyler paused. "I *had* to be locked up," he said. "You *chose* to be." He ordered another beer.

"I figured by now you would have given up drinking," I said.

"Eh, it's whatever. I can handle a couple of beers," he replied. "You're the one who suggested we meet at a bar."

"What was prison like?" I asked.

"Boring, mostly. It was the same shit every day. Get up early as fuck, and there was a sort of roll call. Then we'd have breakfast and watch TV for a while. Then we'd have another head count. Then I'd read car magazines or play board games or whatever. Sometimes more TV, and sometimes work out. They actually started letting me run workout sessions with the other inmates. That was pretty much it, man. Eating, reading, working out—it's fucking tedious. Your whole existence is controlled. Even the lights. Sometimes fights and shit would break out, which broke up the boredom."

"Sounds mind-numbing," I said.

"Having no privacy was the worst part," Tyler replied. "Can't even jack off in peace."

Tom suddenly said, "Tyler, show Rob your tattoo."

I laughed. "No way. You got a prison tattoo?"

Tyler stood up and lifted his shirt. Sprawled across his chiseled abdomen was a flaming skull. "The other inmates made me get this; I didn't have a choice."

"It *was* your choice, in a way," Tom said to Tyler. "You wouldn't have had to get it if you hadn't gone to prison."

I looked at Tyler, but this comment didn't seem to bother him.

"Whatever, maybe it was a choice. It could have been worse." Tyler shrugged. "I saw some really fucked-up tattoos in there."

"What's next for you, man?" I asked. "I know you were making decent money at that car rental place before."

Tyler hesitated. I could tell he didn't want to talk about his employment prospects.

"No place like that is going to hire me now," he said. "I got an interview for carpet cleaning next week. Gotta start somewhere, you know. How about you, man?"

"I got orders—they want me to reenlist and move to Germany."

Tom turned toward me. "Dude, that's awesome. My dad says the beer is way better over there." He held up his glass.

"Rob, you made it," Tyler said. "You keep moving farther away. I don't blame you."

He was right—some part of me enjoyed increasing the physical distance between myself and where I'd come from. I hoped that if where I was *going* was far enough, it could change where I had *been*. So far, it hadn't worked. But maybe, I thought, moving to a completely different country a continent and an ocean away could do the trick.

Tyler tapped my glass with his drink.

I lifted my glass for a toast, saying I hoped Tyler would remain a free man.

"Well, life was simpler in there," Tyler said. "Sometimes, and I know this sounds crazy, but I wish I could go back."

I reenlisted and moved to Germany. Months later, Tyler was arrested for driving while intoxicated. When I heard the news, I had the feeling that this time he'd chosen prison.

In Germany, I realized that my twenty-two-year-old self was living a life that my seventeen-year-old self had chosen. My occupational duties were confining, and I had begun to experience intense bouts of loneliness and alienation. I felt that something was missing or wrong in my life, and that some change was needed to make it worthwhile. Work was often busy enough that it occupied my mind and kept these questions at bay. But when I wasn't working, they were harder to control, and I turned to drinking to subdue my uncertainty and anxieties. The military ceased to feel like an oasis and started to actually feel like a prison.

I'd been in a relationship for a few months with a girl who studied at a nearby university when she invited me to have dinner with her family. We were eating a potato dish that her mother had prepared, and at the dinner table I noticed that she was shooting me odd looks as I ate. My girlfriend saw this, too, and leaned over and whispered to me, "You should use your knife." I looked down and realized I'd been cutting my food with the side of my fork. I'd always eaten that way, first in foster homes and then later with Mom, who used her cutlery the same way. No one had told me it was improper.

Using my right hand, I carefully cut my food, and then switched utensils to use my right hand to eat with my fork. As I continued to exchange my fork and my knife in my right hand, almost certain that I was doing something wrong, I wondered what my girlfriend's mother was thinking. *Does she think I don't know how to use a knife? Does she think I grew up poor and that I never learned proper table manners? Maybe this is simply a cultural difference, and Americans and Germans eat differently.* Was this an issue of class, or culture, or simply a personal quirk?

They asked me whether I'd be traveling home to the US for the upcoming Christmas. I paused, realizing that I hadn't visited home for the holidays in six years. I always told my family it was because I had to work. The military was always the perfect excuse. But it wasn't true—plenty of people visited home for Christmas, but I chose not to.

"I'm not sure," I replied. "I might have to work."

I was promoted yet again and given more responsibility. My professional life was going well, but my inner life was deteriorating. When I'd initially left home, I did very little questioning or searching with regard to my life. I was in "flight" mode, grateful to have left home, and found something to occupy me. For the first couple of years, I'd been untroubled by difficult questions about the meaning of my past and the direction of my future. Lately, though, I'd been reappraising everything I'd gone through. The little kid who was betrayed over and over by parental figures and himself was suddenly seeking expression and validation. It felt like these internal conflicts had come out of nowhere. But the truth was they'd always been there, dormant, waiting until my environment was stable enough for me to process them. The stress I'd muted for years was now demanding to be heard.

I should have listened to these feelings. Instead, I just drank more. I hung out with my friends and would black out to the point where I didn't remember most weekends. When we went out at night, I'd tell my friends I was going to the bathroom. Then I'd sneak over to the bar and ask the bartender for a few shots. They'd naturally assume it was for a group. I'd then pound them one after the other and return to my friends like nothing had happened. On other occasions, my girlfriend would come over to my apartment and I'd drink so much I'd pass out. When I woke up, she'd be gone. I always felt lonely, even though I was seldom alone. Occasionally, I'd think about quitting drinking. But I always found a way to make excuses. *Haven't I been through enough—I can't have a few drinks?* It was easy to think about how bad my life had been and how I "deserved" to drown my feelings away.

My environments suppressed and exposed different aspects of my nature. My childhood experiences inhibited my potential and fostered harmful instincts. Occasionally, though, my latent potential would shine through even amid all that disorder. The military, in contrast, inhibited my destructive impulses and cultivated my good qualities. But now, the darkness within me sought expression. Being in a bad environment doesn't eliminate all the good parts of you, and being in a good environment doesn't eliminate all the bad parts of you. *Who is the "real" me?* I felt beset by contradictions and had no answers.

The holidays passed, and I regretted not visiting home. Out of guilt I bought a ticket to California and looked forward to catching up with Hannah and my friends.

I was in Red Bluff visiting John and Tom, the brothers who I lived with in high school. We'd been hanging out for a few hours catching up and listening to music. "Sad Eyed Lady of the Lowlife" by Alabama 3 was playing in the background. I pulled out my phone and noticed seven missed calls from my sister. I knew her dad and step-mom (Gary had remarried) were out of town, and that she was staying at their house in Red Bluff by herself. She rarely called so many times in a row, so something was obviously wrong. I was worried.

She picked up right away. "I've been trying to get ahold of you for like the past half hour," she said. It sounded like she was crying.

"Is everything okay?" I said, standing up.

"I'm at home. It's an emergency. Can you come?"

"Yeah, okay," I said.

I hung up and looked at my friends.

"I'm gonna go check on Hannah; she's in some kind of trouble," I said, reaching for my car keys.

John shot a glance at Tom, who shrugged.

I drove down the street where Hannah was staying and saw two police cars with their lights flashing parked directly in front of the house. There were two cops standing on the porch by the door. I stepped out of my car.

As I approached the house, the cops locked eyes with me.

"Are you Robert Henderson?"

CHAPTER EIGHT

Potentially Deleterious Effects

My sister stepped out of her dad's house and said to the police officers, "Yeah, that's my brother."

I showed them my driver's license and military ID. The cops explained that someone in the neighborhood called in a noise complaint about two girls fighting outside. When the police arrived at the house, there was a big high school party going on. I peered inside the house and saw a beer pong table set up and red Solo cups strewn everywhere. The cops had already told the guests to disperse before I arrived.

"Your sister explained that your parents are out of town," one of the officers said.

I was about to correct him that we had different parents, or different dads, but I wasn't sure I'd be able to express it coherently, so I just nodded.

"She's lucky you're here," the other officer said. "Your sister is a minor, and she has informed us that she's been drinking. When she mentioned that she had an older brother in town visiting from the military, we told her to call you. We were going to place her in a foster home until your parents returned."

I recoiled when hearing those words—*foster home*. I thanked the officers for telling my sister to call me.

"Make sure it doesn't happen again," they said as they walked to their patrol cars.

"Hey, thanks for coming," Hannah said as I entered the house. "Oh God, my dad's calling."

I went to the kitchen to get some water.

"Here." Hannah extended the phone to me. "He wants to talk to you."

I took the phone.

"Robert," Gary said, "is there anything broken or stolen in the house?"

"Everything is fine," I said, glancing around the messy living room.

"What did the cops say?"

"Just said I had to stay with her until you guys get back. It's no big deal, I was in town anyway," I said.

After the call, Hannah glared at me.

"What? Your dad didn't sound too upset," I said.

"I can tell you've been drinking, Rob," Hannah said.

"I only had a couple of drinks," I lied.

"Did you hear what those cops said? I almost went to a foster home tonight. What if they knew you drove over here drunk like that?" She waited for an answer. "Were you at a bar with your friends?"

"The cops didn't notice anything, don't worry about it," I said. "I'm glad you called. I can't let you stay in a fucking foster home."

Hannah gestured to the fireplace.

"Do you think you could build a fire?" she asked.

"Yeah, okay," I replied.

As the fire came to life, we gazed at the flames.

"I'm happy you came, but still," Hannah said. "You shouldn't be drinking and driving."

I'm used to it. It was funny. The cops planned to place my sister, who was almost eighteen anyway, in a foster home. Then they asked her to call me, a person who drank to forget about his own experiences in foster homes.

"What did my dad say to you?"

"He just asked if anything was missing or damaged."

I hadn't talked to Gary in years, and my emotional response to talking to him was nothing—just numbness. Was this because I was intoxicated, or was this my natural state? It was hard to tell anymore.

When I felt lonely, guilty, or unhappy, I drank to disengage from my feelings. When I felt numb, I drank to release some endorphins to relieve pain and experience a little dose of euphoria. And when I experienced any pleasurable emotions, I drank to quell those feelings, too. There was a kind of twisted logic to it: I didn't feel like I *deserved* to feel good on my own, without being able to attribute it to some external substance. But I didn't enjoy feeling *bad*, either. One reason I drank was to create the pretense that alcohol was to blame for anything I felt.

I looked at my phone and read a text from John asking if I wanted to go skydiving with him and Tom the next day.

. . .

A few years prior, I'd gone bungee jumping with friends in Amboy, Washington. As soon as I leapt off the bridge, it felt like my consciousness caught on fire, a concoction of sheer terror and utter joy. Reaching the end of that two-hundred-foot drop, the elastic ropes tugged on my torso as I bounced at the bottom. I felt alive. I immediately paid the eighty-nine dollars to do a second jump. Then a third.

Skydiving, though, was different. As soon as we jumped out of the airplane, I knew something was wrong. I expected to recapture that same intensity of feeling. But this time, I felt absolutely nothing. I looked around at the scenery, registering the beauty of Northern California, but that was it. My heart rate remained the same. When we landed, John and Tom talked about how exciting it was and how they wanted to make plans to go again soon. I suggested we go to a bar.

When I returned to work, I visited a mental health clinic on the military base. They had me fill out a few forms and arranged for me to speak with a psychiatric nurse.

I told the nurse about how I'd been feeling down lately and didn't know why. When he asked if anything specific led me to make this appointment, I described my blunted response to skydiving and how different it was from when I'd gone bungee jumping a few years ago.

After a few more questions, he mentioned the word *dysthymia*, which I looked up later and found that this was another term for depression. Studies have found that depression afflicts two-thirds of people with alcohol addiction.[1]

I told the nurse I'd been drinking a lot.

He nodded. "Are you taking any medications or drugs?"

"Nothing. Just drinking."

"Have you had any major medical procedures?"

"Yeah. I got my wisdom teeth out when I was eighteen and had corrective eye surgery a couple years ago."

"What did they prescribe?"

"Vicodin, or hydrocodone, one of those. Really good stuff."

He nodded. "Those are the same thing. When is the last time you had a drink?"

I hesitated. He gave me a knowing look.

"Was it today?" he asked.

"Yeah."

"When?"

"About twenty minutes ago. At the E'Club casino across the street."

He informed me that we couldn't continue the appointment while I was impaired.

"You'll have to go to reception and reschedule for another appointment. They can call you a taxi, too."

I asked reception to call me a taxi but didn't bother rescheduling. I didn't want to hear that I might be depressed. I suspected it was true, but talking about it made it more *real* to me. I knew that if

---

1 M. W. Kuria, D. M. Ndetei, I. S. Obot, L. I. Khasakhala, B. M. Bagaka, M. N. Mbugua, and J. Kamau, "The Association Between Alcohol Dependence and Depression Before and After Treatment for Alcohol Dependence," *International Scholarly Research Notices* (2012).

I returned, eventually I'd have to start talking about myself and my feelings, which I wasn't ready to do.

For a while, I'd managed to simulate normality at work and excel at my job. I was good at pretending to be okay—I'd learned how to do that my whole life. But the armor was heavy, and it was slipping.

I used to call home every few weeks; now I seldom called at all. I still texted Hannah regularly every week, but knew that if I called her, she would sense something was wrong. I didn't want to have that conversation.

My girlfriend by this point was directly accusing me of evading her questions about my personal life, which I was. Whenever she asked me about my family or what it was like growing up in America or in California, I never gave her a serious answer and always changed the subject. We could never advance in our relationship because of my fundamental unwillingness to disclose the intimate details of my early life. She believed that my insincerity and out-of-control drinking meant that I was cheating on her. When I scoffed at this, she told me it was over.

I shrugged and walked out of her apartment without saying a word.

I was not a good person to be dating at this point. She was right to end it. Growing up switching families all the time and seeing all the divorces and separations and remarriages had furnished a few lessons about relationships: never get too attached to anyone, be prepared to walk away at a moment's notice, and everyone is replaceable.

I didn't care about the relationship ending, but naturally, it affected me. I decided to take leave to visit my friends in California. I called up John, and we arranged to meet at a bar downtown in San Jose.

I asked how the other guys were doing.

"Cristian was arrested again for beating up his girlfriend."

"Again? I didn't even know he was arrested before. Is she okay?" I asked.

"She had some bruises. It's crazy. Cristian used to call me at all hours of the night saying he thought she was cheating on him, but I never thought he would do something like this."

I didn't either. Cristian was a small, quiet guy and was always more sensitive than my other friends growing up. I thought of Tyler, and how he'd been in prison, too.

"So how is everything with you now?" John asked me.

"Never been better, man, I just got another promotion at work." The first part was false; the second part was true.

"I've been thinking about enlisting too, you know," John said.

"You probably should join. You've been working at the same store for the past six years. Enlisting will break you out of your rut."

"Oh, okay," John said sarcastically. "You don't get into 'ruts' in the military?"

"Let's check out some of the other bars," I deflected.

We talked more and drank more to the point where I could barely see straight. We were outside walking to yet another bar, when a group of four guys and one girl passed us.

I overheard one of them say, "Let's be careful, we don't want to end up at a gay bar."

Another gestured toward John and me, loudly saying, "Hey, isn't that where these two are going?" They laughed together.

"What the fuck did you just say?" John shouted, ready for a fight and not caring that we were outnumbered.

The guys turned back and looked at him. "Yo, you got a problem?"

As John got into a shouting match with these guys, the girl in their group was left standing alone. I walked over and introduced myself. She explained that she didn't speak English very well.

"I just took four shots in a row, so I don't speak English very well either," I said. She understood this joke and laughed.

Encouraged by her positive reaction, I tried to remember whatever Spanish I knew, hoping to keep the conversation going. Suddenly I found myself on the ground.

I looked up and became aware that one of the guys had seen me flirting with this girl, ran over, and sucker punched me. John retaliated by punching my attacker. I got up and kicked one of the other guys in the balls and grabbed another one by the throat, when a third guy took me down. I was in this trashy fight right outside a bar, but honestly, I felt pretty good. Adrenaline kicked in, and the only thing on my mind was survival. On the ground, one of the guys kicked me in the ribs repeatedly. I grabbed his leg and pulled him down and then another one kicked me right in the face. As my ears rang, I knew this was on the verge of ending horribly. At this point, thank God, two large bouncers stepped outside of the nightclub in front of us and broke it up. My nose was bloody, and my eye was throbbing. John's upper lip was swelling; he spat out some blood.

"Wait here," one bouncer said. "Cops are coming."

John and I immediately bolted five blocks down the street and found refuge in a diner.

As we cleaned ourselves up in the bathroom, John looked at me. "You're a fucking idiot."

"Me? You're the one who shouted at those guys," I said.

"You didn't have to flirt with that girl. The guy who sucker punched you, that was probably his girlfriend." John shook his head.

I started laughing. John cracked up, too.

My high spirits didn't last long. The next day John and I met up with my sister for lunch. She looked at my black eye.

"Okay, what's going on with that?" Hannah asked. "Did you get in a fight?"

John nodded.

"John, what happened?" Hannah asked. John told the story.

Hannah looked at me and shook her head. "You're so stupid."

I said nothing. She was right.

About two weeks later, one of my work friends, Wilson, had a going-away party to celebrate his enlistment coming to an end. This gave me an excuse to get as drunk as I could and forget about my breakup, that stupid bar fight, and my sister's disappointment in me.

Afterward, some other coworkers and I went barhopping in Germany until around five in the morning. The next day, we heard that Wilson had missed his flight back home. Over the next few hours, the gut-wrenching story unfolded. After his going-away party, Wilson crashed his car into a tree and walked the rest of the way home. Hours later, his landlord found him in the garage hanging from an extension cord. We had no idea what his reasons were to kill himself. He'd always seemed like a happy-go-lucky guy and always talked about how excited he was to return to civilian life.

After work that night, I drove home and started drinking alone. I thought about Wilson, and how he'd seemed perfectly fine, even jovial, during his final hours with us. I looked in the mirror and noticed some of my hair had started turning white. I'd read that when the body enters a prolonged fight-or-flight state, premature graying can result.[2] A part of me doubted I'd live long enough to see my hair completely lose its color. I reached a dark place—the place where you say, "This is not a good idea. I shouldn't do this. But this is who I am." Already drunk, I went into the kitchen and opened a new bottle of Maker's Mark bourbon. I drank it straight out of the bottle until I passed out.

Three hours later, I came to in my bathtub covered in vomit and cold sweat. I looked up and saw the bottle broken in half in the bathroom sink. Nauseated and shivering, I walked to the kitchen to drink some water but immediately retched it back up. I kept stumbling and couldn't get my balance. I texted Curtis, who left work to come check on me. He arrived with another coworker, and both of them took me to the hospital. When I told the doctor about the bathtub incident, and how much I'd been drinking, she recommended I stay overnight in the ICU.

---

2   Zhang, Bing, Sai Ma, Inbal Rachmin, Megan He, Pankaj Baral, Sekyu Choi, William A. Gonçalves et al. "Hyperactivation of sympathetic nerves drives depletion of melanocyte stem cells." *Nature* 577, no. 7792 (2020): 676-681.

* * *

I awoke the next morning with two IVs in my arm. A woman standing over me explained that she was a psychiatrist and director of the addiction treatment facility in the hospital. She asked me a series of questions. How much had I been drinking? Eight to ten drinks a day, depending on how you count. When's the last day I went without a drink? I honestly don't remember, maybe two years ago. Did I ever experience feelings of worthlessness and guilt? Yes. Did I experience feelings of extreme fatigue? Yes. Had I experienced a loss of interest in things that used to interest me? I had. Did I sleep a lot? Actually, no. I was barely getting any sleep. I constantly drank coffee and energy drinks to mask my permanent fatigue. She reviewed my files from my earlier visit with the nurse at the clinic and diagnosed me with depression and alcohol dependency. Upon hearing those words, I realized that I hadn't felt this demoralized since back when I was a foster kid, learning that I'd have to move to yet another home.

The doctor scheduled me to attend a six-week inpatient program at a treatment facility. There would be no more accolades at work, no more early promotions, and my thoughts of college went out the window. I felt like a failure and couldn't believe I was heading into yet another institution. Before, I entered foster care and the military because others had let me down. Now, I thought, I was entering rehab because I'd let myself down.

At least my commanding officer was supportive. This was in part, I suspect, because we'd just had a suicide in our unit, and he was on high alert for other mental health issues in the squadron. I was embarrassed at the thought of what my coworkers and friends would think. They wouldn't know why I'd suddenly vanished, but I knew rumors would spread.

On my first day at the treatment facility, we had a morning roll call. A woman next to me said she had a question for the counselors.

"I just . . . just . . . just . . . just—" She began jerking her head.

"Hey, she's seizing!" a patient exclaimed, and one of the treatment counselors bolted to alert the doc on call.

"Are seizures common?" I asked.

"It's part of withdrawal," an older patient replied. "If you keep coming back here, you'll see."

That woman was discharged a week later for failing a drug test. She said she needed the drugs to help with her withdrawal. Before leaving, she told me I had a "high bottom," meaning I'd checked into rehab before drinking had caused too much harm in my life. People who had a "low bottom," in contrast, often inflict a lot of damage on themselves or others before getting caught or getting help. My birth mother was a "low bottom" user, I thought.

This treatment center was for military personnel and their families. The patients were service members, spouses, retirees, and adult children of parents in the military. Each day was rigidly structured: morning roll call, group therapy sessions, individual sessions, discussions with fellow patients, visits from occupational therapists, and individual writing assignments.

I had to meet with my counselor, Alan, several times a week. A retired military officer, he'd made a second career as a mental health clinician. He grew up in Compton, California, and, though he was cagey about the details, I gathered that he'd had a tumultuous childhood before attending USC and later joining the military. He'd also volunteered for a few years at a youth detention center. I was pretty sure it was no coincidence that the head psychiatrist assigned me to work with him.

On the first day we met, Alan asked me a simple question.

"Can you tell me how you came to be here, Robert?"

I gave him a rundown of my entire life. Alan's expression changed slightly when I mentioned my birth mother's drug addiction and Shelly's decision to purchase multiple homes in California back when I was in high school. His attention to the former detail made sense to me, but not the latter.

"Okay, Robert," Alan said. "How are you feeling now?"

"Worried," I said. "About telling my mom and sister where I am."

"Why does that worry you?" Alan asked.

"I've known for a while that I haven't been feeling great, but I haven't told my family. Sometimes when I'm around them, it's hard. I'm reminded of all the shit I went through as a kid. It feels like I've been alone with all this pain."

"Are you in pain now?"

"No. I don't know. Sometimes I am."

"Where do you think it comes from, your pain?"

"I can't really pin it on anything specific."

"What's your best guess?"

"I just know that it's fucked up, Alan. My childhood, I mean."

I flinched when I said this. I felt weak for voicing these thoughts. I hated how it sounded like such a cliché, blaming my childhood.

"Look, I'm a grown man," I said. "It feels pathetic to sit here and bitch about it. 'Oh, this poor troubled foster kid, blah blah blah.' But let's be honest. My life was a shit show. My mother was strung out, my father left. All those foster homes. I was a fucking sleepover kid—let's be honest. None of those people truly cared about me, none of them loved me."

Crickets from Alan.

"I just realized something," I said after a pause. "That means I never loved anyone during all that time either."

For some reason, this hit me harder than realizing that no one had loved me. I lost it and started bawling.

"Do you love anyone now, Robert?" Alan asked.

"Yeah, of course. My family. But it's different; I see how other families are. There's a depth of feeling there. I can't say I ever *really* felt that except maybe for my sister. Mostly I've just felt lonely, ever since I was in the system."

I asked Alan, "Is that because nobody loved me as a kid?"

"Early experiences play an outsized role in shaping our lives," Alan replied.

After our first session, I realized that whenever anyone said they loved me, I heard the words but never internalized them. It was the same as someone saying "good morning" to me. Just a nicety.

. . .

If you want to gauge your relationship with yourself and your life, put everything aside and just be alone with your thoughts. Sitting silently in rehab—no alcohol, no phone, no distractions—I found a mountain of unresolved inner pain. I pursued hyperstimulation as a kid to avoid those feelings. The drinking and drugs, the choking game, the bursts of adrenaline that came with putting myself in dangerous situations. Now, I was going through withdrawal. Not just from alcohol, but from every kind of "buzz" I'd sought as a kid. For me and so many of the other patients in the clinic, distraction and extreme sensory manipulation were the aims, whether drugs, alcohol, violence, extreme sports, sex, compulsive eating, obsessive spending, or sleeping all day. The objective was to feel anything but pain or to feel nothing at all.

I drank to medicate my low mood or to increase the likelihood of something exciting happening—like the fight outside the bar in California.

I remembered what my child psychiatrist in LA wrote all those years ago:

> I would recommend finding permanent and stable placement for Robert in a kind and supportive environment as expeditiously as possible, which will go far to mitigate against the potentially deleterious effects of his early experiences.

That "permanent and stable placement" never materialized, and thus, there was no mitigation against the "potentially deleterious effects" of what I'd been through.

After I told Alan I enjoyed reading, he loaned me some of his books. I learned about attachment theory and "monotropy," a fancy way of saying that young children have an innate desire to form a special bond with a parent, usually the mother. I read about "critical periods" in childhood and how kids who don't form close bonds with a caregiver before the age of three are far more likely to have social and emotional problems later in life.

My understanding was that if a kid doesn't feel safe early on, then it is harder for them to ever feel safe later. Other potential consequences of lack of attachment to a parent are lower-than-average intelligence, delinquency, aggression, and depression. It was strange to read this map of my own experiences. I recognized myself in all of it. I'd been a terrible student, got into all kinds of trouble as a kid, and was now depressed.

For much of my youth, I felt mentally anesthetized. There were great floods of pain very early on, like when I cried uncontrollably as a toddler when I was taken from my mother and when I was again taken from my first foster home. But by age four or five, my emotions had gone underground. It took a lot of effort to fully unearth how terrible I'd felt as a kid.

It was odd how, when I thought about the foster kids I knew from school, like the girl who disclosed to me that she missed her parents, both of whom had gone to prison, I would get choked up. But I didn't feel much for myself. Brainstorming with Alan, I came up with two possibilities for why: (1) by not treating me well, adults taught me that my feelings weren't important or valid; (2) I'd managed to escape by joining the military, so I didn't feel justified in feeling sorry for myself. For many kids who had the same kind of life as me, life starts out bad and never gets better. It often gets worse.

While the rest of the facility was overly bright and smelled like antiseptic cleaning fluid, Alan's office was warmly lit and had a faint aroma of leather from the furniture.

"We touched on this before, but when was the last time you felt happy?" Alan asked. I glanced out the window, trying to remember.

"I honestly couldn't tell you. It's like my habit of shutting off the bad feelings dulled my ability to feel the good ones, too."

"Why did you shut off those feelings?"

"To survive. I just learned to switch it all off." I took a deep breath. "If I'd felt the full brunt of losing contact with all ten of the families I'd lived with as a kid, what would have happened? I would have started taking hostages or killed myself, or both. It would have been too overwhelming."

I wondered whether it was a coincidence that Tyler, Cristian, and I found ourselves either incarcerated or in rehab, and none of us had fathers in our lives. In contrast, John, Tom, and Antonio grew up with their dads and never entered such institutions.

I thought I'd found the solution to my problems in the military. And in a way, I did, because it provided stability. It gave me a chance to take a breath and realize something wasn't right. Understanding my inner turmoil held the possibility of self-renewal. But first, I had to come clean with Mom and Hannah.

. . .

As soon as I told her where I was, Mom started crying.

"You always seemed so put together. I had no idea you were struggling, you never talked about it," she said.

"Yeah. I know," I replied. "I got good at hiding it. I even fooled myself."

"I'm glad you're getting the help you need," Mom continued. "And we don't need to tell anyone else about this." She didn't want anyone to know I was in treatment.

After the call, I kept thinking about that and realized Mom didn't want my image as her son who had "made it" to be shattered. It felt like confirmation that, as a kid, I really did have to project an image of strength.

I FaceTimed my sister and explained my situation. She wasn't surprised, because she was aware of how much I'd been drinking. She'd understood the trajectory I was on.

"What's it like there?" Hannah asked.

"It's about what you'd expect." I told her about my daily schedule, and then I said, "I'm just dealing with a lot of stuff I didn't know I needed to deal with."

"I have like no memories from before you were adopted," she said. "To me, you were always my big brother. I forget that you had this other life before. You never talk about it."

She was right—I never talked about my experiences in foster care with her.

"I wanted to forget any of that happened," I said. "Looking back, it was almost as if it happened to someone else, like some other little kid went through all that. And for some reason I'm the one paying the price for it."

"How did Mom react?"

"She was pretty broken up about it. I felt this urge to reassure her that I was fine, even though I wasn't, just so that she wouldn't feel bad."

"If you're not fine, you should say so," Hannah said. "Maybe when you've finished your program, I can come visit."

"I'd like that." Making plans to see my sister lifted my spirits.

I met with Alan later that week. I told him about my phone call with Mom, and how I didn't want to disappoint her.

"It sounds like you learned to disengage from your feelings not only for your own sake, but for your mom's, too," he said.

"Well, she's been through a lot." I felt an urge to defend her, even though Alan hadn't said anything disparaging.

"I'm just going to make two observations," Alan replied. "One is that you were, at least for part of your adolescence, raised by an addict—not a substance addict but an addict, nonetheless."

He was talking about Shelly's gambling habit.

"And for your mom," he continued, "it sounds like you felt compelled to be strong for her; to hide your feelings."

"That's unfair. You don't know them. You've never met them." I didn't like that he was reducing the only parents I'd ever known to poorly drawn caricatures.

"Robert, when your adoptive father left you, you mentioned you pretended to be angry instead of sad."

"I *was* angry. I was sad too. So what?"

"Why didn't you tell your mom how you were feeling?"

Alan was right. It was because I wanted to be strong for myself and Mom. But that wasn't the only reason.

"Mom and Shelly were decent parents. Those five years from when I was nine to fourteen—those were the best years of my life."

"Why did you feel comfortable expressing your anger, but no other negative emotions?"

I paused for about ten seconds and felt my heart palpitate. "Because I didn't want to move again. I thought that if I cried or showed other signs of pain, then maybe they'd put me in another home." Tears rolled down my face. "I know it sounds crazy."

I realized I'd been carrying this belief with me ever since I was three years old, with my face buried in my mother's lap as the police stood over us.

"Robert, it might be time to reconsider that belief. Understand that telling your family, or anyone else, how you feel does not mean they will stop caring about you, or loving you," Alan said. "Drinking to blunt your feelings does not safeguard anything."

"Yeah, I understand," I said. "I told you about my biological mom, too," I said. "She was an addict. Couldn't this all just be inherited from her?"

"That wouldn't explain why you were unsupervised while you were drinking and doing drugs and asking your friends to choke you to get high. Propensity for addiction is, to some extent, genetic. But how it manifests depends on the situation."

Addiction is more likely to arise in a harsh or unstable

environment—especially one where alcohol or drugs are easily accessible. I'd always enjoyed drinking, but, as an adult, it went into overdrive when unlimited access to alcohol collided with the pain I carried. Alan later showed me an article indicating that prescription painkiller abuse among American teenagers has increased more than 40 percent compared to previous generations. The study suggested that this is because of greater availability of prescription drugs in family medicine cabinets.[3] Something as simple as access can cause a massive increase in substance abuse.

I had to excavate my past to understand what I'd been hiding from others, as well as myself, to feel whole again. I came to understand that I was not at fault for what I'd gone through as a kid—the adults in my life were. But those adults weren't going to fix my present situation; only I could fix it.

At this point, I felt compelled to call Shelly.

I didn't have her number. It had been seven years since we'd last spoken, and all I knew was that Shelly lived in Florida now. After I left home, I threw myself into my attempt to achieve complete independence with no need to rely on anyone. Hannah would regularly urge me to return Mom's calls, which I usually did. But Shelly had never once tried to contact me, and I'd long felt hurt by that but would never have acknowledged it until now.

---

3 Amy Novetny, "In Brief," American Psychological Association, February 2013, https://www.apa.org/monitor/2013/02/inbrief.

I found Shelly on Facebook and sent her a message. She replied shortly thereafter, and we scheduled a phone call. I told her about what I'd been through over the last few years, and my experiences in rehab. She said she was proud of me for completing the treatment program, which, strange as it sounds, irritated me. For a moment I thought, *Proud? I was basically born into an institutional system, and going into another one isn't something to be proud of.* I had to take a deep breath and let it go. Those thoughts weren't helping anyone.

Shelly then said that it might have been better that I was dealing with my inner turmoil now, as an adult. She suggested that as a kid, putting my emotions on hold for my adult self to deal with later may have protected me. I felt that she was right.

"Why did you never call?" I asked.

"I could ask you the same question," Shelly replied.

"Yeah, I guess," I acknowledged. Still, I wanted some assurance that the bond I'd had with Shelly wasn't a fluke. When we lost contact, some part of me believed that it had been.

"Look, Rob. It was hard. Hard to have your mom and you kids around, and then have it all fall apart." She paused, and I could hear her holding back tears. "I never wanted you kids to go through anything like that. I thought it would go right this time, but when it didn't, I just left. It wasn't right, I know. And I'm sorry."

This time. I remembered how she had stopped speaking with her daughters all those years ago, before reconnecting with them. She was doing the same thing I'd done—or maybe I was doing what she'd done. Fleeing to forget.

"It's okay, I understand," I said, maybe more to myself than to her.

Shelly then explained that she had met someone in Florida and was happy now.

"And that's what I want for you too, Rob. To be happy. Look, if you ever want to call just to yell at me, or vent, I totally understand."

I've never been much of a yeller or venter and held no ill will toward her. I just said thanks and wished her well.

The conversation was brief, and, while I was glad to have re-connected, I also knew that such phone calls wouldn't be a regular occurrence—perhaps an annual check-in. I dwelled on this thought, remembering the last time I saw Shelly, yelling in the parking lot after her separation from Mom. Shelly, like me, cut off contact with those close to her to subdue her pain. We run from our feelings, and, in the process, hurt others and ourselves. I didn't want to run anymore. I stayed with my thoughts, instead of withdrawing from them, and considered what to do next.

I picked up my phone again and called the education center on base to make an appointment.

CHAPTER NINE

Who Is GI Bill, GI Joe's Brother?

Within weeks of completing the treatment program and returning to my apartment in Germany, I'd noticed the color of my hair had been restored—no more grays. Was it sobriety, sleep, or the absence of stress? In rehab, we talked about how so many slang terms for intoxication are about inflicting harm on ourselves: smashed, hammered, wrecked, plastered, stoned, fucked up, and so on. I'd stopped doing that to myself every day. My mind had been mostly cleared of the rancor of my past, but I knew it would take work to maintain my new state. When something dramatic happens to people and they subsequently attempt to implement positive change in their lives, for the first few weeks it's easy to stand tall and believe in their transformation: this is who I will be from now on. But that transformation requires constant work. Erosion is an inevitability, as New Year's resolutions remind us each year, unless we're willing to put in the effort required to keep things up.

Although people can have a genetic propensity for depression, the risk can be cut in half with healthy lifestyle changes—nutritious diet, regular exercise, predictable sleep patterns, the stuff you'd expect.[1] Since completing the treatment program, I'd read that about three-quarters of people with alcohol dependency overcome their addiction and later resume drinking without experiencing negative consequences.[2] This is especially likely for people who undergo major transitional life events. Perhaps later, when I had my future mapped out, I could revisit the question of sobriety.

It was the spring of 2014, and my enlistment was set to conclude in the fall of 2015, which was when I hoped to start college.

My appointment at the education center was on the calendar. In the meantime, unsure what else to do to prepare, I did what anybody does when they're curious about something: I turned to Google. I searched variations of "Veteran interested in college" and "How to get into a good college as an older student." I decided to aim for top colleges because they would have more resources for me to explore my curiosities. And if I did have potential, I might as well try to aim as high as I could to fulfill it. More practically, there was the matter of age. Back when I was a new recruit, I'd had a conversation with an older coworker.

---

1   Z. Cao, H. Yang, Y. Ye, Y. Zhang, S. Li, H. Zhao, and Y. Wang, "Polygenic Risk Score, Healthy Lifestyles, and Risk of Incident Depression," *Translational Psychiatry* 11 (2021): 189.

2   D. A. Dawson, B. F. Grant, F. S. Stinson, and P. S. Chou, "Maturing Out of Alcohol Dependence: The Impact of Transitional Life Events," *Journal of Studies on Alcohol* 67 (2006): 195–203.

"You ever think about going to college, maybe using the GI Bill?" I asked him.

"Nah, that's dumb," he replied. "Think about it—I'd be so far behind my peers of the same age, it's not worth it."

I spotted holes in his logic—time was going to pass by either way, so why not spend it doing something you found fulfilling? But back then I took his words at face value because it was comforting to believe that my decision to avoid education was the right call. That conversation lingered in my mind, though. I figured if I was going to be a "mature" student, I hoped to at least attend a college where I wouldn't feel like I was starting from square one.

I finally arrived at the education center on base to learn more about my options. The appointment was enlightening, but not in the way I'd expected.

"Okay, man, so you're here to learn about the GI Bill, right?" the education representative asked me. He looked to be in his thirties and was almost certainly a veteran.

"Yeah, that's right," I said.

"Perfect, now is the right time," he said. "You don't want to go back to civilian life and be like 'Uh, who is GI Bill, GI Joe's brother?' Anyway, where you from?"

"California," I replied.

"What part?" He pulled up an online GI Bill calculator on his computer.

"Uh, San Jose," I said. I wasn't *from* San Jose, but that was where Mom lived with her partner.

He typed into his computer, and a map appeared. "Okay, that's right near San Francisco."

He explained that the GI Bill covered college tuition for all veterans who served after 9/11 and it provided a stipend to pay for living expenses. The payment varied based on where you happened to live. Unsurprisingly, San Francisco had one of the highest stipends in the country.

"Check it out," the education rep said. "If you went to college full-time in San Francisco for four years, or thirty-six months in total not including summers—they don't pay you during months you're not enrolled in classes—you'd be getting $3,369 a month, okay? Now multiply that amount by thirty-six months and you get $121,284. That's all tax-free, too."

I looked at him blankly. *What does this have to do with getting into a good college?*

"What I'm telling you is," he said, "the best thing you can do is move back home with your parents and stay in your old bedroom. Enroll in whatever college that will take you and save up that cash. At the end, you'll have a degree and over a hundred grand. Get it?"

I left his question hanging. Not only would this plan not work, but I also didn't like it. Mom worked at a motel and lived in a tiny rent-controlled apartment with her partner, so moving in wasn't an option. And I didn't want to use my tuition benefits to maximize profits, I wanted to use them to get the best education I could.

I thanked the education rep for his time and went on my way.

• • •

As I browsed various online forums trying to learn about college, I came across a book published in 1983 with an intriguing title: *Class: A Guide Through the American Status System* by Paul Fussell. I bought a copy and discovered a new lens to understand education. The book claimed that the criteria we use to define the tiers of the social hierarchy are in fact indicative of our own social class. For people near the bottom, Fussell wrote, social class is defined by money—in this regard, I was right in line with my peers when I was growing up. We thought a lot about money. The middle class, though, believes class is not just about the size of one's pocketbook; equally important is education. The upper class has some additional beliefs about class, which I would later come to learn.

During another of my online searches, I found the Yale Veterans Association website. *Veterans can get into Yale?* I estimated my odds of getting into a school like that were basically zero. But I figured it was worth a shot.

The webpage had an email address. I contacted them, asking for advice on how to write a successful undergraduate application as a nontraditional student.

I was floored when I opened my email the following day. The vice president of the Yale Veterans Association, a graduate student named Kyle, had responded. He recommended I apply for something called the Warrior-Scholar Project, a two-week program designed to help prepare veterans to become full-time college students.[3]

---

3 For those interested in learning more about the Warrior-Scholar Project, visit https://www.warrior-scholar.org/.

After I submitted my application, the program requested a phone interview, stating that they still had seats available at their Yale workshop (they have since expanded to many other locations).

During the interview, I explained that I'd been a poor student but had always been curious, that I read voraciously, and that I felt the program could help fill in some gaps in my knowledge about how to be a successful student and how to apply for college. I didn't want to get my hopes up but felt I did well. I phoned Kyle, and he explained that he would be surprised if I were not accepted to the two-week workshop.

Two weeks later, I received an email, and my heart sank when I read the first line: "*I regret to inform you that we are not able to offer you admission at this stage.*"

My plans were foiled, and I had no idea what to do next.

My sister flew out to visit me in Germany for a couple weeks as I considered my options. I was trying to save as much money as possible from my military salary in case college fell through. I figured I might need extra savings if I didn't have a campus to go to. Still, for the first week, Hannah and I managed to do some traveling around Vienna, Trier, and Heidelberg, staying in cheap hostels.

The second week was spent mostly hanging out at my apartment, watching movies, bingeing *Curb Your Enthusiasm* episodes, and cooking.

We were in the kitchen having coffee.

"When's the last time you visited Mom?" I asked. It was a four-hour drive from my sister's place in Chico to Mom's place in San Jose.

"Um, probably the last time you visited," Hannah replied.

I did a quick mental tally. "You haven't seen Mom in almost a year?"

"Yeah, something like that."

I was taken aback by this. "Why not?"

"I've been busy, with work, with school, all that stuff. I haven't really had time." Hannah had recently started community college and worked part-time as a barista.

"Mom misses you, you know."

"She misses you, too. Why is it a big deal? You haven't been home this whole time either."

"I live seven thousand miles away. You live four hours away."

"That doesn't make me any less busy than you," Hannah replied coldly.

"Fine," I snapped. "But you're still closer."

"So what? Why am I the one who has to visit? You guys are the ones who left! Mom moved to San Jose when we were kids, and then you moved all the way from here to Europe."

"If you don't want to be here, then leave."

I regretted it as soon as I said it. Hannah and I felt guilty for what happened in our family. It wasn't logical for either of us to feel this way for what happened when we were kids, but feelings from childhood are often illogical.

Hannah was glaring at me, on the verge of tears.

"Look, I'm sorry," I said.

When we were kids, all I ever wanted was to leave. But now I realized that for Hannah, all she wanted was for me and our mom to return. I'd relinquished any hope of an unbroken family, while she held on to it.

"Are you going to visit Mom more, when you get out of the military?" she asked. "I will if you will."

"Yes. I will," I replied. "I don't even know where I'm going to live. But I promise to visit more, wherever I end up."

Even if our family wasn't how it was when we were kids, I wanted to make the most of what we had. Not just for me, but for Hannah, too.

"Where do you want to live?" she asked. "Where are you applying?"

"I'm still thinking about that."

"What happened to that warrior scholar thing?"

"I didn't get in," I said. I disappointed my sister a lot over the years, and it never got easier.

"What are you going to do now?" she asked.

"Not sure yet. I'll figure something out."

Fortunately, I didn't have to. About a week after my sister returned to California, I received an email from the Warrior-Scholar Project:

You should now make your travel arrangements for the course.
Come to: Saybrook College Yale University New Haven, CT.

The email went on to provide additional details for the two-week program. I couldn't believe it—I must have been removed from a waitlist.

My commanding officer allowed me to take just enough time off to arrive the day before the program began, which meant I'd be jet-lagged for the first portion of the course. But I didn't care, it was an exciting time.

I scheduled my first ever visit to the East Coast.

Kyle arranged for me to stay with his law-school friend the night before the program began. When I arrived at Michael's residence in New Haven, he introduced me to his cat.

"His name is Learned Claw," Michael said. "We named him after the legal scholar and judge Learned Hand."

I'd never heard of this judge before. My mind jumped to Paul Fussell's book about social class. He wrote that upper-middle-class people often give their cats names like Clytemnestra or Spinoza to show off their classical education. I was glad I'd read that book. Even though I didn't know who Learned Hand was, at least now I knew that he was someone a person with a classical education should know about. I kneeled down to pet the cat, making a mental note to look the judge up later.

As I entered the gates into Saybrook, one of Yale's oldest residential colleges, I immediately felt out of place. The courtyard looked like something out of a movie: manicured grass, spring magnolia trees, and towering gothic buildings. The staff gave me a key and pointed to where I'd be staying for the next two weeks to learn how to apply for college and how to be a college student. My room had stained-glass windows, but otherwise was what I'd imagined a college dorm would look like.

After speaking with the other students and seeing that many of the guys had beards or long hair, I gathered they were all veterans who had completed their enlistments. I didn't meet any other students who were still on active duty like me. This reminded me of my experiences way back during boot camp, where I'd been the youngest guy in my unit. Back then, I'd been in a hurry to leave home because I was on the wrong path. Now, I was in a hurry to get into college because it was the right one.

The program was a fully immersive experience. The coursework centered on themes of freedom and democracy. Days would begin at 8:00 a.m. and conclude fourteen hours later. First, the other students and I met for breakfast in a college dining hall. Next, we attended lectures, followed by lunch conversations about challenges veterans face in college. Our afternoons were spent in seminar discussions and writing workshops.

After these workshops, we spent our evenings studying assigned texts to prepare for the following day or completing our writing assignments. Just being in that kind of environment, with a bunch of other highly ambitious veterans, had a powerful effect on all of us. It made us want to succeed. It re-ignited the curiosity that had always existed within me but had waxed and waned throughout my youth.

• • •

In addition to the academic lessons, the insights I gleaned from the unstructured time throughout the program were equally useful. The tutors at the Warrior-Scholar Project weren't vets—they were civilian students or graduates of top colleges like Yale, Dartmouth, and Vassar. Most interesting for me was learning what television shows they enjoyed, because I'd grown up watching so much television.

I befriended one of the tutors, a recent Yale graduate. One evening, I saw him watching something on his MacBook. He told me it was *The West Wing* and insisted that I watch it. I had never seen this show, nor did anyone I know watch it. But when another tutor overheard him recommend *The West Wing* to me, she nodded vigorously, saying I *had* to watch it. I made a mental note to check it out once I finished the program.

The lessons from the program that I related most personally to my life came from a seminar-style discussion. Led by the eminent Yale historian John Lewis Gaddis, the other students and I discussed the ideas of Isaiah Berlin. Berlin, a mid-twentieth-century philosopher and historian of ideas, contrasted two different kinds of freedom. One is "positive liberty." We have positive liberty to the extent that we are self-determined and can pursue and fulfill our desires. The other kind of freedom is "negative liberty," meaning we are free to the extent that we are not being coerced when we make our own choices. Positive liberty is about the ability to accomplish our aims, negative liberty is about the absence of coercion.

I couldn't help but apply these concepts to my own life. For long stretches of my childhood, I had an abundance of negative liberty, and it simply allowed me to make a lot of bad decisions. The military stripped me of those freedoms; it was a giant coercion machine. It demanded I conform to certain beliefs and behaviors, which, at age seventeen, was beneficial.

Berlin believed people should not be tampered with or coerced. But he went on to say that giving children total freedom means they may "suffer the worst misfortunes from nature and from men." Therefore, he believed, kids need a higher authority who knows better than they do in order to set boundaries. Restricting some freedom is essential for children to grow up, or, in the case of my enlistment, recover from the process of growing up.

In our next seminar, we discussed a quote by F. Scott Fitzgerald: "The test of a first-rate intelligence is the ability to hold two opposing ideas in mind at the same time and still retain the ability to function." Again, I connected this to my own early experiences. I was well aware that dysfunction and deprivation are enormous obstacles to success. On the other hand, I believed that even under such conditions, people still retained agency. People have choices; we're not billiard balls traveling along preordained trajectories with no say in the matter. I thought about what my high school teacher said to me all those years ago, when I'd told him I knew I wasn't going to college: "That is not written in stone. That is a *choice* you are making."

Now, I was making a different choice.

* * *

After I completed the two-week program at Yale to learn how to prepare for college, I returned to Germany to fulfill the remainder of my enlistment. I took the recommendation to watch *The West Wing* seriously. It was, after all, the first show that two college graduates had ever recommended to me. I figured it was an important cultural touchstone. What if I went to college and someone made a comment referencing the show that I didn't understand? It was my attempt to learn more about the culture of a highly influential segment of society by consuming the same media as them.

The hour-long drama aired between 1999 and 2006 and centers around idealistic senior staffers working for a fictional US presidential administration. As I worked my way through the first season, I had an uncomfortable realization: *The West Wing* is not very good. More than once, I thought about pouring a stiff drink after watching an episode. Granted, part of this may be because of the gap between the era in which it was produced and when I was watching it, and the fact that it had originally aired on network television. I suspect if a similar show were made today for Netflix or HBO, it would be better. The show had the pacing of a '90s TV drama, and the way the characters spoke seemed strange to me (I've since grown to enjoy "Sorkinese"; *Molly's Game* was one of my favorite movies of 2017). Still, I kept watching—because I was intrigued by what it told me about the people who'd recommended it.

In fact, *West Wing* creator Aaron Sorkin explained in an interview with *New York Times* columnist David Brooks that the pilot episode generally wasn't well received. But, according to Sorkin, it tested "extremely well" with certain audience segments: households that earned more than $75,000 a year, households where there was someone with a college degree, and households that subscribed to the *New York Times*.[4] I was not a part of any of these groups, which might have been why the show didn't "test well" on me. Still, it held my attention.

I watched two full seasons of *The West Wing* before stopping, but scenes from the series remained with me. The character Josh Lyman (the deputy chief of staff) boasted about how he'd attended Harvard and Yale. C. J. Cregg (the White House press secretary) asked President Bartlet why he'd attended Notre Dame when he'd gotten into Harvard, Yale, and Williams. The show seemed to confirm that education was indeed a necessary ingredient for a better life, and that not all educations were considered equal.

In the meantime, I signed up to take the SAT for my college applications. The evening before the test, I was nervous. This time, unlike when I took the standardized test for the military in high school, I didn't spend the night before playing Xbox and chugging malt liquor. After working a twelve-hour shift, I went straight home, brushed my teeth, and made sure to get a full night's sleep.

The testing location was at an American high school on the US military base. I felt more than a little awkward sitting in a high-school classroom again at age twenty-four, surrounded by a bunch of teenagers. What did these kids here think of me—*who is this old dude sitting with us?* I thought about how if I were to attend college, my classmates wouldn't be much older than them. *Well, at least I don't have gray hairs anymore.* It was the first time in seven years I had

---

4 Aspen Institute, "What's Character Got to Do with It?" [video file], July 1, 2015. Retrieved from https://youtu.be/eucVNYQNGAs.

to sit in one of those classroom chairs with the tiny desk attached. Squeezing myself into it, I thought about how they were smaller than I remembered.

When I wasn't working or watching any number of TV shows (*The West Wing*, *Mad Men*, or *Breaking Bad* were playing in my apartment at any given moment), I was working on my college application essays. I did my best to condense my tumultuous childhood into a few hundred words, while also explaining why my high-school transcript was not a reliable indicator of my academic potential, and how my early life experiences led me to apply for college.

As I worked, my friend Curtis was on my couch nearby watching Walter White pull into his driveway in his 2004 Pontiac Aztek in *Breaking Bad*. The car had a faded factory paint job and was missing a hubcap.

Curtis looked over at me and said, "Damn, dude, this show is actually pretty authentic."

He pointed out how often "regular people" on TV are depicted as better off than their real-life counterparts. We both grew up watching *Roseanne* and thought that Roseanne Conner's two-story house was an example of this. Even more unusual, I thought, was how Roseanne and Dan were married and never divorced throughout the show—a marked contrast from what I saw in Red Bluff, a town not unlike the fictional Lanford.

Shortly thereafter, I sent off my college applications for the 2015–2016 academic year.

. . .

Three weeks later, I scrolled through Facebook and saw something I'd never seen on my feed before: a link to the *New York Times*. I knew of it, obviously, but didn't think I knew anyone who read it. I rarely saw any prominent news links posted—usually it was memes, YouTube videos, or links to music.

The person who posted the *Times* link was Anna Ivey, whom I'd met at the Warrior-Scholar Project. She had been the dean of admissions at the University of Chicago Law School and had visited the program to learn about veterans in higher education. We'd briefly chatted about "Pericles's Funeral Oration," one of the assigned readings, and later connected on Facebook.

I clicked on the link that Anna posted. The newspaper invited aspiring college students to submit their application essays about money and social class. They would select a few of them and publish them online. I paused, considering whether to send mine. Surely, I thought, there were others out there who were applying to college who had more interesting lives than mine. I considered the people I'd met in my life—foster care, my friends in Red Bluff, the military, rehab, and so on. On a spectrum of interesting stories, I would have placed myself in the middle, or maybe a notch or two more "interesting" than the average. *What the hell*, I thought, and decided to submit it.

After sending off my applications, I planned a short vacation to Volterra, Italy, a medieval town near Florence. It was a cheap ninety-minute flight from the airport closest to my apartment in Germany.

The plan was to have a period of recuperation before Yale released their admissions decisions. My appetite for risk-taking had not completely subsided: I'd applied only to what I now know are called "reach" schools, and there was a real possibility that I would not get into any of them. Still, I had my sights set on Yale because of the positive experiences I'd had there.

My vacation was interrupted by a welcome intrusion. I received an email from a *New York Times* editor who informed me that they were publishing my college application essay the following day. I was momentarily taken aback because I'd forgotten I'd even sent it to them. I also felt fear. I used to hate talking about my life, and now my background was going to be widely available for anyone to read. By now, though, I'd realized something: When I ran from my past, I made so many poor decisions. But when I accepted what I'd been through, that was when things started to turn around for me. I signed the agreement forms. The editors sent a photographer to Volterra so that a picture could accompany my essay. They chose a photo of me in the dark looking up at the sunlight.[5]

In the photo, I looked hopeful. But in reality, I was nervous. The clock was ticking on my enlistment, which was set to conclude in less than three months, and I had no idea where I'd be going next.

What if I didn't get in? My mind jumped back to that conversation with Old Joe all those years ago. *You'll be okay no matter where you*

---

5   R. Lieber, ed., "Students and Money, in Their Own Words," *New York Times*, May 21, 2015, https://www.nytimes.com/interactive/2015/05/20/your-money/college-essays -on-money.html.

end up. As an ungainly thirteen-year-old, I didn't fully believe those words. Now, a decade later, I did. By this point, I figured I'd be able to take care of myself, with or without college. I realized how lucky I was. I felt grateful, despite everything. For my adoptive family, for my sister, for the opportunity to serve this great country, for a second chance to be the first in my family to go to college.

At last, I opened an email from Yale admissions. I nearly fell out of my chair when I read the first word: "Congratulations!" I called Mom. She was extremely proud, and together we joked about how happy we were that the GI Bill would cover the tuition fees. I thought about my experience at the summer academic program the year before and couldn't believe it had all worked out. I was ecstatic.

CHAPTER TEN

Problem Child

There were many surreal aspects of my experience at Yale, including the ability to learn from high-profile professors. I took a course on Shakespeare taught by the late Harold Bloom, who has been described as "the most renowned, and arguably the most passionate, literary critic and Shakespeare scholar in America."[1] When I told him about my life, the eighty-seven-year-old professor gently replied, "You were forged in a fire." I also met the psychology professor Albert Bandura—who at the time was ninety-one years old and died in 2021—to chat about a book he had recently written. I was surprised at how late in life many professors worked—some well into their eighties and even nineties. This was a notable difference from the aging adults I knew in Red Bluff, who

---

1 J. Heilpern, "Avon Calling," *Vanity Fair*, April 20, 2011, https://www.vanityfair.com /news/2011/05/out-to-lunch-bloom-201105.

typically looked forward to retirement and preferred not to work longer than they had to, unless it was out of financial necessity.

Before my first classes were scheduled to begin, I was sitting in the courtyard of my residential college when a young woman asked for help lifting some boxes into her dorm room. She introduced herself and told me she was a senior. I explained that this was my first semester.

"What do you think of Yale so far?" she asked.

I was embarrassed to answer. "I keep waiting for them to tell me it was a mistake that they let me in," I said, carrying boxes up the stairs as she guided me. "Walking around, it feels like I'm dreaming."

"That's such a great feeling," she replied wistfully. "Enjoy it."

We entered her room, and I set the boxes down. She opened the larger box and pulled out a large case of pills.

The medication rattled as she set it on her desk.

"Nice stash. Anything for sale?" I joked.

"Yeah, the Adderall is." She didn't appear to be joking.

I thought back to my first day in high school, and how my neighbor offered to sell me drugs. Now here I was at this fancy college, and this senior is offering to sell drugs, too. Later, I'd observe rampant drug and alcohol use on campus. This was at odds with the widespread belief, which I held at the time, that poverty was the primary reason for substance abuse.

Overall, I found that the vast majority of my peers were high performers. One thing many people don't understand is that it's usually not enough to be smart (or rich) to get into a top college—these places reject many smart (and rich) applicants every year. You have to be diligent as well, and I respected their work ethic.

I came to understand that along with the fact that they were generally bright and hardworking, my peers on campus had experienced a totally different social reality than me and had grown up around people just like them.

During my first semester, I felt out of my depth. I had received invaluable guidance at the Warrior-Scholar Project, but that program was only two weeks long.

In my first semester, I took a cognitive science class as part of my major. I'd never read a scientific journal article before, and now I was assigned to read several each week. I had a heavy reading load from other courses as well. I wasn't entirely sure how to handle it and read every assigned text. It was challenging to retain so much information and balance all my assignments. On the midterm exam, my score placed me in the bottom quartile of the class.

I befriended some other students and picked up some tips. We held study sessions, and they showed me how to make flashcards, and how to review PowerPoint slides from the class. One simple approach I learned was to read a slide and then commit the information on it to memory and go through that exercise a few times with each slide. Spaced repetitions. Other students taught me that for the assigned readings, they read a page, and then wrote bullets at the bottom of the page summarizing the most important points. These strategies might sound simple, but for me they were a revelation.

They helped me overcome years of poor study habits and the rust that had developed since high school. Of course, beyond mere memorization and regurgitation, courses required critical analysis—synthesizing multiple ideas in essays and applying what we'd learned to novel prompts in exams. I found that I was proficient at this once I'd learned how to grasp and encode the vast amount of information assigned. I did well on the final exam and received a high score on my final paper.

My classmates taught me that I didn't have to read every single item on course syllabi. At first, I thought if I wasn't reading everything, then I was cheating myself out of my education. This, I discovered, is a common belief held by first-generation college students. I spoke with a variety of students about how they approached coursework and noticed a distinct difference. Students from well-to-do backgrounds, who had parents who were college graduates, seemed to have developed a good sense of how to manage their assignments and understood that reading everything wasn't always necessary. Classmates showed me that we could split the heavy reading burdens by dividing it. We'd write up a summary of our share of the readings and notes.

The following semester, I managed to get into a psychology seminar that was intended primarily for seniors. Here, I realized that my upbringing differed from those of my fellow students in ways that extended beyond the financial status of our families. The professor asked the class to anonymously respond to a question about family background. Out of twenty students, only one other student besides me was not raised by both birth parents. Put differently, 90 percent of my classmates were raised by an intact family. I felt a sense of vertigo upon learning this, because it was so at odds with how I'd grown up. Later, I read a study from another Ivy League school—Cornell—which reported that only 10 percent of their students were raised by divorced parents.[2] This is a sharp juxtaposition with a national divorce rate of about 40 percent,[3] which itself is quite low compared to the families I'd known in Red Bluff. When I explained to a classmate how disoriented I felt when I discovered these differences, she replied that this was how she felt when she learned that seven out of ten adults in the US don't have a bachelor's degree, because that was so out of line with her own experiences.

What? I was surprised that it was *only* seven out of ten, because so few people I'd known were college graduates.

In my first semester, I tried to get into a specific course titled "The Concept of the Problem Child." I read the course description:

Differing visions of good and bad, typical and atypical, children. Reasons why some children are seen as deviant and others as normal. Implications for public policy, medical practice, family dynamics, schooling, and the criminal justice and protective care systems. Sources include public health data, early childhood curricula, and depictions of problem children in literature and popular culture.

---

2   S. Lang, "Children from Divorced Families Only Half as Likely to Go to a Top College, Cornell Research Shows," *Cornell Chronicle*, May 17, 1996, https://news.cornell.edu/stories/1996/05/children-divorced-families-only-half-likely-go-top-college-cornell-research-shows.

3   B. Buscombe, "The Divorce Rate Is Dropping. That May Not Actually Be Good News," *Time*, November 26, 2018, https://time.com/5434949/divorce-rate-children-marriage-benefits/.

For obvious reasons, I hoped to take this course. But it was capped, meaning only a limited number of students could join. Because around one hundred students had applied, many of them seniors, I was wait-listed. *No big deal*, I thought. *I'll take it next time.* I wrote an email to the instructor, Erika Christakis, thanking her for offering the course, and stated that I looked forward to applying again in the future.

I would soon learn this was the last time she would ever offer this course at Yale.

Walking through Old Campus—the oldest part of Yale—I found a flier indicating that NYU professor Jonathan Haidt was visiting campus to give a talk. I'd recently read his bestselling book *The Righteous Mind: Why Good People Are Divided by Politics and Religion*. I figured Professor Haidt would speak about moral psychology, the theme of his book. But instead, on the day of the talk, Haidt discussed the purpose of a university. He urged the audience to consider whether the aim of higher education is to protect students or to equip them with the ability to seek truth, and he was clearly in favor of the latter.

I thought this was a strange presentation. I sat there utterly perplexed. *Why was he talking about this?*

I simply didn't have the requisite background knowledge to understand. This new social environment was so unfamiliar to me that I hadn't realized there was a contentious national debate going on about the very nature of higher education.

Soon, the message of Haidt's talk would become painfully clear. Just as my feelings of being a total outsider had begun to subside, they would suddenly resurface.

Two weeks later, I was sitting on a bench in front of Sterling Memorial Library, reading an email on my laptop by Erika Christakis, the instructor who taught the Concept of the Problem Child course.

"I'm confused, honestly," I said to the student next to me. "I have no idea why people are upset about this."

He sighed. "I knew that email would be controversial as soon as I read it," he said.

The university administration had recently circulated a campus-wide email to students asking them to be sensitive about what Halloween costumes they wear. The idea was that costumes that implied that other cultures or interests were unserious or played into stereotypes might cause discomfort or harm to other students. In response, Erika Christakis wrote an email to the students within her residential college. In her email, she questioned whether the administration should interfere with students' lives—she defended freedom of expression and urged students to handle disagreements about costumes on their own. The social climate immediately changed. Hundreds of students marched throughout campus. They called for apologies from the university and insisted Christakis and her husband, who was also a professor and who defended her, be fired, among other demands.

Because I was older, sometimes students would crack jokes to me about the movie *21 Jump Street*, about two twenty-five-year-old cops who go undercover to pose as students at a high school. Throughout the movie, the protagonists make subtle errors indicating a miniature generation gap. At no point did these jokes feel more apt than when I saw those students marching around campus, demanding the two professors be fired. I felt like they were speaking a language I didn't know.

Even the students who didn't *agree* that Erika's email was wrong *knew* why others thought it was wrong, but I was mystified. I would ask outraged classmates to explain what had been done wrong, hoping to understand.

A student from Greenwich, Connecticut, who had attended Phillips Exeter Academy (an expensive private boarding school), explained that I was too privileged to understand the pain these professors had caused. At first, I was stunned. But later, I came to understand the intellectual acrobatics necessary to say something like this. The student who called me "privileged" likely meant that due to my background as a biracial Asian Latino heterosexual cisgender (that is, I "present" as the sex I was "assigned" at birth) male, this means that I have led a privileged life. However, I also learned that many inhabitants of elite universities assign a great deal of importance to "lived experience." This means that your unique personal hardships serve as important credentials to expound on social ills and suggest remedies.

These two ideas appeared to be contradictory.

Which is more relevant to identity, one's discernible characteristics (gender, ethnicity, sexual orientation, and so on) or what they actually went through in their lives? I asked two students this question. One replied that this question was dangerous to ask. The other said that one's discernible characteristics *determine* what experiences they have in their lives. This means that if you belong to a "privileged" group, then you must have had a privileged life. I dropped the conversation there.

I'd arrived at Yale nervous about the possibility of being intellectually limited compared with my peers on campus because of my impoverished background and poor grades in high school. As I encountered many of their inept ideas, my concerns evaporated.

I was fascinated by this new social reality and avoided discussing my life when contentious discussions erupted. I really wanted to understand what these students thought without risking them being weirded out by someone in their midst who they might have acknowledged as having had a tougher life than them, and who disagreed that words in an email could actually inflict "pain."

That was the language many students used. *Danger* and *harm* and *pain*. Words like *trauma* meant something different for them.

At a party, a young woman told me about her family and how they'd always expected her to get into a top college.

"My mom was super strict growing up," she explained. "Classic Asian mom, I'm sure you know what I mean."

"Well, my mom is Korean," I said. "But my family life wasn't really like that."

"Ah!" she exclaimed. "So, you didn't have a traumatic childhood."

I had an apartment off-campus on Chapel Street. To get there, I had to walk through a lot of poverty—people suffering from drug addiction, homelessness, mental illness, and so on. Sometimes when I'd walk through those areas, I would think about my birth mother, the foster homes I'd lived in, and the people I'd met in rehab. And then I would think about my classmates: At Yale, more students come from families in the top 1 percent of income than from the bottom 60 percent,[4] and here they were ensconced in one of the richest universities in the world, claiming that they were in danger. Broadcasting personal feelings of emotional precarity and supposed powerlessness was part of the campus culture. Conspicuously lamenting systemic disadvantage seemed to serve as both a signal and reinforcer of membership in this rarefied group of future elites.

Many students would routinely claim that systemic forces were working against them, yet they seemed pleased to demonstrate how special they were for rising above those impediments. This spawned a potent blend of victimhood and superiority. It was odd to see relatively advantaged people occupying elite institutions while seeing themselves as somehow beleaguered. Elite universities, in turn, seemed to deliver a double message to the students: "You are the future leaders of the world" and "You are being erased and marginalized." I'd thought that by entering such a place, we were being given a privilege as well as a duty to improve the lives of those less fortunate than ourselves. Instead, many students seemed to be exploiting whatever commonalities they had with historically mistreated groups in order to serve their own personal, social, and professional interests.

I tried to understand the campus protesters, to see where they were coming from. But it was hard for me to sympathize, simply due to the magnitude of the gap between our experiences. Maybe their grievances were a bit overblown, but still, I tried to tell myself,

---

4 "Some Colleges Have More Students from the Top 1 Percent Than the Bottom 60," *New York Times*, January 18, 2017, https://www.nytimes.com/interactive/2017/01/18/upshot/some-colleges-have-more-students-from-the-top-1-percent-than-the-bottom-60.html.

they're young. They're still maturing. Just like my enlisted friends and I were when we volunteered our lives for this country. Just like my friend was when he hanged himself after two deployments. I considered the differences in how fast people are expected to grow up based on how much money their families have. A twenty-year-old at an expensive college is viewed as not much more than a kid. A twenty-year-old in the military is trusted to carry a weapon, repair multimillion-dollar equipment, and make life-and-death decisions.

Frankly, I found that college extends adolescence to a laughably old age. It was surreal to hear people say that college students are adults when they are vastly outnumbered by working-class and poor people who face the full brunt of reality before they even turn eighteen. Interestingly, studies have found that people with adverse childhood experiences—physical or emotional abuse, neglect, poverty, parental divorce, and so on—seem to age faster. Children with stressful lives tend to get their adult teeth earlier, reach puberty sooner, and undergo accelerated changes in their brain structure.[5] This also implies that a very comfortable upbringing might slow maturation. In high school, the guys I grew up with looked older than many of my college peers.

This maturity gap was evident even in small things like seeing my college friends attempt to drive a car. They got their licenses in high school and then spent a few years in college ordering Ubers to chauffeur them around. Living in a college bubble, they were unpracticed at operating a vehicle. More than once I've feared for my

5   A. Gopnik, "What Children Lose When Their Brains Develop Too Fast," *Wall Street Journal*, December 9, 2021, https://www.wsj.com/articles/what-children-lose-when-their-brains-develop-too-fast-11639071752.

life sitting in the passenger's seat of a rental while an inexperienced Yale graduate shook nervously while holding their hands at ten and two.

When I passed through the gates of the university and walked through downtown New Haven, I would occasionally think about how—despite their lofty rhetoric—the people educated at elite universities are often driven more by self-interest than implementing meaningful change. Solving the country's most challenging social ills was a secondary concern.

I remember speaking with a fellow first-gen student at Yale who told me he was against legacy admissions—the practice whereby elite universities give an advantage to applicants with parents or family members who are graduates.

Intrigued, I replied to this student, "You had a harder upbringing than most students here, but you just got into law school, and will probably be very successful in your career. If you have kids and they apply to Yale, should they be favored for admission?"

"Yes," he replied. "But I worked really hard to give them that opportunity."

In other words, he was against legacy admissions in general, but supported it for his own children. He paid lip service to reducing inequality but personally endorsed something that would serve his interests.

Meanwhile, the student protests became a national story. Erika Christakis and her husband, Nicholas, were ridiculed and reviled, with little public support from students, faculty, or the administration.

Privately, many people—perhaps most—were supportive, but they were fearful of openly expressing this. Erika was asked by some of the protesters to announce when she was going into the dining hall so that students wouldn't be triggered. She stepped down from her teaching position at the university, although her husband remained. After those incomprehensible events, I would gaze at the beautiful architecture throughout the university and think about a line I'd read from F. Scott Fitzgerald, describing Gatsby's forever altered relationship with the green light across the bay: "His count of enchanted objects had diminished by one."

I watched students claim that investment banks were emblematic of capitalist oppression, and then discovered that they'd attended recruitment sessions for Goldman Sachs. Gradually, I came to believe that many of these students were broadcasting the belief that such firms were evil in order to undercut their rivals. If they managed to convince you that a certain occupation is corrupt and thus to be avoided, then that was one less competitor they had in their quest to be hired.

But they didn't see themselves this way. They viewed themselves as morally righteous and were surprisingly myopic about the virtuous image they held of themselves.

In December, shortly after the Yale-Harvard football game, one of my peers explained to the rest of the class that she'd seen a group of Harvard students at a New Haven restaurant leave a huge mess at their table.

"I hope the restaurant staff knew those people were from Harvard, not Yale!" said another student.

"I doubt they care," I replied, thinking of my days as a busboy. "They just saw a bunch of spoiled students. Harvard, Yale, it doesn't matter. The mess is the same."

Another time, I was on a social media page where Ivy League students and graduates shared stories about their schools. Someone had posted a story about Yeonmi Park, a North Korean refugee who had graduated from Columbia University. Park described her alarm about how the monolithic culture at her Ivy League school reminded her of her home country. The top-rated comment, the one with the most "like" and "love" reactions: "She should have stayed in North Korea." They couldn't bear the criticism and posted endless mean-spirited comments mocking Park, with some saying she should "go back to Pyongyang."

Ordinarily, the people who visited this webpage would have considered the statement that a refugee should have stayed where she came from to be reprehensible (and it is). But in this instance it was lauded because Park's comments undermined these people's view of themselves as morally righteous. Many students and graduates of top universities are terrified of being seen as what they really are. We don't leave messes for other people to clean up, it's those other elite students from that other school. We're not xenophobic, it's those unenlightened people who didn't go to a fancy college. We haven't cultivated an ideologically rigid environment, go back to where you came from.

In my second year, I learned about a psychology study that investigated moral intuitions. One question asked about incest between a brother and sister. The study found that across different countries, people overwhelmingly stated that sibling incest was wrong. One particular group of people the researchers tested, though, showed a moderate willingness to condone it: students at elite colleges.[6]

After reflecting on this strange finding, I would occasionally ask students this very question to test it myself. Most said yes, sibling incest was fine, assuming no pregnancy. I asked them other questions, like whether it would be okay for an adult to have a romantic relationship with their parent—a man and his father, for instance—and every person I asked said yes. Some were clearly uncomfortable with their answers but could find no reason to object.

The following year, I had lunch with a student from one of my courses. He said he believed in "utilitarianism," which is the idea that moral decisions should be made based on maximizing the overall happiness of the most people. For instance, if two (or perhaps more than two) adult family members could increase their happiness by entering a romantic relationship, then many utilitarians would endorse it. Many utilitarians also believe that sacrificing a smaller number of people for a larger number would be acceptable—the ends justify the means. My classmate and I discussed various moral dilemmas, and he said he would push a man off a bridge to stop a train from hitting five people.

I asked if he would murder his mother to save five strangers. He promptly responded that he would.

I doubted *anyone* I knew outside of college would have said yes

---

6   J. Haidt, S. H. Koller, and M. G. Dias, "Affect, Culture, and Morality, Or Is It Wrong to Eat Your Dog?" *Journal of Personality and Social Psychology* 65 (1993): 613.

to that question. I later read a study that found that upper-class people are more likely to endorse utilitarianism and the belief that "the ends justify the means." One reason for this is that affluent people score relatively low on measures of empathy and favor cold calculations for decision-making.[7] Upon reading this, I thought about how students would sometimes tactically undermine their competitors to get prestigious internships.

I was also mystified at how my peers kept up with the latest news headlines. More than once, someone would ask me what I thought about some trending event covered in the media. When I replied that I hadn't heard of the event, people would look at me as if I were an alien. In the same way that you don't notice how entrenched you are in your specific culture or nationality until you travel to another country, you also don't notice your social class until you enter another one. I had never learned to keep up with the news.

Growing up, Mom and Shelly subscribed to our local paper, Red Bluff's *Daily News*, but they never discussed political or social issues at the dinner table. And we couldn't afford cable, so I didn't watch any of the popular political shows. On campus, though, there was an expectation to know about the issues of the day, and it was common to see the latest editions of the *New York Times* or the *Wall Street Journal* in libraries and residential colleges. The university also offered steep discounts for subscriptions to a variety of periodicals, presumably because these outlets aimed to build lifelong loyalty

---

7   S. Côté, P. K. Piff, and R. Willer, "For Whom Do the Ends Justify the Means? Social Class and Utilitarian Moral Judgment," *Journal of Personality and Social Psychology* 104 (2013): 490.

with students. I came to understand that part of integrating into this community meant having a cursory knowledge of the latest op-eds and fashionable news items.

On campus, it wasn't necessarily important to know about the concrete details of a newsworthy event. Rather, it was more critical to know what to *think* about the event by reading the opinions of others. Back when my life was difficult, I seldom read the news. But now that my life was more comfortable and my future more secure than it had ever been, I was being told that it was important to keep up with it. Being "informed" wasn't important for day-to-day survival, but in this new environment, it seemed to be relevant for social acceptance.

Interestingly, working-class Americans are more likely to read local news, while the wealthy and highly educated favor national and global news.[8] To me, it makes sense to keep up with what's going on in your local community. But there seems to be less practical reason to regularly read about events far removed from you, unless you aim to show others how worldly and sophisticated you are.

Meanwhile, I continued finding myself in situations I didn't quite understand.

In my second year of college, I decided to join a writing team for an on-campus humor magazine. The theme for that month's

---

8   M. Barthel, E. Grieco, and E. Shearer, "Older Americans, Black Adults, and Americans with Less Education More Interested in Local News," Pew Research Center, August 14, 2019, https://www.pewresearch.org/journalism/2019/08/14/older-americans-black-adults-and-americans-with-less-education-more-interested-in-local-news/.

issue was "puberty." In a brainstorming session for satirical headlines, I suggested: "Area male discovers porn goldmine in his front right pocket."

The student editor raised an eyebrow. "Why does it have to be gendered?" he asked. I was mystified. What did "gendered" mean? No one I grew up around ever used this word. No one in the military ever said it. I knew what "gender" was, of course, but why would anyone turn it into an adjective? I grew to understand that there were aspects of social class that can't be quantified or put on a résumé.

Whenever I felt like an outsider, I sought refuge in helping others. Because of the way reading had transformed my life, I volunteered at New Haven Reads, tutoring kids from low-income families with their literacy skills. One boy named Guillermo was in the second grade—the same grade I was in when I'd learned to read. After his mom dropped him off and was out of earshot, he quietly said he didn't think he would ever learn to read. I told him I thought the same thing when I was his age.

He didn't believe me. "I thought Yale students are supposed to be smart."

"I'm not sure about that," I replied. "But it was really tough for me to learn to read."

"My mom says reading is important because she doesn't want me to be like my dad. But I don't know if he ever read, I never met him."

He said it impassively—the same way I would have said it at his age. It conveyed that he didn't feel put upon because his life had always been that way, but he simultaneously wished it were different.

"I never met my dad either," I said.

I told Guillermo about my childhood and how I grew up. He became more eager to learn after I told him about my experiences reading kindergarten-level books when I was in the second grade. In our next session, we learned how to spell his favorite snacks.

I knew what it was like to be in his position. By contributing my time to him and the other kids there, I hoped maybe they would someday know what it is like to be in mine.

But the ideas I would continue to encounter from members of the upper class were, perhaps inadvertently, hindering upward mobility.

CHAPTER ELEVEN

Luxury Beliefs

My childhood habit of visiting school libraries had not abated. I came to Yale to major in psychology, but my generative curiosity soon overflowed the boundaries of my degree. In my attempt to understand class distinctions, I spent a lot of time thinking and reading about class divides and social hierarchies and compared what I'd learned with my experiences on campus. Gradually, I developed the concept of "luxury beliefs," which are ideas and opinions that confer status on the upper class at very little cost, while often inflicting costs on the lower classes. The upper class includes (but is not necessarily limited to) anyone who attends or graduates from an elite college and has at least one parent who is a college graduate. Research has found that parental educational attainment is the most important objective indicator of social class.[1] This is because, compared with parental income, parental education is a more powerful predictor of a child's future lifestyle, tastes, and opinions.[2] In 2021, more than 80 percent of Ivy League students had parents with college degrees.[3]

It is a vexing question whether first-generation college graduates can truly enter the upper class. Paul Fussell—the social critic and author of *Class*—wrote that manners, tastes, opinions, and conversational style are just as important for upper-class membership as money or credentials, and that to fulfill these requirements, you have to be immersed in affluence from birth. Likewise, the twentieth-century French sociologist Pierre Bourdieu stated that a "triadic structure" of schooling, language, and taste was necessary to be accepted among the upper class. Bourdieu described the mastery of this triad as "ease." When you grow up in a social class, you come to embody it. You represent its tastes and values so deeply that you exhibit "ease" within it.[4] This is one reason why, even among graduates of elite universities, parental social class predicts income and occupational prestige. People with parents who are college graduates are often better

1   P. K. Piff, "Wealth and the Inflated Self: Class, Entitlement, and Narcissism," *Personality and Social Psychology Bulletin* 40 (2014): 34–43.

2   J. A. Davis, "Achievement Variables and Class Cultures: Family, Schooling, Job and Forty-Nine Dependent Variables in the Cumulative GSS," in D. B. Grusky, ed., *Social Stratification: Class, Race, and Gender in Sociological Perspective*, 439–457 (Boulder, CO: Westview Press, 1994).

3   "Share of first-generation students in Ivy League schools in the Class of 2026," Statista, October 25, 2021, https://www.statista.com/statistics/940593/ivy-league-share-first-generation-students-class.

4   Bourdieu, Pierre. 1987. *Distinction: A Social Critique of the Judgement of Taste*. Translated by Richard Nice. Cambridge, MA: Harvard University Press.

equipped to gain and maintain status—they tend to be more adept at navigating organizations, smoothly interacting with colleagues, and positioning themselves for advancement.[5] Consistent with this, in 2021 the Pew Research Center found that among households headed by a college graduate, the median wealth of those who have a parent with at least a bachelor's degree was nearly $100,000 greater than those who don't have college-educated parents.[6] This bonus of being a "continuing-generation" (as opposed to a "first-generation") college graduate has been termed the "parent premium."

I don't have the parent premium. For extended periods of my youth, I had the opposite.

It's impossible to say that every individual in a particular class or category has the exact same features across the board. Still, graduates of elite universities generally occupy the top quintile of income, often wield outsized social influence, and are disproportionately likely to hold luxury beliefs that undermine social mobility.

For example, a former classmate at Yale told me "monogamy is kind of outdated" and not good for society. I asked her what her background is and if she planned to marry. She said she came from an affluent family, was raised by both of her parents, and that, yes, she personally intended to have a monogamous marriage—but quickly added that marriage shouldn't have to be for everyone. She was raised in a stable two-parent family, just like the vast majority of

5   L. A. Rivera, *Pedigree* (Princeton, NJ: Princeton University Press, 2016).

6   R. Fry, "First-Generation College Graduates Lag Behind Their Peers on Key Economic Outcomes," Pew Research Center, May 18, 2021, https://www.pewresearch.org/social-trends/2021/05/18/first-generation-college-graduates-lag-behind-their-peers-on-key-economic-outcomes/.

our classmates. And she planned on getting married herself. But she insisted that traditional families are old-fashioned and that society should "evolve" beyond them.

My classmate's promotion of one ideal ("monogamy is outdated") while living by another ("I plan to get married") was echoed by other students in different ways. Some would, for instance, tell me about the admiration they had for the military, or how trade schools were just as respectable as college, or how college was not necessary to be successful. But when I asked them if they would encourage their own children to enlist or become a plumber or an electrician rather than apply to college, they would demur or change the subject.

Later, I would connect my observations to stories I read about tech tycoons, another affluent group, who encourage people to use addictive devices, while simultaneously enforcing rigid rules at home about technology use. For example, Steve Jobs prohibited his children from using iPads. Parents in Silicon Valley reportedly tell their nannies to closely monitor how much their children use their smartphones.[7] Chip and Joanna Gaines are well-known home improvement TV personalities who have their own television network. They don't allow their children to watch TV and don't own a television.[8] Don't get high on your own supply, I guess. Many affluent people now

7   B. Montgomery, "Tech's Rich and Powerful Are So Over Their Gadgets," *Daily Beast*, December 26, 2019, https://www.thedailybeast.com/techs-rich-and-powerful-are -so-over-their-gadgets.

8   J. Juneau, "Joanna Gaines Talks Kids' Screen Time and Says She and Chip 'Don't Have a TV' in Their House," *People*, February 12, 2019, https://people.com/parents/joanna -gaines-doesnt-have-tv-kids-ipad-rules-southern-living/.

promote lifestyles that are harmful to the less fortunate. Meanwhile, they are not only insulated from the fallout; they often profit from it.

Gradually, I would learn the tastes and values of the group that I had not fully joined. I managed to piece together the luxury beliefs concept from my observations and readings to understand what I was seeing. In the past, people displayed their membership in the upper class with their material accoutrements. But today, luxury goods are more accessible than before. This is a problem for the affluent, who still want to broadcast their high social position. But they have come up with a clever solution. The affluent have decoupled social status from goods and reattached it to beliefs.

Human beings become more preoccupied with social status once our physical needs are met. In fact, research has revealed that sociometric status (respect and admiration from peers) is more important for well-being than socioeconomic status.[9] Furthermore, studies have shown that negative social judgment is associated with a spike in cortisol (a hormone linked to stress) that is three times higher than in nonsocial stressful situations.[10] We feel pressure to build and maintain social status, and fear losing it.

It seems reasonable to think that the most downtrodden might be most interested in obtaining status and money. But this is not the

9   C. Anderson, M. W. Kraus, A. D. Galinsky, and D. Keltner, "The Local-Ladder Effect: Social Status and Subjective Well-Being," *Psychological Science* 23 (2012): 764–771.

10   S. S. Dickerson and M. E. Kemeny, "Acute Stressors and Cortisol Responses: A Theoretical Integration and Synthesis of Laboratory Research," *Psychological Bulletin* 130 (2004): 355.

case. Denizens of prestigious institutions are even more interested than others in prestige and wealth. For many of them, that drive is how they reached their lofty positions in the first place. Fueling this desire, they're surrounded by people just like them—their peers and competitors are also intelligent status-seekers. They persistently look for new ways to move upward and avoid moving downward. The French sociologist Émile Durkheim understood this when he wrote, "The more one has, the more one wants, since satisfactions received only stimulate instead of filling needs."[11] And research supports this. A psychology study in 2020 revealed that "Upper-class individuals cared more about status and valued it more highly than working-class individuals. . . . Furthermore, compared with lower-status individuals, high-status individuals were more likely to engage in behavior aimed at protecting or enhancing their status."[12] Plainly, high-status people desire status more than anyone else does.

You might think that, for example, rich students at elite universities would be happy because their parents are in the top 1 percent of income earners, and that statistically they will soon join their parents in this elite guild. But remember, they're surrounded by other members of the 1 percent. For many elite college students, their social circle consists of baby millionaires, which often instills a sense of insecurity and an anxiety to preserve and maintain their positions against such rarefied competitors.

---

11 F. W. Elwell, "Emile Durkheim's Sociology," http://faculty.rsu.edu/users/f/felwell /www/Theorists/Durkheim/index2.htm.

12 C. Anderson, J. A. D. Hildreth, and D. L. Sharps, "The Possession of High Status Strengthens the Status Motive," *Personality and Social Psychology Bulletin* 46 (2020): 1712–1723.

Thorstein Veblen's famous "leisure class" has evolved into the "luxury belief class." Veblen, an economist and sociologist, made his observations about social class in the late nineteenth century. He compiled his observations in his classic 1899 book, *The Theory of the Leisure Class*. A key idea is that because we can't be certain of the financial standing of other people, a good way to size up their means is to see whether they can afford to waste money on goods and leisure. This explains why status symbols are so often difficult to obtain and costly to purchase. In Veblen's day, people exhibited their status with delicate and restrictive clothing like tuxedos, top hats, and evening gowns, or by partaking in time-consuming activities like golf or beagling. Such goods and leisurely activities could only be purchased or performed by those who did not live the life of a manual laborer and could spend time learning something with no practical utility. Veblen even goes so far as to say, "The chief use of servants is the evidence they afford of the master's ability to pay." For Veblen, even butlers were status symbols.

Veblen proposed that the wealthy flaunt these symbols not because they are useful, but because they are so pricey or wasteful that only the wealthy can afford them, which is why they're high-status indicators.

During my first year at Yale in 2015, it was common to see students at Ivy League colleges wearing Canada Goose jackets. Is it necessary to spend nine hundred dollars to stay warm in New England? No. But kids weren't spending their parents' money just for the warmth. They were spending the equivalent of the typical American's weekly income ($865) for the logo. Likewise, are students spending $250,000 at prestigious universities for the education? Maybe. But they are also spending it for the logo.

As NYU professor Scott Galloway said in an interview in 2020, "The strongest brand in the world is not Apple or Mercedes-Benz or Coca-Cola. The strongest brands are MIT, Oxford, and Stanford. Academics and administrators at the top universities have decided over the last thirty years that we're no longer public servants; we're luxury goods."[13]

This is not to say that elite colleges don't educate their students, or that Canada Goose jackets don't keep their wearers warm. But top universities are also crucial for induction into the luxury belief class. Take vocabulary. Your typical working-class American could not tell you what *heteronormative* or *cisgender* means. But if you visit an elite college, you'll find plenty of affluent people who will eagerly explain them to you. When someone uses the phrase *cultural appropriation*, what they are really saying is, "I was educated at a top college." Consider the Veblen quote, "Refined tastes, manners, habits of life are a useful evidence of gentility, because good breeding requires time, application and expense, and can therefore not be compassed by those whose time and energy are taken up with work." Only the affluent can afford to learn strange vocabulary, because ordinary people have real problems to worry about.

The chief purpose of luxury beliefs is to indicate the believer's social class and education. When an affluent person expresses support for defunding the police, drug legalization, open borders, looting, or permissive sexual norms, or uses terms like *white privilege*,

13   J. D. Walsh, "The Coming Disruption," *New York*, May 11, 2020, https://nymag.com/intelligencer/2020/05/scott-galloway-future-of-college.html.

they are engaging in a status display. They are trying to tell you, "I am a member of the upper class."

Focusing on "representation" rather than helping the down-trodden is another luxury belief. Many of the protesters on campus urged for more individuals from historically mistreated groups to be represented among students and faculty, among elite internships and occupations, and in influential positions in society at large. I thought of this as "trickle-down meritocracy." The idea seemed to be that the best way to help struggling communities is to pluck representatives out and put them into positions of power. As long as the ruling class has a few members from these communities, then somehow the advantages they accrue will "trickle down" to their communities. Thus far, there doesn't seem to be evidence that this works. Representation certainly benefits a handful of people who are chosen to enter elite spaces, but it doesn't seem to improve the lives of the dispossessed. In fact, it might backfire. Elite institutions strip-mine talented people out of their communities. Upon completing their education, most of these graduates do not return to their old neighborhoods. Instead, they relocate to a handful of cities where they live alongside their highly educated peers, eroding the bonds of solidarity they had with those they left behind. And who could blame them? It is reasonable to use your talents to advance your career and financial prospects. But if the original intent was to help languishing communities, then this particular solution is failing.

White privilege is the luxury belief that took me the longest to understand, because I grew up around a lot of poor white people. Affluent white college graduates seem to be the most enthusiastic about the idea of white privilege, yet they are the least likely to incur any costs for promoting that belief. Rather, they raise their social standing by talking about their privilege. In other words, upper-class white people gain status by talking about their high status. When policies are implemented to combat white privilege, it won't be Yale graduates who are harmed. Poor white people will bear the brunt.

The upper class promotes abolishing the police or decriminalizing drugs or white privilege because it advances their social standing, not least because they know that the adoption of those policies will cost them less than others. The logic is akin to conspicuous consumption: if you're a student who has a large subsidy from your parents and I do not, you can afford to waste $900 and I can't, so wearing a Canada Goose jacket is a good way of advertising your superior wealth and status. Proposing policies that will cost you as a member of the upper class less than they would cost me serves the same function. Advocating for sexual promiscuity, drug experimentation, or abolishing the police are good ways of advertising your membership of the elite because, thanks to your wealth and social connections, they will cost you less than me.

Reflecting on my experiences with alcohol, if all drugs had been legal and easily accessible when I was fifteen, you wouldn't be reading this book. My birth mom was able to get drugs, and it had a detrimental effect on both of our lives. That's something people don't think about: drugs don't just affect the user, they affect helpless children, too. All my foster siblings' parents were addicts, or had a mental health condition, often triggered by drug use. But the luxury belief class doesn't think about that because such consequences seldom interrupt their lives. And even if they did, they are in a far better position to withstand such difficulties. A well-heeled student at an elite university can experiment with cocaine and will, in all likelihood, be fine. A kid from a dysfunctional home with absentee parents will often take that first hit of meth to self-destruction. This is perhaps why a 2019 survey found that less than half of Americans without a college degree want to legalize drugs, but more than 60 percent of Americans with a bachelor's degree or higher are in favor of drug legalization.[14] Drugs are frequently considered a recreational pastime for the rich, but for the poor they are often a gateway to further pain.

Similarly, a 2020 survey found that the richest Americans showed the strongest support for defunding the police, while the poorest Americans reported the lowest support.[15] Throughout the remainder of that year and into 2021, murder rates throughout the US soared as a result of defunding policies, officers retiring early or quitting, and police departments struggling to recruit new members after the luxury belief class cultivated an environment of loathing toward law enforcement.[16]

The luxury belief class appears to sympathize more with criminals than their victims. It's true that most criminals come from poor backgrounds. But it's also true that their victims are mostly poor. And the perpetrators tend to be young men, and their targets are

14   E. Elkins, "2019 Welfare, Work, and Wealth National Survey," Cato Institute, September 24, 2019, https://www.cato.org/publications/survey-reports/what-americans-think-about-poverty-wealth-work.

15   "Yahoo News/YouGov Race and Politics Survey, June 11, 2020." PDF file. Accessed July 25, 2023. https://docs.cdn.yougov.com/86ijosd7cy/20200611_yahoo_race_police_covid_crosstabs.pdf.

16   Z. Elinson, "Murders in US Cities Were Near Record Highs in 2021," *Wall Street Journal*, January 6, 2022.

often poor women or the elderly. Moreover, because there are many times more victims than there are criminals, to not stop criminals is to victimize the poor. Yet the movement to abolish the police is disproportionately championed by affluent people. A key inhibition against crime is the belief that our legal system is legitimate. Which means that those who promote the idea that we live in an unjust society also help to cultivate crime.

The poor reap what the luxury belief class sows.

Consider that compared to Americans who earn more than $75,000 a year, the poorest Americans are seven times more likely to be victims of robbery, seven times more likely to be victims of aggravated assault, and twenty times more likely to be victims of sexual assault.[17] And yet, as I write this, many affluent people are calling to abolish law enforcement.

Maybe the luxury belief class is ignorant of the realities of who is most harmed by crime. Or perhaps they don't care that the poor will become even more victimized than they already are.

Unfortunately, like fashion trends that debut on the runway and make it into JCPenney three years later, the luxury beliefs of the upper class often trickle down and are adopted by people lower on the food chain, which means many of these beliefs end up causing social harm. Take polyamory, which involves open relationships where people have multiple partners at the same time. A student at a top university once explained to me that when he set the radius on his dating apps to five miles, about half of the women, mostly other

17 US Census Bureau, "Statistical Abstract of the United States: 2011," Table 316, https://www.usgs.gov/publications/2011-statistical-abstract-united-states-0.

students, said they were "polyamorous" in their bios. Then, when he extended the radius to fifteen miles to include the rest of the city and its outskirts, about half of the women were single mothers. Polyamory is the latest expression of sexual freedom championed by the affluent. They are in a better position to manage the complications of novel relationship arrangements. And if these relationships don't pan out, or if kids are involved, affluent adults can more easily recuperate thanks to their financial capability and social capital. Meanwhile, the less fortunate suffer as the beliefs of the upper class spread throughout society as a result of their disproportionate influence.

Most personal to me is the luxury belief that family is unimportant or that children are equally likely to thrive in all family structures. In 1960, the percentage of American children living with both biological parents was identical for affluent and working-class families—95 percent. By 2005, 85 percent of affluent families were still intact, but for working-class families the figure had plummeted to 30 percent. The Harvard political scientist Robert Putnam at a 2017 Senate hearing stated, "Rich kids and poor kids now grow up in separate Americas. . . . Growing up with two parents is now unusual in the working class, while two-parent families are normal and becoming more common among the upper middle class."[18] Affluent people, particularly in the 1960s, championed sexual freedom. Loose sexual norms caught on for the rest of society. The upper class, though, still had intact families. Generally speaking, they experimented in college and then settled down later. The families of the lower classes fell apart.

---

18   R. D. Putnam, Hearing on the State of Social Capital in America, United States Senate, May 17, 2017, https://www.jec.senate.gov/public/_cache/files/222a1636-e668 -4893-b082-418a100fd93d/robert-putnam-testimony.pdf.

This deterioration is still happening. In 2006, more than half of American adults without a college degree believed it was "very important" that couples with children should be married. Fast-forward to 2020, and this number has plummeted to 31 percent. Among college graduates, only 25 percent think couples should be married before having kids.[19] Their actions, though, contradict their luxury beliefs: the vast majority of American college graduates who have children are married. Despite their *behavior* suggesting otherwise, affluent people are the most likely to *say* marriage is unimportant. Gradually, their message has spread.

I've also heard graduates of top universities say marriage is "just a piece of paper." People shouldn't have to prove their commitment to their spouse with a document, they tell me. I have never heard them ridicule a college degree as "just a piece of paper." Many affluent people belittle marriage, but not college, because they view a degree as critical for their social positions.

Here is an example of how this phenomenon works. Before my first year of college, I had never even been to a musical. No one I knew from Red Bluff had ever been to one. But it seemed like everyone on campus had seen *Hamilton*, the acclaimed musical about the American founding father Alexander Hamilton.

I looked up tickets: $400. This was way beyond my budget. So

---

19 J. M. Jones, "Is Marriage Becoming Irrelevant?," Gallup, December 28, 2020, http://news.gallup.com/poll/316223/fewer-say-important-parents-married.aspx.

in 2020, I was pleased to see that five years after *Hamilton*'s debut, it was available to view on Disney+. But suddenly, the musical was being denigrated by many of the same people who formerly enjoyed it, because it didn't reflect the failings of American society in the eighteenth century. The creator of *Hamilton*, Lin-Manuel Miranda, even posted on Twitter that "All the criticisms are valid." This reveals how social class works in America. It is not a coincidence that when *Hamilton* tickets were prohibitively expensive, affluent people loved it, and now that it can be viewed by ordinary Americans, they ridicule it. Once something becomes too popular, the elites update their tastes to distinguish themselves from ordinary people.

In 2015, seeing *Hamilton* was a major status symbol. In 2020, it didn't mean much. And this is why the affluent suddenly turned on the musical. It's a status game, with members of the upper class distancing themselves from something that had become too popular. Once a piece of art becomes mainstream, elites must distance themselves from it and redirect their attention to something new, obscure, or difficult to obtain. The affluent relentlessly search for signals that distinguish them from the masses.

A former classmate recently told me that he didn't enjoy *Hamilton* but never told anyone because everyone at Yale loved it. However, once the musical became unfashionable, he suddenly became open about his dislike of it. I noticed that many Yale students selectively concealed their opinions or facts about their lives. More than one student quietly confessed to me that they pretended to be poorer than they really were, because they didn't want the stigma of being thought rich. Why was it a stigma to be known as rich at a rich university full of rich students? It's a class thing. For the upper class, indicating your social position by speaking about money is vulgar, sharing your educational credentials less so, and broadcasting your luxury beliefs is the least tacky—or most favorable—of all.

Furthermore, it is harder for wealthy people to claim the mantle of victimhood, which, among the affluent, is often a key ingredient to be seen as a righteous person. In fact, researchers at Harvard Business School and Northwestern University recently found evidence of a "virtuous victim" effect, in which victims are seen as more moral than nonvictims who have behaved in exactly the same way. People are inclined to positively evaluate those who have suffered.[20] Plainly, if people think you are a victim, they will be more likely to excuse your detestable behaviors. But ironically, the most well-off are also the most capable of accentuating their supposed marginalization. They can communicate their hardships in a language that other well-to-do people can understand. Prestigious universities encourage students to nurture their grievances, giving rise to a peculiar situation in which the most advantaged are the most well-equipped to tell other advantaged people how disadvantaged they are.

The upper class's drive to distinguish themselves from the masses explains the ever-evolving standards of luxury beliefs. To become fully acculturated into the elite requires knowing the habits, customs, and manners of the upper class. To stay up to date, you need lots of leisure time or to have the kind of job that allows you to browse Twitter. A common rebuke to those who are not fully up to date on the latest intellectual fads is "educate yourself." This is how the affluent block

20   J. J. Jordan and M. Kouchaki, "Virtuous Victims," *Science Advances* 7 (2021): eabg5902.

mobility for people who work multiple jobs, have children to care for, and don't have the time or means to read the latest bestseller that outlines the proper way to think about social issues. And by the time they do, as was the case with *Hamilton*, the cultural fashions will have shifted yet again. Thus, it seems the affluent secure their positions by ensuring that only those who attend the right colleges, listen to the right podcasts, and read the right books and articles can join their inner circle.

Occasionally, I raised these critiques to fellow students or graduates of elite colleges. Sometimes they would reply by asking, "Well, aren't you part of this group now?" implying that my appraisals of the luxury belief class were hollow because I moved within the same institutions. But they wouldn't have listened to me back when I was a lowly enlisted service member or back when I was washing dishes for minimum wage. If you ridicule the upper class as an outsider, they'll either ignore you or tell you that you don't know what you're talking about. But if you ridicule them as an insider, they call you a hypocrite. Plainly, the requirements for the upper class to take you seriously (e.g., credentials, wealth, power) are also the grounds to brand you a hypocrite for making any criticism of the upper class.

But I don't want to give the impression that only the well-to-do care about or react to symbols. Shortly after enlisting, I bought Mom a license plate frame for her 2006 Toyota Camry that read "US Air Force Mom." Cheesy, I know. But she'd been eyeing it at a store on base, and the frame was a way of expressing how proud she was of me. Mom told me that it has gotten her out of more than a few speeding tickets.

"Cops pull me over and ask about it. I tell them my boy is

serving overseas and they let me off with a warning." A ten-dollar piece of plastic probably saved a thousand bucks. Not a bad investment.

Later, Mom told me another story.

"I was wearing my 'Yale Mom' cap at softball practice with the local recreational team. Someone came up to me and asked, 'Is that real?' Pointing at my head, kind of rude about it."

"What did you say?" I asked Mom.

"I just nodded and said yeah. What a strange question!"

To Mom, the hat was just a way of expressing how proud she was of me. Still, we both agreed that it probably wouldn't get her out of any speeding tickets.

I also worked with a former Marine who was interested in attending college. I took a special interest in Daniel because of our similar upbringings. He had been born to a mother who became addicted to crack and, as a consequence, Daniel was placed in foster care as a child. We worked together on his college applications, and he earned admission to Brown University. Seeing him accomplish his educational goals almost made me happier than when I'd done so. In his first semester, Daniel expressed dismay at seeing students on his campus burning American flags on Veterans Day. It seemed like he was having the same misgivings about his new surroundings as I had when I first entered Yale.

Another veteran friend at a different college asked me, "Don't you ever feel like a sucker for serving?"

I paused, unsure what to say. I didn't feel like a sucker. But I would come to understand what he was getting at.

"Something's off about the whole thing. We swear that oath about upholding the Constitution. Then these rich kids who are the same age as us when we enlisted are actively undermining it. Pretty weird."

"Undermining how?" I asked.

"The first two amendments," he continued. "The general opinion at these schools is that the first needs a major overhaul and the second should be completely dismantled. Seems like we basically got duped into believing we are upholding American values while the future ruling class are figuring out ways to undermine them."

I could sense his feeling of betrayal. I grew to understand that, at least within some upper-class circles, patriotism and support for the Constitution marks one as a rube. The irony was not lost on me—students who would burn flags or attempt to silence dissenting viewpoints were being protected by the very principles they despised and the people to whom they felt superior. Even the students from affluent backgrounds who were patriotic and believed in the American Dream seldom publicly expressed it. They withheld their views to fit in and avoid ostracism.

I also found a couple of friends in the ROTC program at Yale. Esteban and Nick didn't grow up like me, but they weren't quite as well-off as many of our classmates. One day we were at Esteban's apartment when we all had the same realization: When we were kids, chain restaurants like Applebee's and Olive Garden were considered "fine dining." That was where people with money went out to eat. Upon meeting real rich people, we realized none of them went to such restaurants, except as a novelty. I later suggested to Nick, Esteban, and some other students that we go to the Cheesecake Factory. One guy asked, "Are we going there ironically?" I flatly said no and ordered some Buffalo Blasts.

I realized that even dietary choices reflected class differences. Yale dining halls had soda fountains that nobody used, save for the one nozzle that dispensed water. The halls also offered "spa water," which was water flavored with cucumbers or strawberries. I'd always associated that with rich people on TV. I mentally contrasted this with my high school, where I couldn't go more than ten minutes without seeing someone carrying a Powerade or a Pepsi. There was a striking absence of obesity among the students—many of them seemed to be preoccupied with their weight and image. I learned a term I'd never heard before: *fat shaming*. It was remarkable that students who seldom consumed sugary drinks and often closely adhered to nutrition and fitness regimens were also attempting to create a taboo around discussions of obesity. The unspoken oath seemed to be, "I will carefully monitor my health and fitness, but will not broadcast the importance of what I am doing, because that is fat shaming." The people who were most vocal about what they called "body positivity," which seemed to be a tool to inhibit discussions about the health consequences of obesity, were often very physically fit.

The luxury belief class claims that the unhappiness associated with certain behaviors and choices primarily stems from the negative social judgments they elicit, rather than the behaviors and choices themselves. But, in fact, negative social judgments often

serve as guardrails to deter detrimental decisions that lead to unhappiness. In order to avoid misery, we have to admit that certain
actions and choices are actually in and of themselves undesirable—
single parenthood, obesity, substance abuse, crime, and so on—and
not simply in need of normalization.

Indeed, it's cruel to validate decisions that inflict harm, especially
on those who had no hand in the decision—like young children.

Before starting my final year of college, I got a position as a summer research assistant at Stanford University. This was an ideal location because it was close to Mom, who lived nearby in San Jose.
At Stanford, I helped with research in developmental psychology,
running studies with young children. I was interested in doing
this kind of research because I'd taken a class with Yale psychology
professor Frank Keil, who, during a lecture, said, "If you want to
understand the mature form of an organism, it helps to understand
its history."

In the evenings at Stanford, I took a GRE prep course, hoping
to score well enough to get into a good PhD program. I figured if
I was going to study psychology, I should go as far as I could and
get a comprehensive education. So I signed up to take the GRE
course, which was about as dull as you'd expect, but the instructor
said something that stuck with me.

"Many of the reading comprehension passages in the verbal
section of the GRE," he explained, "are drawn from periodicals like
The Atlantic or *Scientific American*. This is because graduate programs
believe these kinds of articles are set at the right level for a bright

college graduate to be able to grasp quickly. But they are also *testing for people who read these kinds of magazines.*"

In other words, the instructor claimed the test screens for social class as well as academic ability. *The Atlantic* characterizes its subscribers as "affluent and accomplished." A survey found that 77 percent of their readers have a bachelor's degree and about half have an annual household income of more than $100,000.[21] In contrast, only 32 percent of American adults aged twenty-five or older have graduated from college,[22] and only 25 percent of American households make more than $100,000 a year.[23]

While at Stanford, I discovered another pernicious luxury belief.

I was living in a house on campus with a bunch of students for the summer. I asked a housemate who was working on a start-up how he'd gotten into Stanford and what steps he was taking to build his company.

He paused for a moment and then said, "Ultimately, it comes down to luck."

As soon as he said that, it occurred to me that this mind-set is

21 J. Zhang, "A Systematic Breakdown of *The Atlantic* Magazine," Medium, August 30, 2019, https://medium.com/@josephhhz/a-systematic-breakdown-of-the-atlantic-magazine-aed8ce0725b6.

22 K. McElrath and M. Martin, "Bachelor's Degree Attainment in the United States: 2005 to 2019," US Census Bureau, 2021, https://www.census.gov/library/publications/2021/acs/acsbr-009.html.

23 Heather Long, "Is $100,000 Middle Class in America?," *Washington Post*, October 25, 2017, https://www.washingtonpost.com/news/wonk/wp/2017/10/25/is-100000-middle-class-in-america/.

pervasive at Yale as well—far more common than among the people I grew up around or the women and men I served with in the military. Many of my peers at Yale and Stanford would work ceaselessly. But when I'd ask them about the plans they'd implemented to get into college, or start a company, or land their dream job, they'd often suggest they just got lucky rather than attribute their success to their efforts. Interestingly, it seems like many people who earn status by working hard are able to boost their status among their peers even more by saying they just got lucky. This isn't just limited to my own observations, either. A 2019 study found that people with high income and social status are the most likely to attribute success to mere luck rather than hard work.[24]

Both luck and hard work play a role in the direction of our lives, but stressing the former at the expense of the latter doesn't help those at or near the bottom of society. If disadvantaged people come to believe that luck is the key factor that determines success, then they will be less likely to strive to improve their lives. One study tracked more than six thousand young adults in the US at the beginning of their careers over the course of two decades, and found that those who believed that life's outcomes are due to their own efforts as opposed to external factors became more successful in their careers and went on to attain higher earnings.[25]

Getting back to my conversation with the guy at Stanford, he'd

---

24   J. Daniels and M. Wang, "What Do You Think? Success: Is It Luck or Is It Hard Work?," *Applied Economics Letters* 26 (2019): 1734–1738.

25   M. Van Praag, J. Van Der Sluis, and A. Van Witteloostuijn, "The Impact of the Locus-of-Control Personality Trait on the Earnings of Employees vis-à-vis Entrepreneurs," Tinbergen Institute Discussion Paper (2004): 130.

told me a few days prior that he had a younger sister. So I asked, "If your sister asked you how to get into Stanford or start a company, would you shrug and say 'I just got lucky' or would you explain whatever it was that you actually did—'You have to study, sacrifice, work on the weekends, or whatever'?"

He rolled his eyes before replying, "Yeah, I get it."

Successful people tell the world they got lucky but then tell their loved ones about the importance of hard work and sacrifice. Critics of successful people tell the world those successful people got lucky and then tell their loved ones about the importance of hard work and sacrifice.

By this point, after three years immersed in this kind of thinking, I lost that state of deep curiosity about this environment that I had back when I started college. Now, I felt I had a decent understanding of the social milieu of top universities. But at Stanford, I gleaned some further insights at a top preschool.

As a summer research assistant, I visited the Bing Nursery School at Stanford every morning to help recruit children to be participants in studies for the psychology department. The kids at this preschool tend to come from well-heeled families—much different from the kids I worked with in New Haven. Many things about this Stanford nursery intrigued me, including how many teachers each classroom had (usually at least two), how they encouraged the children's creativity and curiosity, how well-behaved the children were (very), and what they ate at snack time. I didn't see a single Fruit Roll-Up or Flamin' Hot Cheeto. Instead, the teachers served the kids celery with peanut butter, slices of cheese, and pieces of banana. I wondered how my life might have been different if I'd gone to this kind of preschool. Probably not much different, considering how turbulent my home life was.

One thing that surprised me was how attentive these kids were in our research studies. Typically, developmental psychology researchers exclude some children from their analyses if their responses indicate that they misunderstood the questions. At Stanford, we excluded around 10 percent to 20 percent of the child participants. But at schools in New Haven, we sometimes had to exclude more than half of the kids. Considering what a dismal elementary school student I'd been, I almost certainly would have been excluded from these kinds of studies for not paying attention.

Near the end of my internship, I was out in the playground helping a few kids dig a hole in the sand pit. One of the boys mentioned he'd gone out to eat with his family the night before.

"What did you have for dinner?" I asked.

"Arugula salad," he replied. "But usually I get squid ink."

I didn't know what surprised me more—the choice of food or the fact that he pronounced *arugula* perfectly.

One of the other kids chimed in and said she hated squid ink. I asked her what her favorite dessert was.

"Lemon meringue pie."

And here I thought every little kid hated the taste of lemon, just like I had.

Up ahead, I saw that a new kid had joined the playground. It was her first day, and I'd noticed she'd been quiet throughout the afternoon. She was understandably shy in this new environment. She stared at a model wooden car in the middle of the grass. Two other little girls were in the front seat pretending to drive. The new girl tepidly climbed into the backseat of the car.

"Hey," she said to the two girls. "How about I be sick, and you two are the ambulance drivers?"

The two girls in the front seat shook their heads.

"Okay, um, how about I be a bad guy? And you're the cops!"

The two girls again shook their heads. The new girl in the backseat looked over at me, maybe hoping I'd suggest some other ideas.

One of the girls in the front seat whispered a little too loudly, "Look, she's distracted." They both ran off. The new kid looked away from me, apparently hoping I hadn't seen what just happened.

Waves of grief washed over me. I knew what it was like to be the new kid. My response to that kind of social rejection would have been to break something or start a fight with someone or swear at the teacher. This kid just sat quietly.

I handed my shovel to one of the boys nearby, picked up a basketball, and walked over to the girl. I spun the ball on my finger, which I'd learned to do years ago with a cheap rubber ball I'd bought at Walmart.

"Want to learn how to do this?" I asked.

She smiled and tried to take the ball from me. I spun it again and placed it on her finger. Afterward, we sat in the nursery as one of the teachers read *Not Quite Narwhal* aloud to the kids. The story is about a lonely unicorn who is raised by whales and doesn't quite fit in. I glanced at the new girl, who sat completely still, captivated by this story.

I realized: Reading about others who had survived the

vicissitudes of their youth helped carry me through my turbulent childhood.

I'd been hung up on how to communicate how my life had informed my views about childhood, family, and success. Fortunately, I'd been accepted into the War Horse Writing Seminar at Columbia University. The program was designed to help veterans write about their experiences. At first, it was intimidating, because unlike college classes or the Warrior-Scholar Project, this seminar was about *personal*, as opposed to academic, writing. At Columbia, I wrote a rough draft of a personal essay reflecting on my upbringing but didn't let anyone read it.

On the final day of the seminar, Jim Dao, then the op-ed editor at the *New York Times*, visited our class and invited us to pitch him if we ever had any ideas. I approached him later, telling him about how my college essay had run in the *Times* back in 2015. Jim handed me his card and encouraged me to send him anything else I had. I glanced down at the essay I'd been working on, about to tell him about it, and then quietly returned to my seat. I wasn't ready to share it.

Three months later, in May 2017, I sent it to Jim, unsure how realistic it was to expect a reply. To my surprise, he got back to me within an hour, saying that he liked it. Another editor emailed me, saying they would run it soon.

Months later, I followed up. Total radio silence. I wasn't sure how assertive to be in this situation, but I figured I might as well keep at it. I sent follow-up emails every two weeks for the next few months. I didn't receive a response to any of them.

It didn't bother me, though, because in yet another surreal moment, I received notification that my application for a Gates Cambridge scholarship to study for a doctorate at the University of Cambridge was successful. With a 1.3 percent acceptance rate, obtaining the scholarship was even more unlikely than getting into Yale. Applicants had to demonstrate academic excellence, leadership ability, and a commitment to improving the lives of others. Between my college transcript, military experience, and my unusual upbringing, I figured I'd be competitive, but I was far from confident.

Now, I couldn't believe I was going back across the Atlantic yet again.

My final year of college was about to conclude.

After the Yale graduation ceremony, I met with Mom and Hannah for dinner. We didn't realize that the restaurants around campus had set menus for graduation day. At the restaurant we visited, the plates were usually around forty dollars per dish on a regular night. This was a bit pricey, but we figured we could splurge because it was graduation day. But we discovered there was a set menu charging $120 per person, presumably because the restaurateurs knew how little the amount mattered to rich Yale parents. Mom's posture stiffened as she looked at the menu. We all looked up at the same time and laughed.

"Hey, let's go around the corner," I suggested.

There was a Chinese restaurant about a block from my apartment downtown. When we arrived, I checked to make sure there was no "set menu." Plates were priced at a much more manageable twelve to fifteen dollars.

"So, who was that guy?" my sister asked, referring back to Matthew's drunken exclamation before the ceremony that my family had "won the adoption lottery."

"Hang on, sorry," I said. My phone had been ringing all day with an unknown number, and I couldn't answer it amid the graduation proceedings.

I stepped outside and picked up. "Hello?"

"Hello, is this Rob?"

"It is."

"Hey, Aaron Retica here from the *New York Times*. We've published your piece online and just want to ask a couple questions before the print version runs tomorrow."

"Oh, great." We had gone over edits a couple of weeks prior, but they were coy when I asked when they expected it would be published. I was glad they'd run it, but also felt trepidation—because of the fear of judgment, mostly. In my college application essay, I'd been forthcoming about my early life. But in this new essay, I tried to communicate the clarity I'd gained from those experiences. I wrote about the importance of family and responsibility, drawing from my turbulent childhood experiences. Four years ago, I could barely talk about any of this in rehab with Alan, and now I was sharing it with the world. I wondered if I'd made a mistake. *Maybe it'll help someone else out there who reads it.*

I answered Aaron's questions. He mentioned that he'd also

attended Yale, and he asked if it was graduation day. I told him it was, and that I was at dinner with my family.

"Thanks, Rob, and sorry for interrupting. But at least you can say you got a call from the *Times* at your graduation dinner—it'll make a good story."

Through the windowpane of the restaurant, I saw my family inside. Ever since I left home, I'd been focused on trying to escape my past. I'd strived to be independent so that I wouldn't have to rely on anyone. But now, what mattered most to me was to become someone who could be relied upon. I glanced behind me, in the direction of the campus, and it struck me: What is the point of pursuing education and striving for success? The answer, I realized, was to take care of the family who couldn't take care of me. And, for my future family, to be a better dad than any of my "dads" had been to me. The bar, I thought, was mercifully low.

I thought about how the reason I was even getting this phone call—the reason my op-ed was noteworthy enough to catch an editor's attention—was because of how few of these family dinners I'd had growing up. Looking inside the restaurant, I realized that I would have traded this op-ed, Yale, Cambridge, and all the other amazing things that happened over the last few years to have never had to experience so much grief and disrepair growing up, and to have had more of these family dinners as a kid. I just wanted to get back to this one. So, I thanked Aaron and returned to the seat next to my sister.

CHAPTER TWELVE

Twistable Turnable Man

During my first week at Cambridge University, I attended an orientation for new students. The other Gates Cambridge scholars and I were asked by the student leaders to form a circle so we could learn more about one another. In a game they called Icebreakers, the student leaders read from a note card, and, if the statement applied to any of us new students, we were supposed to enter the center of the circle. Later in the game, they asked questions like "Do you speak more than two languages?" and "Have you ever gone on a road trip?"

But the first question they asked was, "Were you a class clown in school as a kid?" I reflexively made my way to the center of the circle. Looking around, I was surprised to see that out of ninety or so new students, I was completely alone. But then I realized, *of course*. To get into a place like this, you have to study hard and get good grades. I looked at my peers and experienced the same feeling I had back when I started at Yale—a feeling of being an outsider. I figured that few, if any, of the other scholars had ever ditched class to go joyriding and shoot paintball guns at pedestrians.

During my first year at Cambridge, I began preparing notes for this book. I had plenty of time to think about what a weird childhood I had—the flashbulb memories of living in a car with my birth mother and seeing her arrested in our cramped apartment, getting dragged away to foster homes, the drama and heartbreak after being adopted, and all the rest. In his bestselling book *The Body Keeps the Score*, psychiatrist Bessel van der Kolk wrote, "Sooner or later most [trauma] survivors . . . come up with what many of them call their 'cover story' that offers some explanation for their symptoms and behavior for public consumption. These stories, however, rarely capture the inner truth of the experience. It is enormously difficult to organize one's traumatic experiences into a coherent account—a narrative with a beginning, a middle, and an end."

With this book, I have attempted to accomplish such a task as honestly as I can.

People who have undergone harrowing events rarely want to discuss them. I had misgivings about sharing my story because I knew many readers would feel pity, which was the last thing I wanted. Whatever sympathy you felt while reading my story, please channel it toward kids currently living in similarly unpromising environments. And then think carefully about the luxury beliefs, practices, and policies that gave rise to their predicaments.

A question I wrestled with in the early stages of writing was "Who is this book for?" Whenever I thought about comfortable upper- and upper-middle-class people reading it, quite frankly, it made my stomach turn.

Instead, I kept thinking about some kid like me out there who might pick this up and draw inspiration, the same way I did as a kid hanging out in my schools' libraries. This reading habit, along with my impulsive decision to enlist, confined my risky behavior within relatively limited bounds until I later experienced the same affliction that plagued my birth mother.

Drinking had merely been symptomatic of unprocessed feelings— a way for me to deal with the sorrow and anger I'd carried since I was a kid. Once I processed the feelings underlying my depression, my alcohol dependency dissolved. My inner conflicts were an indication that I had not fully mined what I'd experienced as a child. There was wisdom stored in the memories of what I'd been through and what I felt, but I didn't want it, because of what it meant I would have to acknowledge.

The most frightening thing was admitting that I felt unlovable and undeserving of love. I'd been betrayed so much as a kid. When adults make children feel like they're incapable of being loved, kids retain those feelings, and they often don't go away. And when children feel unworthy of love, they want to hurt people and do bad things.

Your family of origin is like a rubber band with one end

pinned down. You can distance yourself. But the farther you move, the harder it pulls you. It didn't matter how much encouragement I got later from Mom or Shelly or my teachers or coaches or anyone else. Deep down, because I'd been abandoned and mistreated as a kid, all that encouragement felt hollow. My birth parents left me, and each time I had to live with yet another foster family, it was further proof that I was worthless. Children believe that if a family loves them, then that family won't let them be taken away. Adults understand on an intellectual level that this isn't true—the foster system works the way it works—but little kids don't fully grasp this.

Wordsworth's "The child is father of the man" conveys the idea that the experiences we integrate into our character as children remain with us into our adult life. To some degree, this is consistent with psychological research. Studies have indicated that in the first five to seven years of life, children develop an understanding of how predictable their environments are, to what extent they can trust others, and how much they can rely on the enduringness of close relationships.[1] Kids who learn that their environments are unstable and that their relationships with adults are unreliable become more likely to act out and do things that harm themselves or others. Marital discord, missing parents, frequent relocations, and unreliable caregiving create an "insecure or mistrustful internal working model" of the self, others, and relationships. In these circumstances, kids often have difficulty believing anyone truly cares about them.

---

1 J. Belsky, L. Steinberg, and P. Draper, "Childhood Experiences, Interpersonal Development, and Reproductive Strategy: An Evolutionary Theory of Socialization." *Child Development* 62 (1991): 647–670.

Sadly, this internal model often freezes in childhood, and requires a lot of work in adulthood to undo.

I avoided my feelings as a kid. If you're in the midst of disorder, as I was, dwelling on it is not necessarily the best idea. Growing up, I'd been ensnared in chaos and didn't have the capacity to make sense of it all. At the time, fully reflecting on it would have made my experience of it worse. As I grew older, part of me was still stuck in those earlier experiences. There was territory I had traversed as a kid that I hadn't fully mapped. So, my emotions were trying to tell me something: There's unprocessed danger here. But I didn't want to dig into it and unpack it.

We create maps of our inner lives when we update our perceptions or behavior so that those previous detrimental events we went through won't happen again. That's the practical purpose of memory—to avoid making future mistakes. For me, that meant understanding that many of the choices I made as a kid were simply feeble attempts to receive care and love. Later, I thought I could simply escape. I was unsophisticated in my thinking. I thought I needed to leave where I'd come from. You can leave something, but often, it won't leave you.

I sought relief by ignoring my own feelings. To survive my early life, I had to believe it wasn't as bad as it really was. But such intense stress and neglect of one's inner life inflicts costs. When faced with a high level of uncertainty, your body prepares for anything, which is physically and mentally taxing. I burned through a lot of physiological resources as a kid: anxiety, rage, despair. Later, I tried to use alcohol to quell the flames, but instead they grew. The human mind is a remarkable contraption, great at keeping us psychologically buoyant in periods of chaos and allowing us to pay the price later, once the storm has settled.

How did I escape, both physically and mentally, from those deprived and dysfunctional circumstances? According to some schools of thought within psychology, very young children are implicitly preoccupied with three questions.[2] First, am I a lovable person who is welcome here? The answer kids perceive from those around them is critical for how they feel about themselves. If the answer is no, then their self-esteem is thwarted. Kids long to earn that gleam from their parent's eye. If they don't receive this, then they have difficulty cultivating a sense of vitality and self-worth.

Later comes a second question: How can a small, inexperienced being like me cope with this vast world and all these overwhelming feelings? If kids have parents that are calm and reliable, then they will develop an internal sense of security as they reach maturity. If not, they often find harmful ways to cope as a means of escaping awareness of their own vulnerability.

And finally, the third question: Am I like other people, and am I accepted by them, or am I weird and unacceptable? When kids are in a stable environment with reliable parents and predictable patterns, they feel integrated into a social environment and find it easier to befriend peers who want the best for them.

If these three needs aren't adequately met, then kids often go

2   E. Arble and D. Barnett, "An Analysis of Self: The Development and Assessment of a Measure of Selfobject Needs," *Journal of Personality Assessment* 99 (2017): 608–618.

on to face severe challenges later in life. These unmet needs become a driving force in a person's life, as it was for mine. I got into stealing, drugs, drinking, the choking game, drunk driving, vandalism, fistfights, and more to escape my pain. As is the case with so many other people, much of my self-defeating behavior was rooted in self-loathing and trauma.

Not all my coping responses were detrimental. As a child, I found inspiration by reading nonfiction stories of others who had grim childhoods. I was capable of identifying good advice, even if I didn't always implement it. I tried to draw on those stories to make sense of my life, and while they helped, I wished there had been more stories of real-life orphans or foster kids who rose above their environments. But true stories were hard to come by.

This is at odds with the pervasive trope of *fictional* orphans: Tom Sawyer, Oliver Twist, Jane Eyre, Harry Potter, Don Draper, Rapunzel, Mowgli, Cinderella—not to mention all the comic book orphans like Clark Kent, Bruce Wayne, Peter Parker, and so on. This preoccupation with parentless protagonists extends beyond Western cultures. The anthropologist Manvir Singh has written that such characters are "everywhere—not only deeper in time than Disney or Victorian novels, but stretching from the Arctic to New Guinea, from Igboland in Nigeria to the Kachin Hills of Myanmar."[3] This universal interest in orphan protagonists reflects every child's nightmare of losing their parents—a unique, elemental fear. In *The Body Keeps the Score*, Dr. van der Kolk writes, "Children are programmed

---

3   Manvir Singh, "Orphans and Their Quests," *Aeon*, October 8, 2019, https://aeon.co/essays/what-makes-the-sympathetic-plot-a-universal-story-type.

to be loyal to their caretakers, even if they are abused by them. . . . I have never met a child below age ten who was tortured at home who would not have chosen to stay with his or her family rather than being placed in a foster home."

Fictional orphan stories tell the audience that people are capable of surviving their nightmares. But in reality, few parentless children live out a Cinderella story.

Real life isn't a fairy tale or a comic book.

In Red Bluff, I knew a couple of older kids named Paul and Nina in a nearby town. They had lived in foster homes and were adopted; Mom was friends with their adoptive parents. I remember they had a big house, and both of them got good grades. Paul, as an adult, got a tattoo that read "Mom" inside a heart on his right shoulder. A couple years later, he had a child with a woman he barely knew and abandoned both the woman and their child. His mom thought the tattoo was stupid, and his abandonment of his family even stupider. Nina got married to a guy who couldn't hold a job, and they divorced less than a year after their wedding. Last I heard, he was dodging child support payments to Nina. Though Paul and Nina had a few good years with a stable family, I am certain they had a stressful early childhood in the foster system. Living in such instability can often redirect a kid's trajectory regardless of their interests or capabilities.

In fact, childhood instability has a much a stronger effect than family socioeconomic status for a variety of important outcomes, including education. This is clear when comparing children living in poverty with children living in foster care. In the Los Angeles County foster care system (where I grew up), for example, only 64.5 percent of foster kids graduate from high school. But the graduation rate for students categorized as "socioeconomically disadvantaged" is 86.6 percent, the same as the overall average in LA.[4]

What about college? In the US, 11 percent of kids from families in the bottom income quintile obtain bachelor's degrees, compared with less than 3 percent of children who have been in foster care.[5][6] In other words, a poor kid in the US is nearly four times more likely to graduate from college than a foster kid.

Instability also has negative effects on long-term social and health outcomes for children. A 2021 study led by Amir Sariaslan at Oxford University found that, compared with their siblings who were never placed in foster homes or other types of out-of-home care, kids who are placed in care are four times more likely to abuse drugs, four times more likely to be arrested for a violent crime, three times more likely to be diagnosed with depression or anxiety, and twice as likely to be poor as adults.[7] Placement instability—that is,

4   2017–2018 Los Angeles County Civil Grand Jury Final Report, Los Angeles, CA: Los Angeles County Civil Grand Jury.

5   P. J. Pecora, R. C. Kessler, J. Williams, K. O'Brien, A. C. Downs, D. English, J. White, E. Hiripi, C. R. White, T. Wiggins, and K. Holmes, *Improving Family Foster Care: Findings from the Northwest Foster Care Alumni Study.* Seattle, WA: Casey Family Programs, 2005.

6   J. B. Isaacs, I. Sawhill, and R. Haskins, "Getting Ahead or Losing Ground: Economic Mobility in America," Brookings Institution, 2008.

7   A. Sariaslan, A. Kääriälä, J. Pitkänen, H. Remes, M. Aaltonen, H. Hiilamo, P. Martikainen, and S. Fazel, "Long-Term Health and Social Outcomes in Children and Adolescents Placed in Out-of-Home Care," *JAMA Pediatrics* 176 (2021): e214324–e214324.

frequent relocations—appeared to be largely responsible for these detrimental outcomes.

This is not to say that children should never be placed in the foster system. In my case, my birth mother was clearly unable to care for me properly. Foster care is often crucial for keeping children safe. Still, the system is far from optimal. The findings from the 2021 study show that on average, kids who are placed into care do worse than their siblings who are not. This highlights the importance of considering out-of-home care placements as a last-resort intervention. And if possible, limiting the number of placements.

In my own case, it is impossible to disentangle every contributing factor to my own experiences with addiction, depression, and risky behavior. But living with nine different families before my eighth birthday almost certainly played a major role. A solid, two-parent home is critical for a child's future. There is simply no shortcut.

Other research has found that foster children are 2.7 to 4.5 times more likely to be prescribed psychiatric medication than non-foster children.[8] Infants younger than one year old are twice as likely to be prescribed a psychiatric drug compared to non-foster children.[9] For many people, if they are taking care of a baby that isn't "theirs," they will be more likely to sedate them out of convenience. This

---

8 T. M. Burton, "Foster Kids Are Overly Medicated, Report Says," *Wall Street Journal*, December 2, 2011, https://www.wsj.com/articles/SB100014240529702043977045770727 43861074270.

9 M. Abdelmalek, B. Adhikari, S. Koch, J. Diaz, and C. Weinraub, "New Study Shows US Government Fails to Oversee Treatment of Foster Children with Mind-Altering Drugs," *ABC News*, November 30, 2011, https://abcnews.go.com/US/study-shows-foster -children-high-rates-prescription-psychiatric/story?id=15058380.

also seems to be true for older children. Among adolescents in foster care, 66 percent take at least one psychiatric medication.[10] Taken at face value, this means that the best predictor of having a mental health condition—better than family history or genetics—is being a foster child. If you tell me that everyone else in your family, including your identical twin, has a mental health condition, I won't be able to tell whether you have one. My odds would be no better than a coin toss. But if you tell me you're a foster kid, then two out of three times, I'd guess "yes" correctly.

In all likelihood, though, these drugs are not always indicative of an underlying condition. I suspect that medications are over-prescribed for foster children because it is an easy way to numb their pain or dampen behavioral expressions of their pain such as substance abuse, violence, and other self-defeating behaviors.

A while back, I listened to an interview of a professor who said many academics study the lower classes because for them it is an unfamiliar and interesting group. But this particular professor came from humble roots and studied the upper class, because for her that was an unfamiliar and interesting group. But perhaps another reason academics seldom study the upper class is because they don't like the scrutiny. As I mentioned in the previous chapter, upper-class membership includes (but is not limited to) anyone who has at-tended an elite university who has at least one parent who graduated

10   J. M. Zito, D. J. Safer, D. Sai, J. F. Gardner, D. Thomas, P. Coombes, and M. Mendez-Lewis, "Psychotropic Medication Patterns Among Youth in Foster Care," *Pediatrics* 121 (2008): e157–e163.

from college. And indeed, the vast majority of academics at elite colleges earned their degrees from other elite schools.[11] More than 70 percent of professors have a parent who graduated from college, and professors at top universities are nearly fifty times more likely than the general public to have at least one parent with a PhD.[12]

Incredibly, as I was in the process of writing this book, a Yale dean emailed me asking whether I would be "gentle" in my discussions of the university. She had heard from a couple of other alumni that I was writing a memoir and was aware of my criticisms of elite colleges.

When I received that email, I thought about how little contact people at top colleges have with the kind of people I grew up around, like my two best friends from high school who were incarcerated.

One of my best friends in college, Bryan, had served in the Marine Corps. We discussed how all our friends on campus, including the ones who, like us, served in the military, were raised by both of their parents. He observed, "If my parents had gotten divorced when I was a kid, I'd definitely be in jail right now." Bryan explained that when he was in high school, he just barely avoided getting into serious trouble because of his stable and loving family, and how even though his parents weren't as rich as most of our Yale classmates, they created a good home for him and his brother.

Later, at Cambridge, I told a fellow graduate student about my

11   A. Clauset, S. Arbesman, and D. B. Larremore, "Systematic Inequality and Hierarchy in Faculty Hiring Networks," *Science Advances* 1 (2015): e1400005.

12   A. Morgan, A. Clauset, D. Larremore, N. LaBerge, and M. Galesic, "Socioeconomic Roots of Academic Faculty," *Nature Human Behavior* 12 (2021): 1625–1633.

friend Antonio, who could have been recruited to play college football. All he had to do was attend makeup classes for two weeks and get a B. He went for the first week only and then bailed.

My Cambridge friend replied, "Maybe it's good he didn't go to college. If that's who he was and what he enjoyed doing, maybe he wasn't meant to go."

I asked if that was her son, what would she have done.

"Forced him to go to class and threaten to kill him if he didn't."

We now live in a culture where affluent, educated, and well-connected people validate and affirm the behaviors, decisions, and attitudes of marginalized and deprived kids that they would never accept for themselves or their own children. And they claim to do this in the name of compassion. It's fine if Antonio and I skip class and ruin our futures, but it's definitely not fine if *their* kids do so. Many of the people who wield the most influence in society have isolated themselves and their children from the world I grew up in, while paying lip service to the challenges of inequality.

The reason I got where I am is because I had something I was running away from and something I was running toward. I was running away from the turbulence of my youth and running toward social mobility—money, education, esteem. I managed to channel my energy to striving to accomplish my goals. Upon obtaining a few totems of achievement, I came to realize that they are flawed measures of success.

External accomplishments are trivial compared with a warm and loving family. *Going* to school is far less important than *having a parent who cares enough* to make sure you get to class every day. But it is important to remember that even if every foster kid graduates from college, that wouldn't necessarily make them happier. A 2018 study found that people typically pursue higher levels of education because they believe it will lead to more leisure time. But, in fact, more educated people tend to have *less* leisure time.[13] They earn more money, but also work more hours. This upends their expectations and ends up having a net zero effect on overall happiness.

In contrast, there is evidence that familial adversity in childhood reduces happiness in adulthood. Interestingly, though, people who grow up in poor families are not more likely to be unhappy as adults. But people who feel they were unloved as children are significantly more likely to be unhappy.[14] For happiness, it's better to be poor and loved than rich and unloved. Of course, the worst is to be poor and unloved. A similar pattern has been found for health—childhood instability, but not poverty, is linked to poor physical and mental well-being in adolescence.[15] In short, to grow up to become a healthy and happy adult, having a loving family as a kid is at least as important as having money.

Childhood trauma isn't bad because it leads to lower graduation rates or lower incomes. It isn't bad because it leads to higher rates

---

13   I. Kristoffersen, "Great Expectations: Education and Subjective Well-being," *Journal of Economic Psychology* 66 (2018): 64–78.

14   L. J. Freeman, D. I. Templer, and C. Hill, "The Relationship Between Adult Happiness and Self-Appraised Childhood Happiness and Events," *Journal of Genetic Psychology* 160 (1999): 46–54.

15   B. H. Brumbach, A. J. Figueredo, and B. J. Ellis, "Effects of Harsh and Unpredictable Environments in Adolescence on Development of Life History Strategies," *Human Nature* 20 (2009): 25–51.

of addiction or crime. It's bad because of the firsthand, phenomenological experiences of the kids going through it. In other words, it's bad because it's bad. Frankly, even if stable and secure homes for children had *no effect* on future educational attainment, occupational success, crime rates, addiction, and so on, they are still worth promoting. A safe and loving childhood is a good in itself.

Today, I am immensely grateful for how my life has turned out. Really, it feels like I've woken up from a nightmare. People have told me that my story has brought them to tears. That's never been my intention—I don't want pity. I'm one of the lucky ones. There are many kids who have suffered far more. Some of them never recover from what they've endured.

I've lost touch with most of my high school friends, but here is the last of what I know of how their lives turned out. My friend Cristian has been released from prison and, as of three years ago, was unemployed. Tyler cleans carpets for a living. Two years ago, he posted an Instagram photo of himself with a facial disfigurement because he had wrecked his motorcycle again. I recently told him he's not a criminal anymore, he's a "justice-involved person" (a replacement term suggested by the luxury belief class). He replied, "Yeah, okay, and you're not a college grad anymore. You're a 'classroom-involved person.'" It's possible that my friends were never going to go to college. But if they'd had different upbringings, they wouldn't have wound up in prison.

Antonio has one kid out of wedlock and another with a different woman on the way. John joined the military at age twenty-four, served for six years, and is now working at a restaurant and taking community college classes. Tom lives with his girlfriend and was recently fired from Walmart.

A couple months ago, I spoke with two of Mom's friends who asked me for advice. They view me as a responsible adult—they see someone who was honorably discharged from the military and attended top universities. This would have stunned the seventeen-year-old Rob, to learn that someday people would look at him and *that* is who they see.

Mom's friends were worried that their son isn't talking as much as other six-year-olds. They, like many parents, were concerned with how "smart" their kid is.

"Should we be reading to him more?" they asked me.

I thought of how lonely I felt trying to teach myself how to read as a foster kid.

"Yeah," I replied. "But not because it will expand his vocabulary. Read to him because it will remind him that you love him."

ACKNOWLEDGMENTS

I would like to thank my agent Dylan Colligan at Javelin for recognizing the potential for a book in my 2018 *New York Times* op-ed. Additionally, I am grateful to my editors Rebecca Strobel, Maggie Loughran, and Natasha Simons at Simon & Schuster for their editorial guidance, and for their patience as I slowly came to understand what this book was really about once I'd started writing it.

I owe special thanks to Professor John Lewis Gaddis, who was the first to read and critique early versions of the manuscript. His confidence in the writing and the story helped to quell my initial doubts when starting this project.

Additionally, I am indebted to Emily Yoffe, Molly Schiessl, Steve Hely, Katharine Birbalsingh, Will Storr, Jim O'Shaughnessy, Esteban Elizondo, Drew Pinsky, Nicholas Christakis, and Jake Fischer for reading drafts and supplying critical feedback. I also benefited from conversations about writing with James Clear, Margi Conklin, Jim Dao, Tucker Max, J. D. Vance, Tara Westover, and Alicia Wittmeyer.

I am grateful to my family for many reasons, not least for their support in helping me to rekindle long-dormant memories.

Lastly, I owe thanks to Carmen Hui Jing Lim, for her wisdom, her warmth, and her insight.

ABOUT THE AUTHOR

Rob Henderson grew up in foster homes in Los Angeles and the rural town of Red Bluff, California. He joined the US Air Force at the age of seventeen. Once described as "self-made" by the *New York Times*, Rob subsequently received a BS from Yale University and a PhD in psychology from St. Catharine's College, Cambridge. His writing has appeared in the *New York Times*, the *Wall Street Journal*, the *Boston Globe*, and more. His weekly newsletter is sent to more than forty thousand subscribers. Learn more at www.RobKHenderson.com.